Jo Frost is one of the UK's most trusted and leading childcare and parental guidance experts and she is the most recognisable face of parenting on television. Jo's books and TV projects have received huge international acclaim and are seen and written in many languages throughout the world.

For further information on Jo and her work, please visit www.jofrost.com.

This book is dedicated to my niece, Isabella.
I love you.
Hugs and kisses,

Auntie JoJo
xoxo

Jo Frost's
Confident
Toddler Care

First published in Great Britain in 2011 by Orion Books,
An imprint of the Orion Publishing Group Ltd
Orion House, 5 Upper St. Martin's Lane,
London, WC2H 9EA
An Hachette UK Company

5 7 9 10 8 6 4

A CIP catalogue record for this book is available from the British Library.

ISBN: 9781 4091 13348

Printed and bound in China

The Orion Publishing Group's policy is to use papers that are natural, renewable
and recyclable products and made from wood grown in sustainable forests. The
logging and manufacturing processes are expected to conform to the environmental
regulations of the country of origin.

*Note: All children are unique and this book is not intended to be a substitute for the advice of
your doctor or health visitor who should be consulted on toddler matters, especially when a child
shows any sign of illness or unusual behaviour. Neither the publisher nor the author accepts
any legal responsibility for any personal injury or other damage or loss arising from the use or
misuse of the information and advice in this book.*

PICTURE CREDITS:
Daniel Pangbourne: viii, 7, 8, 12, 47, 74, 98, 131, 152, 165, 177, 188,
208, 220, 224, 231, 265, 280, 282
Author's own: i, ii, 91, 199
Illustrations by Helen Flook

CONTENTS

PART III: A Day in the Life of a Toddler

PART IV: Useful Resources

GRATITUDE LIST

Mary Jane Ryan, my co-worker, my friend. Our time together on this book has been a pleasure indeed. Your support and strong work ethic continues.

Daniel Pangbourne, yet again you have captured the true spirit and heart of these little darlings.

To all the parents and children in this book – such a fun day!

Sarah Kate Thorne and Natalie Chesterman.

Dr Mark Furman – thank you for the thumbs up, again.

Eugenie Furniss, a true cheerleader. Thank you for making this happen, you old soul. I look forward to many more.

To the girls in the literary department at WME and Orion Publishing, true team work and dedication every step of the way.

Last but not least, a huge big bear hug and gigantic thank you to my family and close friends who continue to nourish me on every level. Your love and support I couldn't do without.

P.S. Dad…you're a Grandad! xxxx

INTRODUCTION

These wonderful (but sometimes crazy) years

(Oh yes and there are many!)

Welcome! For years, parents have suggested that I need to write a book solely focused on toddlers, and it's easy to see the reasons! That's why I am so excited to welcome you to this book – and to this wonderful stage of your child's life. After all, you've often seen me on the telly helping parents cope with this phase of their children's lives.

The toddler years are filled with so many milestones: learning to walk, talk, eat and even dress. It's also a time of meltdowns and, needless to say, confusion – for you and your toddler. You should think of it as a grand expedition with wondrous sights to behold; however, along the way you'll be doing a lot of hard work. That's not to say it won't be fun. When I think of my time as a nanny working with toddlers, a smile is always at the forefront of my thoughts.

How do you do it?

How can it be fun when it all seems so frustrating? How can you help your child develop with the right kind of care and attention to ensure her proper development? How do you teach life skills, such as potty-training, using utensils, and abiding by your rules? That's the advice and help I'm going to give you in this book. A sibling to my *Confident Baby Care* book, *Confident Toddler Care* is going to guide you through the next four years – from when your child begins to walk at around 14 months, right through her fourth year, when she's getting ready to start school.

If your child has just started walking, congratulations! You're thinking ahead. You're going to become more knowledgeable about this important stage of your child's life than you ever imagined. You've now entered a whole new phase of your child's life.

You're going to learn new tools and techniques, and better understand your toddler's emotions and state of mind – and your own. You'll become more observant and in tune with her – which I believe is crucial – and come to realise your value in her life.

And if you've picked up this book because your little one has already sprouted into a toddler, and is pushing for independence, and you're thinking: 'I don't know what to do! *Arghhhhhhh*!', this book is for you, too. It will all be OK. You're not going to be alone. When have I ever said something that I haven't followed through? I'll be with you every step of the way, and you can trust me on that. Armed with this book, I know you will enjoy this amazing period of your child's life. You can't not.

It's a whole new world

What's the difference between babies and toddlers? Well, throughout the first year of your child's life, you were focused on nurturing and meeting his every need for sleep, food and love. Once you figured out a schedule to meet those needs, it was pretty easy because babies just fall into the programme. Now, suddenly, you're the parent of this little person who is walking around and pointing out what he wants – and what he doesn't. He's at a newfound stage of relating to the world around him from a (literally) different height. His personality is becoming more defined and his independence is growing. You'll no longer be doing everything for him, and you'll be teaching him how to do things for himself. He's calling out *Mama* and *Dada* for the first time, and you're all made up about that, too.

New parenting skills

This phase requires a whole new set of parenting skills. Note: this Nanny Jo doesn't come with fairy dust to help you magically solve everything you'll encounter. But what I do have is the knowledge and experience to help you prepare for your journey, with a backpack full of essential tools to pull out when you need them: *Confidence, Patience, Discipline, Perseverance, Energy, Commitment, Plan Ahead, Perspective* and *Humour*. In Chapter 1, I go into these tools in detail, to prepare you for raising your toddler well throughout these years.

You'll need these tools whether you're dealing with tantrums in public, toilet-training, or getting your toddler to eat at the table. Don't worry though; I'll prompt you along the way with a 'Backpack required' symbol to remind you to put these tools in place. And PS: You're the one who'll be carrying the backpack, not me.

Using this book

To help you better understand your little one, and the best way to meet the challenges and savour the joys of the toddler years, I've structured this book into four parts so that it's easy for you to negotiate. Let's face it: time management is key when you have toddlers. I know that one. This is about me teaching you so that you can teach them.

Part I: Parenting Every Day, Every Hour looks at your emotional journey as the parent of a toddler and offers specific advice for working parents to help you cope with childcare, guilt and much, much more. There is also a chapter that provides an overview of exactly who this little person is – and how she thinks and develops. This will give you the background you need to understand why she behaves the way she does, and what to expect as she grows from the age of one through to the age of four. This chapter also includes a section on the importance of teaching the crucial life skills that your toddler must master.

In *Part II: The Big Issues in the Toddler Years*, I'll look at the foundation issues that you must deal with when raising a toddler, including safety, discipline, the importance of play and stimulation, positive transitions, getting out and about, establishing proper eating habits, and, of course, potty-training. Yes, it can be done in one week and I'll show you exactly how!

In *Part III: A Day in the Life of a Toddler*, I'll take you through an average day, from when your toddler wakens till she goes to sleep. Routine is very important to a toddler – and it makes your life easier, too! You'll also find all the information you need to get her up and dressed, having a fun-filled day and – that all-important one – getting her to go to bed and stay there! We need our rest, too, so I know you are keen to hear that one. I can feel your smiles.

Finally, *Part IV: Useful Resources* is the section to go to for nursery rhyme and book ideas, useful contacts or if you need no-nonsense medical advice, fast.

Confident Toddler Care is intended to be read from beginning to end, as well as used as a reference book throughout the toddler years. The index can lead you to any specific topic, if you need some tips in a hurry. In fact, throughout the entire book, you'll find boxes with how-to tips and techniques, as well as lots of other signs to watch out for all sorts of different topics, problems and concerns If you've read any of my other books or watched my TV shows, you already have a sense of my philosophy and approach – no-nonsense and practical, with a good dose of fun. I don't beat around the bush. Quite frankly, who's got time for that? I say it how it is.

As a nanny, I started off looking after babies and progressed organically to looking after toddlers – over and over again. It's a challenging time for some, as there is so much going on at once. I haven't just gone through potty-training once; I've been through it more times than I can count. Plenty of nappies have passed my nose. I've dealt with more tantrums than any supermarket would welcome and recited more nursery rhymes than Humpty Dumpty himself. So, hey, now you're getting my decades of experience.

Confident toddler parenting

Scared or nervous? I've had parents confess that they are afraid they are going to screw up their toddler, and this is a pretty normal concern. But, have faith in yourself, because your toddler does! He's ready to follow you anywhere. Yes, you *are* wearing many hats – and a superhero cape or two. What you do will make a truly massive impact in your toddler's life. And you will be laying down a foundation that sets standards and precedents for when he's older.

When I work with parents, I always ask, 'What do *you* think?' There is so much parenting advice out there, so many dos and don'ts, that many people feel that what they are doing is not good enough. And this leads to a serious lack of confidence.

I'm here as your parental guide, giving you support along the way, but I'd like to bring you to a place where you have the confidence to make choices for yourself, that will make you happier about the parent that you are and want to be — not what others want you to become — so that you are empowered as a parent.

Feeling confident in your ability to help your child through the toddler years is important for two reasons. The first is so that you feel good about what you're doing. That doesn't mean you do everything perfectly (what is that anyway?), just that you know you are doing a good job. The second is because confident parenting during this stage of your child's life helps him feel secure and that builds trust — a foundation between you. While he stretches for independence, deep in his little heart he feels the need for reassurance. And when you're confident, he knows that you're firmly in control and feels protected. This can prevent a lot of acting out and other such nonsense behaviours.

Parenting with confidence is not something that is formed out of willpower. Rather, it grows through understanding, experience, communicating with your partner, friends, and parents — and, most importantly, practice! Trust me: you'll get lots of that, whether you want it or not.

The wonder years

The toddler stage can have its difficulties on many levels, but it can also be so emotionally rewarding. For the first time, you're actually having a relationship with your child that goes two ways. When you say something and it registers, you can see his little mind processing. And then, when he comes back and throws you these out-of-the blue comments, it's absolutely delightful. He's got his own distinctive walk, his own character and personality — and who can resist it when those little chunky hands reach out for a hug and pat you back.

I'm always so moved by a toddler's pure innocence — no filter, nothing conditioned or tainted — and the wide-eyed wonder with which he sees the world. I love the toddler years so much that, even now, I still miss the joy of helping two-, three-, and four-year-olds grow over time. Don't get me wrong: it's wonderful to reach out to so many parents now. It's the delight of these years that inspired me to write this book.

PRESERVING MEMORIES

If I could go back to the days when I worked with toddlers as a nanny in a family, I wish I'd kept a book of those little moments that touched my heart or made me laugh. It would be a seriously large book! That's why I'd like to encourage you to write down the moments that really touch you. The toddler years bring so many of these moments, but they can be easily forgotten in the bustle of daily life. Preserve them – they're a precious treasure that you can share with your toddler when he gets older.

If somebody said to me: 'Paint the toddler years', the result would be a colourful, organised mess! And so much fun! It's these years, which you are about to experience, that light you up as a parent.

Rising to the challenge

You'll be challenged and pushed in ways that you would never dream possible. Hey, I'm a realist. But the toddler years don't have to be difficult if you adopt a practical, consistent, loving approach, with realistic expectations. Toddlers can bring out the best in you, even when you fear they're bringing out the worst. You're responsible for this little cherub that you love immensely and you will start to think through things in a way that you've never done before. And thinking – rather than just reacting – is the first step towards being the confident, successful parent you want to be.

As hard as some moments may seem, the reality is that the toddler years should be seriously prized. Each phase goes by so quickly. Cherish the special moments. Be willing to be surprised. Find the magic and get ready for the ride.

Enjoy!

PART I

Parenting every day, every hour

TOUCHSTONES FOR THE TODDLER YEARS

1 Communicate clearly

2 Adopt a positive mindset

3 Repeat, again and again

4 Be consistent

5 Give encouragement

6 Establish routines

7 Have realistic expectations

8 Set boundaries

In this section, I'll explore the journey you'll be going on as you parent a toddler, as well as let you know how your toddler will be growing and developing between the ages of one and four. I'll also begin to provide you with a foundation of understanding that will help you to cope with the issues and situations you will be experiencing in your daily life with your toddler.

Touchstones for the journey

Your tasks as parents of a toddler are made easier when you're armed with my top eight 'Touchstones for the Toddler Years'. In brief, they give you all you need to raise your toddler to be a healthy, contented child – and allow you to enjoy your time with him. These tips are so important that I suggest you copy them and put them somewhere where you can see them on a daily basis. I can't tell you how important it is to embrace these concepts. They will hold you in good stead and help you to help your child develop.

Your emotional journey

You're the parent of a toddler and, in case you didn't notice, your child is beginning to experience a whirlwind of intense, contradictory and sometimes even explosive emotions – up one minute and down the next. And what about you? One minute your heart is breaking over the cute things she says, and the next you're tearing your hair out with frustration because she won't listen to a word you say! Impatience, fear, anger – at some point you'll feel all of these. And you are both learning! While she's learning how to be independent, you're learning how to set limits. She's learning to say 'no', and so are you – and actually mean it!

When I was raising toddlers, I, just like you, had to learn to adapt to situations – to think on my feet, to compromise when necessary, and to stick to my guns. I had to think smart, use common sense and always make a decision. Through practice and loads of experience, I became confident in my ability.

So will you as a parent.

From the adversity of dealing with the first temper tantrum or when she tests you and then tests you again, you'll gain confidence in dealing with her.

I'm not saying it will always be easy. For instance, there are going to be times when you've put your toddler to bed, and she's crying. You *want* to go into the room. You *want* to pick her up, because comforting is an inborn instinct.

But then you say to yourself: 'If I don't do this, how am I going to teach her to go to sleep on her own?' So you stick to it. In order to follow through with discipline and some of the other techniques I suggest, you have to become a bit detached in order to be objective in what you are teaching. If you're completely emotionally attached when all is kicking off, you can't see where you need to go and what you need to do. There's no clarity. That doesn't help anyone.

A wealth of emotions

In this chapter I'll offer insight into the different emotions you'll be experiencing and provide tools to support you along the way. I've sat next to parents, and comforted and reassured them when they have been fearful and overwhelmed, and felt like throwing in the towel. I've felt what they've felt and, as a result, I truly believe that if you know what to expect along the way, you'll be less worried, less impatient and less fearful. The more first-hand experience you gain, the more your confidence will grow and the less intense the roller-coaster of emotions will be.

That's what this chapter is all about – giving you the insight, reassurance and comfort in knowing what to expect in your own parenting journey, and how you can deal with your emotions throughout the process. You'll also find tips on finding balance with your partner, what to do when you don't agree on parenting issues, and even how to revive that good-old date night so that you're keeping your own relationship alive. Remember, the one that got you here in the first place?

The blessings of the toddler years

You're in a constantly evolving relationship with your child, spending time with her, and getting to know her as she gets to know you. She'll be learning new things and you'll remember from your own experiences how much fun and silliness there is out there. You'll see the joy in her face and remember the joy of exploring. She's impacting you just as much as you're impacting her.

As the parent of a toddler, you learn to put things into perspective, set limits and stay firm but loving. You have the chance to grow more patient and to have more fun – to become a more compassionate and realistic adult.

If you're questioning whether you're enjoying this stage of your child's life, ask yourself why. Do you feel that you're not getting what you thought you would from it? Is it not how you imagined? You now have a little person interacting with you. She's got her own thoughts. She notices things about you – and about herself – that are really funny and quirky, and comes out with the most honest observations. How can you truly connect with your child and bridge the gap between yourself as an adult and this tiny person walking around?

Some parents tell me that they find it really difficult to connect with their toddlers because they don't know how to loosen up and have some fun. If you relate to this, try to see the next few years as a blessing. Go into them with an open mind, and discover how much you can learn about yourself along the way. How could you grow in yourself throughout this time? How could you enjoy it more? What's needed?

We tend to parent our children the way we were parented. As your child heads into these active years, think about the way you were raised. What do you want to pass on? What do you want to do differently? Have you talked to your partner about his or her thoughts on this? I encourage both of you to take a few moments to do the following exercise.

WHAT'S IMPORTANT TO YOU?

Take a minute and write down how you would finish this sentence, 'During the toddler years, it's important to me that I'm … '
    Here are some examples:

- **having fun with her**
- **focusing on the stage she's in now, and not always looking ahead**
- **teaching my core family values**
- **really involved and committed with time**
- **helping her with her developmental stage**

Use this exercise as a way to start conversations with your partner about what's important to each of you. Having this focus can help to guide you in making confident decisions in a variety of situations.

Embrace the responsibility

Raising your toddler is one of the most important and gratifying jobs you'll ever have. I say 'job' because jobs come with responsibilities. You're the one supervising and looking after his every need, 24 hours a day, seven days a week, even if you use childminders or another form of childcare. You're listening. You're watching. You're doing. You're responsive to everything, and that is a huge responsibility. But it is not an impossible one.

A high-powered person in a corporation does not take his responsibilities lightly because what he does has a huge impact on every employee, from the boardroom to the postroom. The situation is similar to yours throughout the toddler years because, over this period of time, you're responsible for your child on every level: socially, mentally, emotionally and physically. It's your responsibility not just to protect him from harm, but also to help him grow into the individual he'll become. For your child, these years are all about learning through play, and through your instructions on the basic life skills. It's not a time when you can coast, but you certainly need pit stops to refuel. You'll undoubtedly gain a new maturity, as you're now more aware of the impact of everything you say and do.

All of this responsibility takes an enormous amount of energy and focus. And, while it is your job, it shouldn't seem like hard work or a chore. Embrace the responsibility! Allow it to bring out the best in you. This will help you to approach parenting with the right mindset.

Make a decision

So many times I see parents failing to make decisions because they're afraid to screw up. Even worse, they ignore the situation and the little problems they encounter become really big. Don't be afraid to make decisions. You can only learn from your mistakes if you make them in the first place. And the truth is that the majority of people don't know how to deal with toddlers before they become parents.

Let's bring it back to basics – you make decisions every day. You look outside and see what the weather is and decide whether to wear a jumper or a shirt. You decide whether to have cereal or scrambled eggs and bacon. So, why wouldn't you make decisions that involve your children's growth and development? You can't afford to hesitate simply because you're afraid! Have an open mind and try the appropriate techniques and give them a chance to work.

> **What's the worst that can happen?**
>
> When you're having trouble making a decision, ask yourself: 'What's the worst that can happen?'
>
> You make the wrong decision! So what! Then you can change it.

Packing your backpack for the journey

Remember the backpack I talked about in the Introduction? We're going to put it together with eight different coping skills to help you to navigate the next few years, as you go on this journey with your toddler. Think of these qualities as mantras, which you can use daily during the toddler years – and beyond. I suggest you print them out and put them on the fridge as a daily reminder.

These tools are interconnected. You need: *Confidence* because it enables you to make decisions and gives your child stable ground; *Patience* to keep your cool because whatever you tell or show him won't sink in the first time or maybe even the first 50 times; *Discipline*, or the mental ability to understand what is necessary to create change; *Perseverance* to be consistent; *Energy* and *Commitment* to tackle challenges and stay the course; and the ability to *Plan Ahead* so you can provide the structure that toddlers crave, and also avoid problems. *Perspective* helps you to see the big picture and know that this phase of your child's life is not going to go on forever. Finally, know that during these years your greatest coping skill is your sense of *Humour*! Find the humour in the repetition of it all, because it's the counterbalance to the monotony of routine.

TOOLS FOR THE JOURNEY

- ◆ Confidence
- ◆ Patience
- ◆ Discipline
- ◆ Perseverance
- ◆ Energy
- ◆ Commitment
- ◆ Plan Ahead
- ◆ Perspective
- ◆ Humour

Getting enough sleep

In addition to packing your backpack with the proper attitudes, the biggest advice I can give you for these years is to get enough sleep. Everything feels overwhelming when you're not rested. Proper sleep is critical to feeling good. When you're rested, you're less likely to lose your temper and you'll have more energy to interact fully with your toddler. You can't have enough patience, perspective, energy or humour without enough sleep.

When you don't get enough sleep, it's like only partly charging your batteries. It affects your skin, your nails, your hair and your hormonal levels. Can you expect eight hours from your mobile phone if you've only charged it for 30 minutes? You can't. Equally, you can't expect to have the energy you need when your batteries are only partly charged. That's just one reason why it's important to get your kids back to sleep when they waken in the night. You *need* to sleep. Sleep is a priority for your kids; you need to make it a priority for you as well.

What winds you down? What do you need to do in order to get into that place? When you get enough sleep you have more energy. You'll see things differently. And you'll enjoy parenting more because you won't feel so dragged down all the time. You'll have more energy — not just for yourself, but also to give to your kids and the other relationships in your life.

SORTING YOUR SLEEP

How many hours of sleep are you getting a night? Experts say that adults need between seven and nine, with seven being the absolute minimum.

If you're not getting enough, how come? Are you trying to squeeze in housework after the little ones are in bed? Watching telly? Getting up in the night with a wakeful toddler?

Figure out what is standing in the way and then put a plan into action: turn the TV off in the bedroom; share more of the load with your partner; prioritise and pace yourself with housework (remembering that not everything has to be done every day); turn off the lights earlier; use my 'Staying in Bed' technique with your child. Do what you need to in order to get enough rest.

Don't just do, *be* in the moment

Do you remember when you first had your baby? Every smile, every laugh – you took it all in. You were doting, observing every little detail. You could say, 'She's like this' or 'He does that' because you took the time to notice.

Now that you're chasing your toddler around, it's easy to become so focused on the tasks that you can lose sight of what's most important. If your main aim is to rush your toddler off to childcare the moment he wakens, you can miss the funny side of him trying to pull his pyjamas over his head – watching him get stuck and ending up looking like a nun in a habit. If you miss these moments, then you miss the whole point.

The truly special moments occur when you least expect them. And it's these moments and quiet times that tug at your heart in a pleasant way.

You watch her unwrap a present with infectious excitement and enthusiasm, her eyes aglow; you see her sleeping like a little angel. Even if you're trying to get her out the door, work on seeing each moment as a chance to connect, rather than something you have to rush through in order to get to the next thing. Maybe she's managed to fasten her Velcro shoes for the first time, or get her jacket on the right way. Stop and take note: these are firsts that are every single bit as important as those first steps and words.

HOW WAS IT FOR YOU?

Try to remember what it was like for you when you were little. Childhood is about learning, being creative and having fun without the responsibility of adulthood. When you stop and recall your own childhood, it's easier to remember what your toddler needs, and you'll find it that much easier to be responsive. This is, of course, what he needs most of all. Draw on your own wonderful experiences:

- ◆ **What do you remember being good at?**
- ◆ **What do you remember learning?**
- ◆ **What kind of things did you enjoy doing?**

Take it one issue at a time

◆ **Energy**

It's so easy to get overwhelmed! She won't listen, she acts out, you discipline her and the tears come. You feel like a failure. Take a step back and try to figure out what's at the root of the issue. Is she tired? Has her Daddy been working a lot lately and she's missing him? Break it down so that you don't make it bigger through worrying – or not taking steps to resolve it. Rather than wasting your Energy worrying, keep it in your backpack and use it to solve the problem.

If you're in a car and need to get somewhere, you don't sit and think: 'I'm in West London and need to get to North London. Oh no, how will I ever get there?' You get out your *A–Z*, switch on your GPA, or look it up on MapQuest. It's the same when you face a situation with your toddler. When I work with parents, we first discuss the situation and what we want the end result to be and why. Because if you don't know why you are doing something, you'll never follow through. With a starting and ending point in place, together we come up with a plan of action.

You can do the same thing. Be realistic and pace yourself. If I had sleeping, picky eating, and potty-training to deal with, then sleeping would be first thing I would want to get in hand for the simple reason that if the whole family is sleep deprived, no one has energy to do anything else. Once you get the sleeping back on track, she'll start eating better, and then you can tackle potty-training. If she's eating and sleeping regularly, potty-training will be easier because you can see patterns and potty-training goes more smoothly.

Thinking out loud

You need to think it out loud – and step-by-step – because you can only juggle so many balls without dropping one. When you drop one, the others follow; you're not only setting yourself up to fail, but actually arresting your child's development.

News alert

Toddlers have an enormous capacity to learn quickly. If you consistently teach them something, they get it! Even if they've already been taught bad habits, their brains and behaviour can be retrained swiftly. I like to think of rewiring because it's easy for their brains to learn. Millions of you have seen me do this time and time again.

> ## Make a plan and follow through
>
> When you face a challenge with your child, take a moment and break it down. Where are you trying to get to? What's the first step? Do you need additional help finding your way? Look up the topic in this book, then come up with a plan and start addressing it. Ignoring it will usually only make it worse.

Lead by example

Who made an impact on your life as you were growing up? Was there one person who inspired you and the way you act today? We teach our toddlers by the things we say, but they also learn from what we do. Are you modelling positive behaviour?

In the eyes of your toddler, you are everything. Day in, day out, you are the person he refers to and admires, particularly since he hasn't been influenced by any other teachers or coaches just yet. You are his go-to person for everything, from table manners to how to deal with emotions. He learns from you – full stop.

As his hero, you are leading by example – whether you are conscious of it or not. This is great for teaching correct behaviour; however, unfortunately, toddlers also tend to learn things and ways of doing things that are not so good. For example, we lose our tempers but tell our kids to 'stop having temper tantrums'. Or we turn around and shout, 'Stop shouting!'

I'm going to say it outright: it's natural to feel sad and angry. The emotions you experience belong to you. But it's how you handle these feelings that make the difference when modelling good or bad behaviour.

Dealing with frustration

How can you show him that there are other ways to deal with anger and frustration than shouting? Don't shout. If you are angry, tell him you're angry, but also tell him what you're going to do to feel better. If you get really angry and you feel you can't control your emotions, take a deep breath and walk away.

The 'Naughty Step' technique (which I go into detail in Chapter 5; see page 108–110) is for your child *and* you. It gives you space to calm your emotions and gather your thoughts so you don't lose control of yourself.

Children give unconditional love. You have to be mindful of this fact, because kids forgive you no matter what. I've worked with families where there have been countless difficulties that the parents have had to work through. Regardless of how they've acted, their kids love them unconditionally. There's a loyalty there, but there will be no trust if this behaviour continues.

Share feelings, carefully

It's also important to be mindful of what you're saying and doing because toddlers are perceptive. They see, hear and feel everything going on around them. I understand that there are times when parents just feel so overwhelmed. They don't want to panic their kids even more by letting them see their feelings, so they try to protect them by hiding their emotions. However, because kids are so connected to their parents, they instinctively know when something's not right.

Has there ever been a time when you've been feeling a little bit sad and, from nowhere, your toddler comes up to you and gives you a hug, or pats your back like you pat his? And you think: 'I needed that. That was lovely.' In the last ten years, researchers have discovered a brain structure called 'mirror neurons'. These special brain cells literally mirror the feelings of the people around them. If you're angry, your child feels it. He feels your sadness, your impatience, your happiness and your joy.

I'm not saying that you need to open the chat lines and tell him everything that's going on for you. There are a lot of things that aren't appropriate for little ones to know. Most importantly, your toddler should never feel that what's going on is his problem. That's why it's important to acknowledge your feelings, but also let him know things are going to be OK. If he's not reassured, your emotions can leave him on wobbly ground.

If you're sad, tell your child, 'Mummy's a little bit sad today, but it's going to be all right.' You are telling him that his perception is correct – which is an important thing for him to understand – but that you are more than capable of handling the situation.

Dad's involvement

One of the biggest areas of family change I've witnessed over the years has been the level of involvement of Dads in their children's lives. With more and more women either choosing or having to go back to work, there's been a shift in roles and responsibilities. The 21st-century Dad is more actively involved in his children's lives, on a day-to-day basis, as well as from an emotional perspective. I think this involvement is critical in the well-being of a family, whether it is traditional or not. It's a win–win situation for all involved.

Household management

During the toddler years, housework can be such a stress point. One of the first things I tell parents with whom I work is to prioritise what *truly* needs to be done, using my 'Do, Dump, Defer and Delegate' technique. Work out with your partner – or, if you are a single parent, create your own schedule – how to pace chores throughout the week so that you're not overwhelmed.

Prioritise what's important. Do the sheets need to be changed every day? Probably not. But, keeping your floors clean might be a priority, as your toddler will be playing down there, and constantly picking things up. The reality is you can't obtain perfection in your home when you have a toddler. This is not about you living in the Victoria & Albert Museum. Your priorities have to be different when your children are small. Just stating this as a fact can relieve an enormous amount of stress for parents who feel they need to keep everything in order all of the time.

If I go into a house and see that it's spotless, it makes me pause. A parent who obsessively cleans is probably highly stressed and trying to control another situation. If you're spending all your time cleaning, when are you spending time with your toddler? Your house might be messier than you like, but that's OK for now. Prioritise your time.

DO, DUMP, DEFER AND DELEGATE

To avoid overload, break down the tasks you have into four categories and deal with them that way:

◆ **Do: you're going to do it.**

◆ **Dump: let it go altogether. Does the garage really need to be cleaned?**

◆ **Defer: wait until later. Sorting the photos into albums can happen another time.**

◆ **Delegate: give to your partner or someone else.**

Balancing the load between you

There may be times during the toddler years when you or your partner feel like you're carrying too much. This can lead to frustration and resentment, and put a strain on your relationship.

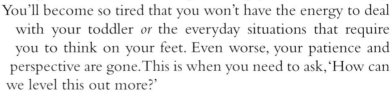

If and when this happens, I encourage both of you to take a step back and see what you can do to work together more efficiently. Being able to support one another and balance the responsibilities helps you both stay connected and sane. If one of you is feeling like things are all right, but the other is feeling drained and totally exasperated as a result of looking after your toddler, then tensions will arise. Trying to do everything at the same time – the parenting, running the house and working – is simply too overwhelming.

You'll become so tired that you won't have the energy to deal with your toddler *or* the everyday situations that require you to think on your feet. Even worse, your patience and perspective are gone. This is when you need to ask, 'How can we level this out more?'

●　●

Remember: when your partner gives you a break, express confidence that they can take care of your toddler just as well as you can. They might not do things the way you do, but it's important to let them step in and do it their way.

●　●

Getting your own time with your toddler

Some parents tell me that balancing the load is hard when a toddler only wants Daddy or Mummy to do particular things. There are certain activities, like going to bed, where your toddler finds it most comforting to have it done by the same parent who usually does it. However, when it gets to the point where it's bothering one partner, then it's not just about your child's needs, but yours, too. It's all about balancing responsibilities, as well as giving balance to the special times each parent wants to have with his or her child.

I know this is particularly true of working parents, when one travels a lot or puts in many hours per week. When you return home, your toddler wants you to do everything! Alternatively, if Mum is at home all the time, your toddler will want Mum and only Mum to take over. It's important to remember that toddlers are creatures of habit, and given free rein they'll make sure they have the same routine over and over again. But that isn't necessarily right for you and your partner. Mum needs a break and Dad needs to be allowed to step in. If Dad is tired, it's Mum's turn. And so on!

Make sure you figure out what you and your partner would like to do in these situations, so that you don't fall into the trap of letting your toddler run the entire show. For example, even if your toddler always demands one of you at bath-time or for the bedtime ritual, it's important to give the other parent a chance to participate in these activities. Both of you need to enjoy the experience, and your child needs to see that she can enjoy the experience with both of you. Otherwise, one of you will feel left out. My 'Step Out, Step In' technique can help.

STEP OUT, STEP IN TECHNIQUE

◆ When bath- or bedtime rolls around, go to another part of the house so that your toddler can't chase you.

◆ First time round, it might be easier if you pop over to your neighbour's for half an hour, or go out for a walk. This gives your partner the chance to step in, knowing that your child will have to rely on him or her.

◆ Before you disappear, it's important to explain to your child: 'Daddy's busy tonight, so Mummy's going to do it'.

Relationship strain

Every relationship takes work to maintain it at a place where you're both content. That's ongoing. But there will be times when your relationship will feel extra stressed. Chances are it will be tested on every level during the toddler years. You both need to be on the same page so you can present a united front. If you're not, you need to figure out how to resolve your differences. And quickly!

The moment your relationship becomes strained – and the more you string out resolving it – the more time your toddler spends in the middle of it. Even if you tell her that everything is OK, she's got a sixth sense that something's not right. Remember those mirror neurons.

If you feel you're here already, the first step is to talk. The worst thing you can do is stop talking, and that's what I find most couples do when they don't have the answers. You have to make time to come together and work it out. Otherwise the strain will be the wallpaper around which your child is raised. I worked with one couple who had long stopped working on it. They had spent months punishing one another and, as a result, had a toddler who was hitting, kicking, fighting and yelling. They sat there, both naively saying, 'I don't know why his behaviour is this way.' They were both wallpaper hangers.

Do not underestimate the environment you create for your little ones. Toddlers mimic what they see and hear, and they feel energy that cuts like a knife as we all do. They just don't verbalise it. Toddlers show how they are feeling through their behaviour.

Communication and respect

It's important to your relationship and your overall parenting that your communication is honest and open so that you can talk about your disagreements. It's also important to recognise that when each of you has stated your opinion, you both get busy proactively resolving the situation. If you do it at work because your job depends on it, why wouldn't you do it at home?

I once worked with parents who had lost respect for one another because neither one felt they were being heard. They became consumed by simply surviving and eventually drew up divorce papers. They told me that they had no choice. I said, 'No, you choose to divorce or you choose not to. Is this the choice you want to make?' They started to talk to one another and open up. For the first time, they began to listen to one another and their relationship improved.

The first step in communication is listening. Feeling unheard or unsupported can be a very lonely place to be. If you feel like you're on your own and not working together, it's hard to move forward. Anything swept underneath the rug is going to come back up again and again, until you handle it in a way that makes both parties happy. No one wants to get to a place where divorce seems the only option. For this reason, I'd like to suggest the 'Talking Box' technique to redirect your focus.

THE TALKING BOX TECHNIQUE

- ◆ **Create a box and fill it with blank cards.**
- ◆ **Both you and your partner write what you would like to discuss, one item per card.**
- ◆ **Spend half an hour each night going through the box. Cap the time, so you don't go around in circles.**
- ◆ **Don't move on to the next card until the previous one is resolved.**
- ◆ **By focusing on the question in the box, and not each other, it's easier to let go of the fear of how the other person will react.**
- ◆ **The important thing is to listen to how the other person feels, talk about a resolution, and then move on.**

Can I get some 'me' time around here?

Whether you're the one working or the one at home with the kids – or, indeed, doing a bit of both – you both need a break. It's not about who's doing what because the truth is that it's all challenging. It's too easy to get so caught up in the everyday tasks of raising your family that you forget that you are your own person, too. Don't feel selfish for wanting some time to yourself; it doesn't mean that you are disregarding your family. It is healthy to pursue your own interests, too. When you make time to do things you love on your own, it brings much to your parenting, too. Why? Because you're more fulfilled and have had a little respite from toddlerhood.

Don't feel like you need to spend money on expensive activities such as massages or golf. Being given the space to go for a walk by yourself or have a relaxing bath is sometimes all it takes to feel energised again. We live in a society where there is a forced admiration for managing to do so much – to be Supermum or -dad. But if you feel you're juggling too many plates while riding an elephant, you've missed the point. It's not how much you do in a day, but the purpose of what you do and what you get out of it.

Reviving date night

A young mother of triplets once confessed to me in a humorous way that she couldn't remember the last time she'd gone out and had fun with her husband. As funny as she made it sound, I knew that this young mother – in her mid-twenties – was feeling the pinch of balance. She and her husband were going through the motions of parenting, but not personally connecting. Her kids had hit 18 months, so it was clear this young couple needed to go out on a date night and get their sexy back.

Do make time alone together a priority if it's what you both want. Just like it's so easy to get caught up in the everyday tasks of taking care of your kids, it's easy to forget to nurture your relationship as a couple. Date night gives you time to be together – just the two of you. Even if you end up just talking about the kids, at least you're having an uninterrupted conversation! The same is true for those of you who are raising children single-handedly. Be sure to give to you, so you can give to yours.

> ### *Alternative babysitting options*
>
> I once worked in a neighbourhood where eight families set up a system of trading babysitting tokens with each other. What a great idea. If you're worried about the expense of a babysitter, see if you can trade nights with other couples in your area.

Parenting solo

Whether you decided to have a child on your own, are divorced and your former partner isn't co-parenting, or you become a temporary single parent because your partner is away, at war or in prison, there's no question that single-parenting has its challenges. It's all on your shoulders, and you don't have support living under the same roof.

I don't want to dwell on the negatives, because I've known many a successful single parent, and I see a lot of people embrace the responsibility beautifully. In fact, because you are on your own, you soon realise the importance of routines and prioritising, and get into the swing of things more quickly, because you have no one else to rely on. Similarly, the fact that there is no one around to give you a break can also encourage you to reach out and make friends with people who can take on a bit of the childcare when you need some time off. You'll need some help, and you'll most definitely appreciate it when you get it.

Solo parenting does mean playing both bad and good cop, which can be exhausting at times; however, you won't spend any precious time and energy arguing about who's going to do what – or how! Most single parents develop wonderfully close relationships with their children, and while the toddler years can present a challenge to *any* parent, single or not, it is possible to establish an understanding early on and use your closeness to encourage the behaviour you want to see.

The bottom line is that you should embrace your role as a parent, get as much help as you can, and know when it's time for a break. Find ways to take up offers of help whenever you can; there's no reason to be proud when a little time off can ease the stress and help you to feel more relaxed in your parenting role. You can do it!

Dealing with multiples

In this chapter, I've equipped you with the emotional skills you need to parent your toddler, and explored how you and your partner can work together *and* have alone time. But what happens when you're dealing with multiples and everything is times two, three, or even four?

Get help, help, help. Whether you need extra help from your partner, your parents, your extended community, or hired help – make sure you get the support you need. Taking care of multiples is a lot of work, requiring a tremendous amount of Energy from your backpack. Until you teach your toddlers basic life skills, such as dressing, feeding and toilet-training, you're doing it *all*, times two, three or even four. Take heart. Because you are teaching these skills multiple times, you learn quickly what works and what doesn't. You're constantly getting practice and honing your skills. Think of it as an intensive parenting course where you gain the experience to lead the class! And don't forget that precious 'me' and 'we' time.

◆ **Energy**

> ### *For parents of multiples, adopted children, and siblings close in age*
>
> Throughout the book, I will be pointing out when and where to modify my suggestions based on your special circumstances.

2

Working parents

This issue has earned the right to its own chapter because now, more than ever before, more and more couples are working and raising small children. This brings up all sorts of issues – not to mention emotions – from practical concerns about childcare and spending time with your toddler, to finding peace on an emotional level, as you come to terms with the idea that you won't be with him 24/7. This chapter offers my help on all these levels.

Shifting priorities

When you have children, your priorities shift. The date that you go back to work, the type of work you do, and the number of hours you work all come up for examination. Before children, you may have had a plan, but now you may feel differently. Work may have been your focus in the past; however, with children in the house you may find that it is no longer the be-all and end-all. Your focus is on your little ones.

Take a good look at your situation. Perhaps you can work part-time or a shorter number of hours per day. Perhaps you can work flexibly, so you are around for more of your child's waking hours. It may also be possible to downsize, so that you don't have to work at all. Or the reality may also be that your commitments mean that you *must* work full time.

Whatever your situation, thinking it through and making peace with your decision is crucial so that you can focus on your toddler and what he needs for his development, rather than being stuck in guilt that results in overindulgent parenting and poor peace of mind. It's a matter of balance. You need to figure out how to work, get your toddler's needs met, and have time as a family. It can be done – it simply takes creativity, planning and structure.

I worked once with a very young couple with small children. They owned a coffee shop with a children's activity centre. He went to the shop every day and worked long hours. She stayed home and took care of the shop's accounts. The kids bounced between the two places with no set routine and very little interaction with their parents. I had them switch jobs for a few days. Not only did that give them each a new respect for what the other did, but it helped them to get on the same page in terms of what was important for their kids. He saw the importance of not keeping them at the shop too late, as it made them cranky when they didn't have a set bedtime. They needed routines, rules and boundaries, and discipline when the rules were broken.

They also realised that they needed to create time to do things together as a family. They didn't have the money or time to spend on trips, so they became very imaginative, and had a great time playing together in their garden. They created more balance between work and being together, which worked really well once they got their priorities straight.

As a working parent, you have to be really good at time management. You have to able to juggle five balls at once. You have to be able to realise what needs to sit on your plate and not give into the urge to keep filling up that plate. You have to become an adult who says 'no' to things that are being asked of you.

And, in order to do that, you have to recognise what's important to you – and what's not. Is it having a house that looks like it has come straight from the pages of a magazine? A garden that is perfect? Or is it having time for fun with your toddler? Getting clear on what matters to you will help you to know which balls you need to juggle.

> ### What really matters to you?
>
> You only have 24 hours in a day. Get clear on your priorities and be realistic, so that you can make a schedule that matches. Talk to your partner about what kind of family life you want to have, and how to make that happen – starting now. It may mean letting certain things go to have time for what truly matters.

Routine is your friend

Working parents in particular always ask me how to manage a schedule with a toddler. Time with your children is so precious, as you have a limited number of hours each morning and night – if any at all. A set schedule actually gives you more time with your kids. Preparation and organisation is half the battle.

I helped my neighbour, who is a working mum with a three-year-old and a six-year-old. Every night she would come home, open her fridge, and try to decide what to make for her kids. Just trying to figure it out wasted half an hour, causing crabbiness all around. I helped her to come up with a menu for the full week. Now, on Saturday she sits down, looks at her budget, goes through her cookbooks, and comes up with a plan for the week. She makes her list and then goes to the supermarket. If she knows it's going to be a crazy week at work, she even cooks one or two meals on Sunday and freezes them. It's cost-effective, healthy and homemade – yummy.

Having a schedule also helps toddlers understand that although Mummy and Daddy go off to work, when they come home, it's family time. Toddlers don't understand the concept of work, but they can understand that their parents go to a place they *call* work. And when they come home, they get to be together. I can't overstress the importance of routine in your lives, so as your first priority, you'll need to create one that you can all live within (see pages 225-228).

Guilt and working mums

The majority of working mums to whom I speak say the same thing – no matter what job they do, they feel guilty. They feel guilty because they feel they're missing out on key experiences in their toddler's life. Women who choose to work might not carry the same baggage, because they have consciously made the decision to do so; however, women who *have* to work and would rather be at home may have a more difficult time because they feel like they don't have a choice.

If you can relate to this, think about what your work does for your family. Does it put bread and butter on the table and a keep a roof over your head? Accepting your circumstances frees up your energy to focus on work at work and on your kids at home. You need to come to a place of acceptance, so you can begin to feel better about your circumstances. Of course there will be times you feel short-changed, but refocusing on the time you can spend together will help to balance it out.

Some things remain a fact: you're not going to be there during working hours, and right now you simply can't change that. It doesn't mean that circumstances won't change, but it is what it is for the time being. Finding a way to make peace with that is what will allow you to experience less guilt. Finding more harmony and enjoying the time that you do have with your younger ones allows you to enjoy your role as a parent. Having those fun experiences goes a long way to helping you find the balance you need to parent well.

You've also got to learn to let go of certain things as well. A big one for many working parents is not being around when their kids are sick. They feel that they should be looking after them if they're not well. Again, it's about recognising the reality of your life and accepting it. You may feel a tug on your heartstrings, but you also need to realise that your job is making it possible to keep afloat, and that's important, too.

Mums worry, 'am I doing any damage by not being around in the toddler years?' I truly believe that as long as your carer is responsive, and meets the needs of your toddler on every level, there is no damage being done. I know this for a fact, from my time as a nanny and spending years working alongside professional women who were on the road.

In particular, parents question whether the two hours a day that you see your child during the week and the 24 waking hours you have to spend with him over the weekend are enough during the toddler years. The truth is that if that's all the time you have, that's enough – as long as he's getting your attention when you're home. He's getting you and what you bring to your parenting – your values, your humour, your loving ways. You have to grow into that skin and feel comfortable with it. And I believe that you only come to terms with it through doing it and seeing that your child is actually OK.

Beyond guilt

◆ Instead of focusing on all the time you are not there, ask yourself 'What are the little things that I could do when I'm home that it would feel good to give?'

◆ What is your toddler into right now and how can you enjoy that with him? Dinosaurs? Get some dinosaur books out of the library and take a trip to a museum on the weekend. Cooking? Get a mummy-and-me cookbook and try a recipe this weekend.

◆ Put boundaries on your home time: limit work calls, texts and emails – except for emergencies or after bedtime.

◆ Maximise together time on weekends.

◆ Make exceptions to bedtime on certain days – such as Friday or Saturday evenings – making them half an hour later so that you can have more time together. But don't get into a habit of doing this every day. You know what your toddler is like if he doesn't get enough sleep. When you weigh it up, it's not worth it.

◆ Can you take time off when your toddler is sick? Tending to him when he's ill might make you feel that you are there when it's most important.

A toddler is a toddler

As issues come up with your toddler – such as separation anxiety, tantrums and pushing boundaries – it's important to remind yourself that every other toddler is going through the same things. It's *not* because you're away during the day. It's *not* because you are working. It's because she's a toddler and these are the issues in the toddler years. As a working parent, it's really important to realise that when your toddler goes through these things, there is a toddler with a stay-at-home mum who's going through the same things right now, too.

This is very important to bear in mind, or hurtful guilt can lead you to find excuses to succumb to negative behaviour – such as not disciplining your toddler, or overindulging with toys. In these circumstances, being a working parent becomes an excuse: 'I do what I do because I feel guilty.' If this sounds like you, it's time to take a good look at yourself in the mirror. If you have to work, you have to work. But what kind of parent are you going to be when you are home?

The biggest issue I come across with working parents is trying to substitute material things for time. *Things* cannot be substituted for time – for nurturing, caring and emotional connection. What's replacing *you*? There shouldn't be anything replacing you apart from a very competent carer who is able to meet the needs of your child while you're at work. There is only one of you, and that is what your child needs – you. This one Mummy and this one Daddy.

Only you know whether you are giving your child toys as a treat. Is it because you were somewhere new and saw something wonderful – or because you feel bad that you are away? You know how to tell? If you bring back something *every* time that you go. *Every* time you go. If you know in your heart that what you are doing is not acceptable, but you find excuses to allow it to be OK because you work, then you know you have to change.

The same is true about failing to put in place proper rules, boundaries and discipline. If you know, deep down, that you are not giving your toddler the structure she needs, please read the chapter on discipline and get started on being consistent on rules (see page 99).

Re-entry issues

There is one special circumstance that working parents encounter, which other parents don't: misbehaviour the minute you come in the door to get your attention. That's the biggest issue that I've seen. Everybody wants to see their toddler running to the door in excitement when they come home. Because that's how you feel, too – excited to be with her. But then you get the cold shoulder – or worse. Working parents report that they almost feel like they are being punished by their toddler because they've been at work all day.

Of course it feels bad when your little one treats you like this. But if you feel apologetic for working and pacify that behaviour, you are only setting yourself up for ongoing problems. What works is to be yourself, stick to your rules, and let your toddler find her balance with you.

Get down on the floor

One of the best things you can do to ease re-entry and reconnect with your toddler is to get down on the floor and doing something that she wants to do. She may just want to climb on you, and that's fine as well. I've seen many a Mum come in from work, drop her bags, lie on the floor in the living room and let the kids crawl all over her. It's a time for kissing and holding and 'What did you do today?' before you start dinner, make that last work phone call or check your texts.

If you've been having trouble with misbehaviour when you come in the door, giving your undivided attention first thing can help with that, especially if you make it fun.

Stay connected

If you are away, keep connected. Skype or call – maybe on a lunch or dinner break. Find out what they've been up to. Why? Because it will help *you*. Your kids are fine! They're out there playing. They're getting on with their day. In all my years of nannying, I never had a four-year-old say to me, 'Jo Jo, I was just wondering if Mummy's OK while she's in that meeting.' Your kids are fine. It's important to stay connected for *you*, so that you can feel comfortable in the knowledge that she is fine. Can you come home at lunch and see your child for 30 minutes? Great! If not, call. Your peace of mind is important.

Quality time

I often say to Mums that if you can give consistent, focused attention for only 30 minutes, it's better than being random and giving a minute here and there over two hours. That's what we mean by 'quality time'. When we use the word 'quality', we mean that it's fulfilling. We feel that we both have enjoyed the time. It doesn't need to be filled up with something that's really active. I can have quality time with my child by doing nothing, just being. It's our undivided attention that's key.

To do this you need to learn how to be in the moment – to concentrate on enjoying where you are right now, rather than thinking about what you're going to do tomorrow or in an hour. I don't think you can stop those thoughts from happening but, when they do, you can notice and say to yourself, 'Let me just concentrate on the now.'

Finding the right childcare

Of course, one of the most helpful ways to deal with your feelings about working is to find the best childcare situation for you and your family. You can use a relative, hire a nanny or childminder, or find a playgroup, preschool or day nursery. When you know your child's needs are being met at every level, it's easier to have peace of mind.

Here are some factors to consider:

◆ Do you need full- or part-time care?

◆ Do you want your child cared for in your home or somewhere else?

◆ Would you like her to be alone, with one other child, or in a group?

◆ What's your budget?

Your answers to these questions will determine which option fits your situation. Here are my thoughts on the typical options, adapted from *Confident Baby Care*. For help with easing your toddler's transition to one of these options, take a look at my 'Goody Bag' suggestion on page 44.

A LITTLE HELP TO FIND THE RIGHT CARER

Once you know what kind of situation you are looking for, a good place to start the search for the right place or person is through the government's website (www.childcarefinder.direct.gov.uk). Once you have the name of a centre or childminder, you can then go to OFSTED – the Office for Standards in Education, Children's Services, and Skills (www.ofsted.gov.uk), to review inspection reports. They do not, however, have recommendations for nannies.

Relatives as caregivers

You may be in a situation where your parents or other relatives are caring for your toddler all or part of the day. It goes without saying that you need to be on the same page as much as possible regarding discipline, diet, sleep and virtually every single other aspect of your child's care and upbringing. This is particularly important if you all live under the same roof.

It really is crucial that you have these conversations, because looking after a grandchild, for instance, does not give a grandparent licence to do things their way, and ignore your parenting decisions. Make sure you are clear about how you expect her to deal with your toddler. Any relationship that you're having with a person looking after your children has got to be one of the best relationships you have. After all, she's looking after your child. Use the 'Talking Box' technique (see page 27), if you need help.

One family with whom I worked was a classic example of parent and carer not being on the same page. The carer was an aunt who felt that because she took care of her nieces all day for free, it gave her the right to make up the rules and not support her sister's (their Mum's) ideals. Not only was it very confusing for the children, but it made it incredibly difficult for Mum because she was with her children for less time than that her sister was.

I helped Mum understand that the one with the expectations and rules should always be the parent, while the carer should always be the one supporting those clear expectations. That is crucial for the well-being of the children. This doesn't mean that the carer never gets an opportunity to suggest something – in fact, she may well have experience that the parents don't. But, ultimately, at the end of the day, it's her job to back up the parent. These issues generally come up more with relatives, because if a hired caregiver isn't doing what you want, you can simply find someone else.

In this situation, the mother finally decided that, despite her attempts to communicate her rules, her sister was not willing to respect them. So she arranged to work part-time so that she could assert her way of doing things with her kids.

If, like this Mum, you are having issues with a relative in care-giving, there's probably a lack of respect in the adult relationship. The relationships should never be about winning and being in control, but about mutual respect and compromise – mutual respect in understanding what's important for the wellbeing of the child involved. In the case above, that simply wasn't happening, so Mum had to find a different solution.

On the other hand, make sure you're not taking advantage of your relative. Don't wear her out! Be clear about the hours she's minding. Just because she's volunteered to help, don't take it for granted. Show some appreciation. It wouldn't hurt to come back with a little card or gift to show how thankful you are. Think of ways you can help her, as she is helping you.

Nanny or nanny-share

If you can afford it, nothing beats the one-on-one home care a nanny gives. Come on now, what did you expect me to say? Nannies are experienced in giving toddlers 100 percent of what they need, including stimulating activities, as well as taking care of the needs of any other children. She's been checked by the Criminal Record Bureau (CRB) and certified in CPR. I would suggest you look at a nanny who has the 12-hour paediatric first-aid certificate. I also suggest you look for a nanny who is OFSTED-registered, as you can claim money back for childcare. And if you get along well, she'll do the local dry-cleaning run, too!

Some people with one toddler find another family with a toddler and share a nanny. Either way, it's crucially important to find an experienced nanny. I always say, 'Pay peanuts, get monkeys.' Don't be stingy when it comes to your kids. The finances of domestic help still seem to be dinner-table talk. One is not in Morocco bartering for a leather handbag. This is about your children and you need to feel completely confident about the choices you make.

There are two ways to find a great nanny – word of mouth and reputable nanny agencies. And there are two kinds of nannies: those who are formally trained and have certificates, and those who have had lots of experience in the field. It's a matter of personal choice but, either way, be sure to check all references.

When interviewing a nanny, you need to pay attention to how she interacts with your child, but it's important that you feel good about her, too. You need a nanny who can do what is required, but also share a good relationship with you. For this reason, it's important always to have more than one interview – to be sure that the two of you can gel.

Any person coming into your life to spend 12 hours (or more) a day with your child should be able to answer a few questions to your satisfaction. These include:

◆ What's her experience with toddlers?

◆ What's her opinion on nutrition? Does she cook? What's her favourite dish?

◆ Does she class herself as sociable? What are her hobbies?

- Would she be interested in meeting with other nannies and Mums so that your toddler will spend time with other children?

- Is her timetable flexible? Can she do occasional babysitting?

- What are her attributes?

- Is she timely?

- Has she looked after multiples, if appropriate?

- Does she like travelling and is she open to the possibility of going on holiday with you if you would like her to?

- What are her thoughts on discipline?

- Is this a short- or long-term assignment for her?

- What (if any) is her religion and how does that play into yours and her work as a nanny?

- If this is a nanny-share, could she give you a verbal example of what a daily routine would be?

- What does she like most about the toddler years?

- Is there anything additional she'd love to share?

Ultimately, you are looking for somebody you can welcome as part of your family because this is an incredibly important, intimate situation. I've had amazing relationships with the families that I've worked with and keep in contact with them even now, 20 years on. Trust your gut.

Get clear on the rules. Are you going to have her on a three-month trial? Will she be paid monthly or weekly? Is it necessary to sign a confidentiality clause? Be clear about her holiday entitlements and any other perks. Remember, you are hiring a nanny for the reasons why she does the job, not for what she can get. Try to get all the issues on the table in advance. Write up a contract including the needs of the child and what you expect, so there are no surprises down the line. If you use an agency, they will take care of these legal procedures. There will, however, be an introduction fee plus an added fee of one month of the nanny's salary.

Hopefully the rest is history. With her experience and support, and your direction and willingness to learn, it's a win-win situation.

Daycare centre or nursery

If you're considering this option, look at every daycare centre or nursery within your home or work vicinity. Check out exactly what the staff-child ratio is. Make sure they're licensed so that all the safety issues are taken care of. Are things nice and clean? Is it a happy, colourful environment? You don't want a sober, grey environment. Do the other children seem happy? You want to feel good about taking your child there and know that she's going to be happy there. Get references from other parents.

There will undoubtedly be a routine that you can see in action, but find out the basics:

- Do you provide food or do they?

- What are the ages of the children?

- What activities do they do? Do they offer a balance of stimulating activities and play, crafts and quiet time?

- What educational toys are available?

- What's the educational philosophy of the director? Does there seem to be good communication between the people who work there? How will they communicate with you about what's happened with your toddler that day?

- Does your child have to be potty-trained to be admitted?

In the end, just like when you walk into a house that feels great and you know you want to live there, you'll want to experience a 'feeling' when you walk into a childcare facility. You'll want to *know* it's right for your child. For this reason, I would recommend always visiting unexpectedly – not just on 'open day' – so you can see it in motion when they're not expecting visitors.

Take into account that with any sort of communal childcare, when one child gets a cold or another bug, they all get it. And, generally, you can't bring a sick toddler to daycare or nursery. So, you are going to have to stay home to care for him. New parents often don't expect that, but it is a reality of institutional care.

Free care is available

Throughout the UK, 12.5 hours a week of free early education, for 38 weeks a year, is available for this age group. All sorts of private and public options qualify – nursery schools and classes, day nurseries, playgroups and childminder networks.

THE HANDOVER TECHNIQUE

Whether you use a sitter, childminder, nursery or daycare, I believe strongly that you always need to have a solid form of communication between you and your carer. You can talk, or keep a notebook, or fill out a form, whatever is easiest for you both. This is where you pass along information about your toddler that the other person might need to know – for example, she hasn't had lunch and she's been off all morning, she went to sleep later last night and she's a bit crabby, she's upset about not seeing her Dad this morning. Anything that affects your child and her well-being and health is worth mentioning.

I call it the 'Handover' technique. It helps with the transition because the person coming in gets up to speed quickly and has a better idea of how to interact with your toddler. It brings you both onto the same page and that's where you need to be.

Childminder

Another option is a childminder. This is usually a woman alone or with an assistant who cares for a few babies and/or toddlers in her home. Make sure you see all of her credentials to be sure that she has the proper safety precautions, educational toys, child–adult ratios, etc. In other words, you want to be sure that she and her house are equipped to safely meet the needs of the children in her care.

As you would with a daycare centre or nursery, ask:

◆ Exactly what do you do with the children all day? Is there a timetable or routine?

◆ Can I have a diary of what my toddler does each week to track her progress?

◆ Do I provide food or do you?

◆ Are you open during holidays or will I need to find alternative help? What is your sick policy?

◆ How many children do you look after during the day? At what times? What ages are they? What does the law say about that? How many kids are you authorised to have? She should know the laws and relate them to you.

◆ What experience and training do you have, and what about your assistants?

◆ How recently was your home inspected?

Make sure that you also notice what she's like as a person. As with a nanny, character is important, and a good relationship between you is key. It's your prerogative as a parent to ask as many and whatever questions you like. No childcarer should ever feel offended. Most parents will tell me that they go with their gut feeling. So if it feels right…

THE GOODY BAG

One great way to encourage a successful transition is to create a goody bag. Here's what to do:

◆ **Get a goody bag and fill it with little age-appropriate toys that your toddler loves. The bag lives at Grandma's (or the childminder's, etc.) and every time your toddler goes, he gets his goody bag.**

◆ **This is particularly useful because it allows your child to play with his familiar toys in what is perhaps an unfamiliar environment. This is particularly good for two- to three-year-olds!**

Other carer issues

There are plenty of potential issues that can crop up over the coming years, and it's a good idea to be prepared for them. Bearing them in mind can make it that much easier to find solutions.

Feeling jealous of your carer

I can't tell you how many working Mums have asked me how to deal with the jealousy they feel that someone else gets to have fun with their child. It's completely natural to feel frustrated that you spend long hours working and your carer gets the good stuff. However, it's not a healthy place to be. If you feel this way, it's important to have a conversation with yourself. First of all, jealousy and envy are two different things. Are you jealous that your child is becoming close to somebody else? Does that make you feel insignificant in your child's life? In that case, it's important to identify what you are in your child's life and recognise that this cannot be replaced. Or are you envious of the time that your carer gets to have with your child? That may draw home the importance of finding more ways to enjoy the time you *do* have together.

Feeling jealousy or envy will not create a good working environment for any carer looking after your child. Rather than focusing on her, work on finding that wholeness in yourself and doing what is fulfilling with your child. Anything else doesn't fit the reality of the situation that you're in right now. It's about how you think as well. Be grateful that you have someone to look after your child while you're in your current circumstances. Look at the positives, otherwise you'll drive yourself insane.

Inconsistent discipline

Another issue I often hear is 'My child behaves with my carer and not with me.' If this is the case for you, there's a message in there! First of all, pay attention to what your carer is doing – and how. There may be much to learn from someone who is experienced in the job of dealing with toddlers, and, more importantly, your toddler will respond better if he's getting the same messages both at home and with his carer.

Next, take things on board and get on with it. You may find that you are allowing your toddler to get away with things because you are not around. You think, 'I've got a couple of hours with her. Discipline is the last thing I want to be doing.' But the reality is that unless you create rules and boundaries and stick to them with discipline, you are not giving your toddler what she most needs. Consistent discipline makes her feel secure, and her behaviour will improve immeasurably. That makes the time you have with her all the better.

The choice is yours

You may have no choice but to work full-time when your child is young – and that's tough. But you still have a choice to make the best of the time you have. You still have a choice about how you wake up and how you deal with things – how you go about your day and what you do when you come home. You may be in a particular set of circumstances, but you still can focus on the choices you do have and the situations you can control. If you choose not to, then you choose to do nothing about it. I hope this chapter has given you some perspective on good choices and some tips on what you can control. The rest of the book has loads of tips and techniques to help as well. I know you can do it.

3

Your little person

Sometime after her first birthday and after she starts to walk, you'll come to recognise that your child is no longer a baby – mostly, perhaps, because babies don't have screaming meltdowns! Maybe you got some crying when she was a baby, but not like this. You tell your child she can't have whatever it is she wants, and suddenly she's on the floor kicking around – and you see lungs on her like Pavarotti. There you are thinking: 'You've got to be joking', trying to convince yourself that this is not your daughter. But it can actually be scary for some parents to see their child have a temper tantrum for the first time. I have seen parents react in all different ways, from wanting to leave their child on the floor to shaking with embarrassment.

But the signs of toddlerhood aren't all that scary. What about when she does something like pull a funny face that makes you laugh? She realises she's making you laugh and does it again. She's understanding humour for the first time. What a great moment. Then comes the belly laugh ... contagious! Over these four years, your child will blossom into her own little being. She's already learned to walk (that's what makes her a toddler) and is learning to talk. Over the next few years, she'll be potty-trained, learn to dress herself, interact with other children, hold a pencil and draw, kick a ball ... and the list goes on and on.

This chapter explores the development stages your toddler will go through over the next four years, and includes my thoughts on temperament, gender differences, and the importance of teaching life skills during this phase of your child's life. At the end of the chapter you'll find a table of developmental milestones to use as a reference.

Your child's development depends upon you

As you think about your child's development, take some time to appreciate what a huge impact you have on your toddler. The brain is an incredibly complex organ with all kinds of parts that need to work smoothly together. Brain scientists tell us that it is through your relationship with your child and the experiences to which you expose him that his brain actually wires up and becomes connected. In other words, you actually shape your child's brain.

Interaction creates the wiring so that your child learns and develops emotionally, physically and mentally, especially during these crucial years from one to four.

This interaction is so important that I can tell instantly when there hasn't been enough of it in a household – for example, when I go into a home with a child who is two and a half or three, and his speech is delayed. This toddler and his parents haven't played enough together and his parents haven't talked enough to him. Unintentionally, these parents stopped something in this child's brain from connecting up. It's almost like the brain is like the stroke of a match and it doesn't light up if a parent or other caregiver doesn't spend a lot of time interacting with the child.

This can often be seen in bigger families, where the parents are spending so much time just keeping the household together that their toddler isn't getting the individual attention he needs to ignite these sparks. No matter what your family size, you need to understand that research shows that the key to healthy child development is the amount of time children spend with loving adults – having fun and learning experiences.

The tasks of toddlerhood

Besides being the time in which a great deal of brain-wiring occurs, the toddler years are all about:

◆ reaching for independence despite being physically unable to do all that he wants to

◆ learning to regulate emotions, particularly the negative ones (that's why discipline is so important at this stage)

◆ learning life skills through play and repetition

Your job is to provide the experiences and routines to promote healthy development, and that's why you need to keep your parenting backpack filled with *Confidence, Patience, Discipline, Perseverance, Energy, Commitment, Plan Ahead, Perspective* and *Humour*. Because it can be monotonous to say the same thing over and over again, until you're tired of your own voice – or to play Snakes and Ladders over and over, or say 'no' again and again. However, when you realise that through repetition you're actually helping your child to develop at a healthy rate, it becomes easier to carry on with the same relentless routine, because you understand why it's necessary.

◆ **Confidence**

◆ **Patience**

◆ **Discipline**

◆ **Perseverance**

◆ **Energy**

◆ **Commitment**

◆ **Plan Ahead**

◆ **Perspective**

◆ **Humour**

Understanding your child's temperament

Children's temperaments vary. Some are more active, others more reticent. Some are calm, some bold, others more fearful. Some have trouble with change and are more prone to stress, others love newness. Some are more wilful, others more willing to do what you want. There was a study done at Harvard University where people were tracked from birth through to adulthood. It found that each person's temperament was seen from the onset, hardwired in the brain and the autonomic nervous system. Midwives I work with don't need scientists to tell them this. They say you can tell a child's temperament from the minute he's born.

Parents of multiples are often aware of how different one is from the other. But how many times are parents surprised when their second child is different from the first? Why do you expect him to be the same? They may have the same DNA, but they've certainly got different temperaments, as the particular mix of Mum and Dad's genes show up.

An individual approach

What type of temperament does your child have? It's important to bear this in mind as you go through the different solutions I suggest for each situation you encounter during the toddler years. Understanding your child's temperament will help you know when to put your foot on the pedal and when to ease it off. Know that every child will have a meltdown, for instance. Some kids will adhere to the rules after just a warning, others will test, test, test. You adapt your response to your child's temperament.

Temperament can also affect development, with more risk-taking children pushing earlier to walk and climb, for example. That's why you'll see that I give wide age ranges for various behaviours. Because temperament is inborn, it's your job to understand and support whatever temperament your toddler has, rather than try to turn him into someone else. This is not to say that you don't encourage a shy child to interact, for example; it simply involves recognising that he may need more help in a new environment than a more outgoing kid.

If, for instance, your child has trouble in new situations, you'll want to take more time to help him feel comfortable with his surroundings and offer help: 'Let's go over together and say hello.' Or perhaps you have a child who retreats when he does something wrong and gets stubborn about re-engaging. You may need to help him by saying something like, 'Can you help me in the kitchen?' so he can see that you are inviting him back in.

The genetic link

Temperament is very genetic, so you may see yourself reflected in this little person –which can be both painful and funny. If you have a wilful temperament, you may be facing an equally strong child. Or, if you hang back, your child may, too. Remember when you were young and your mother said, 'Wait until you have your own child.'? Well, now you do and the shoe is on the other foot.

You need to be aware of the effect that this reflection of yourself is having on the way you respond to your child. Do you accept too much because you secretly enjoy his defiance? Do you push too hard because you don't want him to be shy like you? Your job is to separate out your preconditioned responses and ask yourself what your child needs to become a happy, high-functioning version of himself.

If your child has the genes of your partner, you've got to accept and work with that temperament, too – even if it's different from yours. If you've got a slow mover and you're a fast-paced person, give him a little more time in the morning to get ready, instead of being frustrated all the time. Don't try to force a square peg into a round hole. Parenting is never about control and force, because that's damaging.

Watch out for boxes!

While I understand that temperament exists, I feel strongly that we should not use it to put a child in a box – to be labelled 'the shy one' or 'the independent one'. This creates pigeonholes in your mind, limits her from developing her full potential, and may produce unnecessary tensions between siblings. Labels can also diminish a child's self-esteem. Toddlers get a lot  of reassurance from knowing that their parents believe they can accomplish something: 'You can do it! Come on!' Don't let labels get in the way of believing in your child and his abilities.

Above all, I want to encourage you strongly to observe and learn what's easy and difficult for your child. The more you pay attention to who your child is and what her challenges are, the more you can support her development throughout her childhood. I can't suggest strongly enough that you need to observe your toddler, to know what he's like, to understand what he needs. Parents complain that they haven't got time, but when I ask them to tell me things about their toddler, some definitely know and others don't. The truth is that if you don't know, you haven't made time to make it a priority.

The importance of observation

Keen observation is critical because toddlers are emotionally volatile and can really test your boundaries. I have learned much from sitting on the sidelines and observing as well as being involved. I can't tell you how much less frustrated or worried you'll be if you accept your child for who she is and work alongside that. Watching and understanding your toddler helps you to become more in tune with her, which enables you to be able to balance emotion with logic. If you deal emotionally with every issue your toddler has during these years, you'll be a wreck and so will your child. There's got to be some logic along with your feelings – your mind and heart working together to create a middle ground of common sense. From there you can deal more calmly with whatever your child does – and not take it so personally.

QUESTIONS FOR OBSERVING YOUR TODDLER

Learn to read your child, and become in tune with her. Here are some things to pay attention to:

- **Is she particularly sensitive to sounds?**
- **Does she have trouble with transitions?**
- **How well does she interact with other people?**
- **Does she hold herself back? Or is she one of the first to jump in?**
- **In a group of toddlers, what does she do when someone takes something she wants?**
- **How talkative is she? Does she primarily express herself with words or with actions?**
- **When you say no, how does she deal with frustration?**
- **Is she stubborn or is her personality more easy-go-lucky?**

Boys versus girls

I was once asked if I noticed a big difference between toddler boys and girls. While there are subtle differences in how they play, overall I would say that toddlers differ more in temperament than by gender. I've seen very passive little boys, and I've seen really wild, rambunctious little girls. Based on my experience, I've noted a few gender generalisations:

- Boys are more emotionally needy than girls when it comes to play. They tend to require more interaction in general – and more of your attention. Girls don't necessarily need you to be as involved. However, this doesn't mean that you should give her less attention.

- Boys will make noises more often than girls while playing – like car and monster growling noises. Girls don't, really.

Again, I am in favour of understanding and supporting your toddler in becoming himself, rather than making gender generalisations. Everywhere we look, we see conditioning – boys should play with cars and girls with dolls, for instance. It's important to help toddlers, regardless of their gender, to broaden their imaginations, to develop their nurturing and caring side, and creatively make those experiences fun. In the 1940s you would never have given your toddler boy a Hoover to play with, but now we do. And we now see adverts where girls are playing with trains. All toddlers will benefit from freedom to explore whatever's on offer, and develop different parts of their brains and personalities in the process.

Developmental stages

One of your most crucial jobs as a parent is to understand the unique needs of your child at each developmental stage of the toddler years. Knowing what to expect can help you to guide your child to reach her potential. However, while it is important to refer to the table at the end of the chapter as a loose guideline, don't get caught up in worrying about whether your child holds a crayon at the same time your friend's child does or when he talks in sentences. Every child develops at his own pace.

Unless there is a medical issue – and as long as you are providing the kinds of experiences you'll learn in Part II – the stages of your child's development will happen naturally. As the doctors say, as long as your child is developing within the age range on the table, everything is likely to be fine. However, if you are seeing a six-month to one-year gap between what your child is capable of doing and what is perceived to be the norm for the average child, be sure to consult your GP.

I feel so strongly about not comparing obsessively that I even hesitated to include a list of developmental stages in this book. I'm appalled at how a child's development is used by some parents to gloat over others. Equally, however, it is important to have this list as a rough gauge, so that you can know when to consult your GP or health visitor if your child's development is significantly delayed.

One of the other reasons why understanding the developmental stages of toddlerhood is important is to enable you to recognise what your child's brain is capable and incapable of doing. For example, he's unlikely to be able to kick a ball at 18 months. That awareness does not, however, prevent us from starting the process by having him play with a ball. We know that a toddler is not going to be able to do a complicated puzzle straightaway, because his brain has not sufficiently developed to do so; however, that shouldn't stop us from doing it with him! Shadowing him is just as fun and he'll learn loads from the experience.

Toddlers learn over time. No matter how high your expectations are, you can't force development. You can't force how the brain grows and everything connects. It happens when it's ready. You can, however, stimulate your child to develop at the appropriate time, and that's where the fun comes in.

A lightbulb moment

As you know, repetition is key. You read stories over and over and then one day you open up the book and he already knows what's on the page because he's memorised it. You've stimulated him to learn a new trick, and set him firmly on the road to understanding language and reading! During the toddler years, you'll be doing lots of things to build a foundation for developmental milestones that show up weeks, months, or even years later. This can be really frustrating for parents, because you'll often feel like your toddler isn't getting anywhere! You show him how to put on his shoes over and over again, and he just can't get it. That doesn't mean you don't continue to show him, but that you have Patience and recognise that his development is not yet there. When you do it over and over, his brain begins to understand and remember. Then one day it clicks in.

- ◆ **Patience**
- ◆ **Perseverance**
- ◆ **Commitment**

Being realistic about development can also help you to have more patience with all the teaching and coaching you must do. When you know that you actually help develop your child's brain – making it able to learn tasks – it gives you the stamina to carry on showing and telling because you're feeling great about your involvement.

For parents of adoptive children

In terms of developmental stages, you may find your child is a bit behind if she was neglected or abused in infancy, or adopted as a toddler. Use the guidelines in this chapter to see where your child is emotionally, physically and mentally, and ensure that you have realistic expectations. Then begin to provide a lot of stimulation. The great thing is that through all the time and attention you pay, you'll be bonding even more strongly. If you have any concerns, see your GP, and don't hesitate to contact any one of the wonderful support groups for parents in your situation (see Further Help page 330).

Development of multiples and children who are very close in age

I recently worked with a family who had a four-year-old and twin three-year-olds. As I told the parents, even when your kids are born close together – nine months or a year apart – or are multiples, you still have to identify where each is mentally, physically and emotionally, and support their individuality.

So, for example, if you have a three-year-old and a two-year-old, you'll have to make sure you have your oldest child's skills up to a three-year-old level. It's all too easy to keep one behind for the other! Do different kinds of activities with your two-year-old than you do with his sibling. You'll also need to avoid comparing kids and using another child's achievements to egg your little one on. Saying 'Come on, your brother can do that' is very bad for the self-esteem of the child being pushed, and sets up sibling rivalry.

Even though you may have become comfortable managing your multiples as a unit – with the same clothes, games and activities – there will come a time when allowing each to express her individuality becomes important. Of course there will be many times when you must do things simultaneously, with all of them together; however, you want to ensure that you give each child individual attention and the ability to express her preferences in clothes, food, toys and everything else. It's fine to be the same as infants but, as toddlers – especially as they reach three or four – each needs ways to be unique. Although it's easy to dress your kids all the same, let them be different. This will encourage individuality and the expression of their own unique personal characteristics. Concentrate on the inner of each child, not the outer.

Balancing the developmental stages of toddlers and older siblings

If you have more than one child, it's very important to understand that your children are different ages and should be treated as such. For example, your toddler may want to be involved in what the seven- or eight-year-old is doing, and you may just give in and allow it. In fact, I've seen parents turn to the older child because he's more mature and rational and say, 'Oh, just let her be involved'.

This puts enormous pressure on your older child. We tend to ask older siblings to exercise patience with toddler siblings; however, we do need to balance this with the older child's need for independence and uninterrupted play. He may have been focusing on creating something – a sandcastle, for instance – while your toddler is bulldozing everything. While it is definitely easier to encourage your toddler's involvement, it simply isn't fair. Sometimes it is important to take your toddler away and make it clear that this 'game' isn't appropriate for him, and give him something else to do. If he pitches a fit, simply ignore it. Only if he's destroying the tower after you said 'no' would I discipline him.

Establishing a balance

Of course, you also need to encourage things that your older child can do with the younger sibling. It's all about balance. Perhaps your older child is painting and your toddler says, 'I want to do!' You can get her some felt-tips and put her somewhere she can't get her hands on the other one's stuff.

Remember that toddlers have no major impulse control and we have to expect them to act impulsively from time to time. Part of what they are learning is to control their impulses. Sometimes toddlers intentionally want what the older child has. In this case, you need to be the boundary line for your older child. It's a matter of fairness.

Mini me, the caretaker

Parents, please think carefully before you put an unrealistic burden on your older child to be the caretaker of your toddler. I'm not saying that every now and then you can't say, 'Please go get me the toys for your sister...'; however, your older sibling is not meant to be a crutch for you. 'Watch your brother for a minute' is very different from 'Go entertain him for an hour while I work on my computer.' Remember, he's not your babysitter – yet.

Teaching life skills

A life skill is a practical skill that your child will learn to become more competent in doing things independently. These years are all about helping toddlers learn the basic life skills: eating with utensils, using a cup, dressing and undressing, going to the potty, brushing teeth and hair, verbally expressing what they need and want, playing independently for short periods of time, opening and closing doors, tidying up – the list goes on and on.

When you teach your toddler life skills, you are moving him from one step on the ladder of human development to the next, helping him to grow mentally, emotionally and physically.

Teaching life skills creates a wonderful sense of achievement for your toddler. It really is a big deal for a child to be able to put on his shoes and pick up the toys and put them in a bucket. All the things we take for granted are big deals for a child when he can actually do them himself.

Your child will give you signs when he's ready to learn particular life skills. The clearest one is when he says, 'I want to do that'. Take him seriously – he's telling the truth. Equally, he may say nothing and just try on his own, without you being aware. This may result in a big mess to clear up, but it's a sign of independence – and a sure sign that he's ready for something new. Try to bear that in mind as he squirts lotion all over the bathroom! Rather than getting angry, understand he wants to learn. In that circumstance, for instance, have him help you clean up, and then show him how to put lotion on himself. And then put the container where he can't get at it without your permission!

Breaking life skills into parts

As much as toddlers want to be independent – and may say 'me do' or something similar – it's obvious that we have to teach them how to do almost everything.

The trick is to enable them. Allow your toddler to try even if she can't do it, and set her up for success by breaking apart the task in hand. For example, she might not be able to do up her buttons yet, but she can learn to pull off her shirt. Almost all children learn to take clothes off before on. It's just easier.

Secondly, coach him through what she needs to do. If she's trying to put on her shoe and can't get her heel in, say: 'Stand up and push your heel down' while you do it for her. And don't forget the encouragement. A smile stretches a long way. So does a 'you can do it'.

Teaching her the ropes

What about things she can't quite manage? Have her do it with you. Let her brush her hair and then you do it. Or put your hand on hers and do it together. Once she's mastered something – eating with a spoon, for example – move on to the next skill: eating with a fork. Don't wait until she's a particular age. Move on to the next thing and know that if she's not doing it well, she just needs more time to get there. You'll find my specific tips for teaching life skills throughout this book – particularly in Part III: A Day in the Life of a Toddler, when I take you from waking your child up in the morning to helping him stay in bed at night.

You can increase your child's ability to learn life skills through games and activities. For example, threading beads on a string helps with hand-eye coordination and pincer control for eating, buttoning, etc. In Chapter 6, you'll learn lots of activities that will help with life skills.

Remember: It's faster to do almost anything yourself, but your toddler will never learn if you have this mindset. Take the time up front to teach him. He needs that from you.

How to talk so toddlers will learn

♦ Be clear in your instruction. Don't mumble.
♦ Encourage with enthusiasm and be affectionate with your language. The more you sound excited about what you're asking her to do, the more willing she'll be to do it.

Frustration is part of learning

You may see your toddler get frustrated at his inability to do something. That's a good sign! Frustration leads to determination not to quit. He really wants to do this! In his mind, he's already there. He knows what he wants to achieve, but doesn't have the motor skills quite yet.

Coach him to calm down: 'If you get really angry and go *Ahhhh*, you can't put that through, OK? So just calm down and try again.' To help him zone back into focus, I speak more slowly, use eye contact, become even more specific in my instructions, and encourage him to go right back and try again. That way I defuse the anger that is a result of his frustration, so he can focus and finish. When he finally gets it, the experience of success will be a breakthrough for all.

Practise new skills with your toddler and then let him try himself. If he tries a few times and gets frustrated, you have to look again and assess the situation. Can you do part of it for him and let him finish? When he finally gets it, whether it's today or next week, he'll experience such a sense of success! It's a breakthrough.

Take the pressure off

You have to be out the door in 20 minutes or you'll get stuck in a traffic jam, and you decide that this is the day to teach your child how to button up her coat. That's not good timing, is it? It's like having an important meeting in 30 minutes, and having to create a press kit for 20 people when you don't know how to work the copier. As an adult, you may work well under this kind of pressure, but for a toddler it's too much stress.

You've got to be in a non-pressured situation when you're teaching life skills because you don't want to pressure your little one. To learn any life skill, your toddler needs dexterity and that takes concentration and practice. When a child is being rushed with 'Come on, come on, come on', it is simply unfair. She will already experience frustration in trying to achieve a particular skill because she knows what she wants to do, but her hands won't do it. If you're getting frustrated and angry with her on top of that because you have to be somewhere else, you're just adding fuel to the fire.

♦ **Plan ahead**

TIPS FOR TEACHING LIFE SKILLS

◆ **Do it when you see a moment in your day when you have 30 to 45 minutes to spare – on the weekends, in the afternoon, whenever you see a window.**

◆ **Make sure your toddler is well rested and fed; he'll be more open to learning.**

◆ **Adopt a sense of excitement about learning something new.**

◆ **Encourage effort.**

◆ **Get out your backpack. You'll need it!**

Helping your child learn

Besides repetition and coaching, patience and perseverance, what can you do to help your child master the basic life skills she needs to know between now and when she goes to school?

◆ *Offer lots of reassurance.* Say things like 'You can do it!' as she's trying something new. If she doesn't get it, remind her that she soon will!

◆ *Use plenty of praise.* It really helps her overcome frustration. In fact, scientists have discovered that the brain uses praise as a way of deciding what to carry on doing. If it doesn't receive positive feedback, it 'decides' that the activity in question is not worth the bother. So when your toddler is learning something new, pour on the 'well done' and be detailed in your praise.

◆ *Don't praise her for things she's already learned.* Too much praise has been shown to create an over-inflated sense of self in the long run. If she's been undressing for a while now and you want to help her learn to dress, compliment her when she puts the shirt over her head rather than taking it off.

◆ *Don't rescue too soon.* It's natural to want to prevent your toddler from getting stuck or making a mistake, but it's actually how she learns.

Remember how many times she fell before she learned to walk? If she's in physical danger, of course you need to intervene; however, when you jump in and fasten the snap after she's been trying for half a second, you are interfering with her ability to do it for herself. Watch for a bit and see if she can get it. Then, if needed, show her again or do it with her. Not rescuing is particularly hard when you can see that she might be in a tight spot – say getting out from under a table. When you let her try first, her body starts to work out what coordination is needed and she develops a greater sense of spatial relations.

Moving your child on

The table on developmental stages on pages 66–70 can help you to decide if and when you should be helping your child move on in her life skills. If you're still feeding your child at four, for instance, you need to know she can certainly do it by now.

Failing to move children on is a real problem. Over the past few years in particular, I've noticed that essential life skills are not being taught at the right time. Toddlers' development is being delayed because they are being spoon-fed, and kept on bottles and in pushchairs for longer. Parents are literally extending those baby years by doing *everything* for their kids. I've seen five-year-olds with beakers.

And don't get me started on two- and three-year-olds with dummies! A dummy is meant to be used to help infants sleep, not as method of keeping a toddler quiet. It can arrest speech development and cause problems with teeth. If your toddler still is using a dummy, please use the 'Dummy Fairy' technique immediately (see page 63). This really works. One little girl whose parents used the technique found a dummy a few weeks later under a chair. Rather than try to save it for herself, she came running to her Mum, saying there was one more to leave out for the dummy fairy.

●●

When children don't learn life skills at the right time, no one wins. Children don't develop as they should – and parents end up having children who are dependent for far too long! This in turn causes toddlers to become frustrated and impatient because they want *to learn to do these things. Ultimately you are making your child lazy because you're teaching her that she shouldn't even bother.*

●●

Why don't parents understand the necessity of their toddler learning these life skills? It's not about feeding her so that food will get in quickly. It's about encouraging her to feed herself. It's getting your child to start brushing her teeth, get herself dressed and learn to put her toys away. Of course you can do it better and faster. But that's not the point! She needs to learn and she only learns by doing.

This doesn't mean that you never dress your four-year-old or carry her backpack because she's developmentally capable of doing it herself. There are lots of little things that parents do for toddlers as part of love and affection. But make sure that she knows how to do it!

As she starts to do things for herself, she'll experience a sense of accomplishment. What's more, she'll do better in school as well if she has her basic life skills in place – she'll arrive ready to focus on academics! – and it will help with self-esteem. Towards the end of the toddler years, toddlers look at what other kids are doing and begin to mimic. At this point, they become more aware of what they can and can't do in relation to other toddlers, and may feel frustrated when they can't do what others can.

Trust me: life will become easier for you, too. If you move your toddler along with her life skills, by the time she reaches school age, your day-to-day life will run smoothly. This is particularly crucial when you have a toddler and a newborn. Once you discover you are pregnant again, you have a good part of nine months to teach your toddler the skills that will make life a little bit easier for you and for her when the new baby arrives. Don't wait till you're trying to breastfeed the newborn to teach your older child how to get herself dressed!

THE DUMMY FAIRY TECHNIQUE

◆ Tell your toddler that 'The Dummy Fairy's coming tomorrow to take the dummy!' and explain why. Parents come up with different stories, such as: 'You're a big girl now . . .', 'They need them for the babies . . .' and so on. Make it short and sweet (in other words, *not* that her teeth will stick out and it will cost thousands of pounds in orthodontic fees to set them right later on). Toddlers don't understand this kind of reasoning.

◆ Collect the dummies with your child and place them in a gift bag.

◆ Hang the bag on a doorknob or place in a sitting area.

◆ Leave a note for the fairy to take the dummies.

◆ When she's asleep, collect the bag and put them *all* in the bin outside the house (no chance of you saving one).

◆ Leave a small gift inside the bag.

◆ If possible, sprinkle a few coloured feathers and some glitter around the bag as evidence that the Dummy Fairy has truly visited.

Blankies and lovies

Many toddlers are attached to an object that pacifies them on an emotional level. They seek comfort from wrapping themselves up in a blankie or fiddling with their bunny rabbit's ears. It's something they've done from the time they were a baby, and so they've become attached to it.

Watch for the object getting in the way of his ability to interact. I once worked with twin boys and one of them had a blankie. When he got bored or upset, he'd wrap himself up in it and stay on the sofa for an hour! That's not OK. He should have been playing and having fun. So I made a rule that it was only for sleeping.

Having said that, as long as the beloved object is not interfering with your toddler's ability to play and interact, I believe it's not a problem. Kids tend to grow out of them on their own by school age. (Although I know some teens that still have theirs on a shelf!) However, if you feel you want to transition your child away from it before then, that's your choice. I'm not here to tell you that you are wrong.

I do see parents all the time who allow their child to take his favourite object everywhere because they don't want a tantrum. Then they get angry at him when he loses it. Two-, three-, and four-year-olds can't be responsible for losing things. If they drop something, they don't remember where they dropped it and you can't expect them to. You've got to make decisions based on their developmental stage. And that means being in charge of where your little one's lovie goes. Make a rule that it stays at home to avoid trouble.

THE BLANKIE BYE-BYE TECHNIQUE

If you are absolutely dead-set against your child having a blankie then, over a course of three weeks, this is what I suggest. This also works for comfort objects – without the cutting, of course.

- **Cut it in half and let him use that half for a week.**
- **Cut in half again and let him use that quarter for two weeks.**
- **When it's a small scrap, announce that the Blankie Fairy is coming that night to take it away.**
- **Have him say goodbye. When he wakes up, it's gone, with a toy left in its place.**
- **Make sure that the toy you choose is not a replacement for the blankie; a puzzle, truck or car that is more interactive is better than something that could become another comfort item.**

Setting healthy boundaries

During the toddler years, there is a really fine line in recognising what your child needs from you developmentally – and whether what she is asking for is not actually healthy or necessary. In some cases, toddlers are at a perfectly normal stage of development, but simply want to invade your space!

For example, a child who constantly wants to climb all over you may actually be quite happy going off to play. She wants to invade your personal space because you're on the phone or talking to a friend; in other words, she doesn't have your full attention! All toddlers want their parents – your food, your attention, your body and your bed! However, by the age of three onwards, you need to start to curb this behaviour and build spatial boundaries. You create space by having her sit next to you rather than on top of you. You tell her she has to eat her own food before she can have something from your plate or a sip of your drink. You teach her to say 'Excuse me' before she can talk to you when you are in a conversation with someone else. You put her back in her bed when she gets out.

To create appropriate, healthy boundaries, you have to learn to tell the difference between times when she's just trying to take everything that you've got and those other times when her behaviour is coming from a nice place of just sharing. Normally you'll know this, because you'll be doing something and she's interrupted and it didn't feel genuine. In other words, she was happy doing something else before you started to do something that caused her invasive reaction.

Power plays

Power plays are part of normal toddler development. They're trying to figure out who's in control – you or them. That's why you may find fights for control over what they eat, potty behaviour, bedtime, etc. It's up to you as a confident parent to recognise which things are no big deal and which things that they can't have leeway on. These power plays take time – and sometimes a lot of time. Parents find excuses, 'I don't have the time' so they give in. It may seem easier, but in the long run you're just making life harder for you and them. You have to find the time if you are to move them from any transition, teach a life skill, or to overcome any challenge. The good news is that once you win, the issue generally goes away. You don't have to keep fighting over potty-training or eating veggies because he now does it. That's why your backpack is so important!

DEVELOPMENT STAGES OF TODDLERS

1–2 YEARS

Motor development

Walks forward and backward
Walks up steps using two feet on each step
Can climb into an adult chair and turn around and sit

Development

Holds crayon in his fist and scribbles
Puts an object in a cup
No longer puts everything in his mouth

Language development

Babbling turns into words
Uses about 50 words by age two and can put two words together
Approaching two, is able to follow directions and be helpful – understand
    simple requests like 'please hand me your socks' – even if not talking much
Names four to five body parts
Points to five simple pictures that you name ('Where's the dog?') in a book
Makes animal sounds
Knows own first name
Points to objects he wants

Social and emotional development

Can have temper tantrums
May develop separation anxiety; is clingy and possessive of parent
Is very possessive about toys
Routines are important
Starts to exhibit emotions such as shame, jealousy, pride
May be more fearful than when an infant
Is easily redirected by an interesting distraction

Life skills development

Plays alone for a short period of time
Takes shoes and socks off

Drinks from a beaker, then from an open cup approaching age two
Feeds himself with a spoon

2–3 YEARS

Motor development

Kicks and throws a ball
Jumps off a step
Runs, marches
Can stand briefly on one foot and on tiptoes

Development

Unscrews a jar
Builds a tower of six blocks
Copies a vertical and a horizontal line
Holds a crayon or pencil properly
Threads big beads on a string

Language development

Starts to use short sentences
Uses more than 200 words
Enjoys music, sings songs
Understands 'in', 'on' and 'behind'
Knows full name, age and gender
Starts to ask why – *a lot!*

Social and emotional development

May have temper tantrums and other strong emotions
Asserts himself with the word 'No'. Try to give a couple of simple choices
    instead of asking closed questions.
Likes to imitate adults
Is easily frustrated
Is still clingy and possessive of parent, but less so
Begins to have a sense of self
Begins to read facial expressions and social cues
Has a short attention span
Is possessive about toys; plays alongside other children, not with them

Loves repetition; may insist on sameness of routine

Likes to make choices but has trouble doing it. Give two, not five options.

Life skills development

Towards age three, begins to able to be toilet-trained

Can take off clothes

Can put on shoes and socks

Is able to pour from a pitcher

3–4 YEARS

Motor development

Stands on one foot, plays jumping games, jumps to the side

Rides a tricycle

Goes upstairs putting one foot on each stair

Loves playground equipment

Can bounce

Opens doors – so you must remain vigilant about safety

Development

Builds a nine-block tower

Does puzzles and pegboards

Copies a circle; draws a face and maybe a stick body

Shows hand preference

Turns pages one at a time

Cuts with blunt scissors (not necessarily well)

Language development

Names eight pictures in a book

Asks questions: 'Why?', 'What is…?'

Counts to ten

Speaks in sentences; tells simple stories; recites nursery rhymes

Answers questions

Social and emotional development

Is eager to learn

Needs clear rules and consequences for breaking them

Learns by doing

May develop fear of the dark or monsters

May have an imaginary friend

Becomes curious about body parts, including genitals, which he finds hilarious

Starts to play with other children rather than in parallel

Likes to help – picking up toys, carrying laundry, etc

Life skills development

Able to undress himself and dress with a little help (but needs help with buttons and shoelaces)

Washes and dries his face

Is able to go to the potty alone, including wiping (you may need to check on thoroughness)

Is dry in the daytime, but may still not be dry at night

Is able to use a fork

Still needs help with brushing teeth and combing hair after he's done it

4–5 YEARS

Motor development

Pumps himself on swing

Gallops and skips

Throws a ball overhand

Development

Draws recognisable objects

Uses a knife

Likes zipping, snapping and buttoning

Makes designs and crude letters

Language development

May use profanity and silly words

Understands basic concepts like number, size, weight, colour

Uses complete sentences and can follow a two-step command: 'Get the bag from the kitchen and put it in your room.'

Knows over 1500 words

Asks seemingly endless questions

Social and emotional development

Is able to play well with others and understands sharing

Can be bossy

Is typically very talkative

May still have a security blanket or comfort toy, etc

Likes to play pretend: doctor, mum, postman, etc

Moods may change rapidly, may boast, exaggerate, name-call

Is highly social – enjoys being with and playing games with other children

Has friends, but may be aggressive in play

Is imaginative, dramatic

Shows concern for others

Can help set or clear table

Still needs constant supervision outside

Life skills development

Brushes teeth and hair with supervision. Bathing still needs supervision.

Is able to go to the potty unsupervised

May still wet bed at night due to lack of bladder control (14 percent of five-
   year-olds still have this problem)

YOUR CHILD'S 'I CAN DO' LIST

The 'I Can Do' list helps you to know what you can expect from your child rather than doing everything for her.

- **Now that you've read about the development stages of a toddler, think about the age of your child and make a list of the life skills you want to focus on teaching over the next period of time. For example, climbing stairs, using a spoon, putting on underpants or trousers.**

- **How can you make her a little bit more independent? Create a list for your child by cutting out pictures from magazines or download some from the Internet.**

- **Post your colourful list somewhere and encourage her to tick off her achievements as you go along.**

PART II

The big issues in the toddler years

TOUCHSTONES FOR THE TODDLER YEARS

1 Communicate clearly

2 Adopt a positive mindset

3 Repeat, again and again

4 Be consistent

5 Give encouragement

6 Establish routines

7 Have realistic expectations

8 Set boundaries

In this section we'll look at the seven key issues for toddlers: safety as they become more mobile; discipline as they learn boundaries and how to regulate their feelings; the importance of play and stimulation during these years to foster healthy development; how to create positive transitions both small; potty-training; creating healthy eating patterns; and going out and about with your little ones. You'll learn my best tips for coping well in each of these areas, so that life with and for your child is fun and trouble free as possible.

4

Safety first

Having a toddler brings safety to the forefront of my mind full stop. You now have this mobile, extremely curious little one who is ready and willing to get into everything. Creating an environment that your child can explore but still be safe in may feel overwhelming when you start to think about all the things that can happen. Most accidents happen at home – not outside, where you are more likely to be on guard. Try not to worry: with some precautions in place, you can toddler-proof your environment and make it the ideal place for your child to learn and grow.

You do, however, have another job! Just like everything else, a toddler is *learning* to be safe for the very first time. It's not something with which he is instinctively born. So keeping your toddler safe means you not only have to make your home a safe environment, but also begin to teach him what danger means and what he needs to be aware of and avoid. This means teaching him everything from not touching a hot stove ('Hot! Owie!') to explaining why you need to hold his hand crossing the street.

In doing this, you must balance being overprotective and letting him have the freedom to explore and learn. You've got to allow an element of risk-taking – within *reason*. If you're hovering over him saying, 'Don't go there, you'll fall off', you'll get in the way of his learning and make him nervous. This doesn't mean that you don't shadow him on the equipment in the park, for instance, or come to his rescue if he's in true danger; but, you need to find the balance between protection and freedom to help your toddler develop.

- ◆ **Discipline**
- ◆ **Perspective**
- ◆ **Plan Ahead**

Safety is an on-going process

Toddler-proofing should be seen as an ongoing process rather than simply a one-off event. Your child will develop and change tremendously between the ages of 18 months and four, and so too will his needs. The gate that worked great for your two-year-old may become a very unsafe climbing gym the next year.

Throughout this chapter you'll find a wide range of safety factors to bear in mind. The suggestions I make are meant to provide information and raise your awareness. Like all of my suggestions, you need to customise them according to what's right for your child and family.

Whether you are at home or out and about, the number-one thing you can do to keep your toddler safe is to supervise her at all times. Out of sight should *never* be out of mind. You need to know where she is and what she's doing. I never leave a two- or three-year-old out of sight or unattended, even for a moment. Unless I know she's in the safe environment of her playroom (which I'll constantly check), I always keep her within sight and sound. If I can't hear her, I am instantly suspicious. Because if it's quiet she's either concentrating on something or up to mischief! Deadly silence is a clear giveaway that something's going on. Either way, we both know that one, right?

Household safety

If you've read *Confident Baby Care,* then you'll see toddler-proofing as a natural extension of baby-proofing your home. You're just taking it to the next level because now he can walk, grab, climb and get into anything and everything. In the event that you *haven't* safety-proofed your house, it's urgent that you make your environment safe *immediately.* The diagrams on pages 78–79 shows you the danger spots throughout the house and what you should do to make them safer.

* *

When you start to think about toddler-proofing, get down on your knees and crawl around, looking at your space from his level. What's within reach? What looks like something fun to climb onto, or pull down? What things in the environment do you need be mindful of?

* *

I'm not necessarily suggesting that you make your house into a monk's cell. But if you have special treasures, put them out of reach. It's unfair to expect your two-year-old to understand the importance of Granny's heirloom china. Kids do need to learn boundaries and to respect their surroundings, but if you put away dangerous and precious items, it will help you avoid saying 'No' 10,000 times a day. Be realistic.

Poisonous items (cleaning products, medicines and all poisons) *must* be locked away out of reach. Medicine, including vitamin tablets, can be especially dangerous, as pills look like sweeties. Remember, too, that your handbag, or a friend's handbag, can hold many forbidden items: pills, toiletries, choking hazards such as coins, safety pins or hard sweets. Put these away where they can't be reached.

Think about your toddler. Is she a climber? It doesn't matter if you put things up in a cupboard if she figures out (and she will) that putting the chair against the work surface will enable her to clamber on and get what she wants. Bookcases and chests of drawers become toddler ladders, and can easily be tipped over. I'll never forget a little boy who put a bike onto a washing basket to reach up and open up a cupboard, because the cupboards were where all the games were. Fixing bookcases to the wall will ensure that they don't topple over when the inevitable climbing takes place.

If you have stairs, make sure they are gated so she doesn't fall down. And don't forget to teach your little one how to climb – and climb down – steps, as one of her life skills.

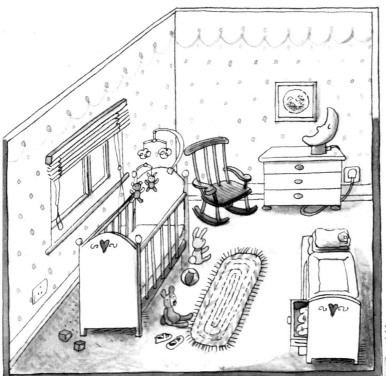

How Much Do You Know About Keeping Your Toddler Safe at Home?

How many dangers can you spot in each room?
The answers are on page 80.

BEDROOM

KITCHEN

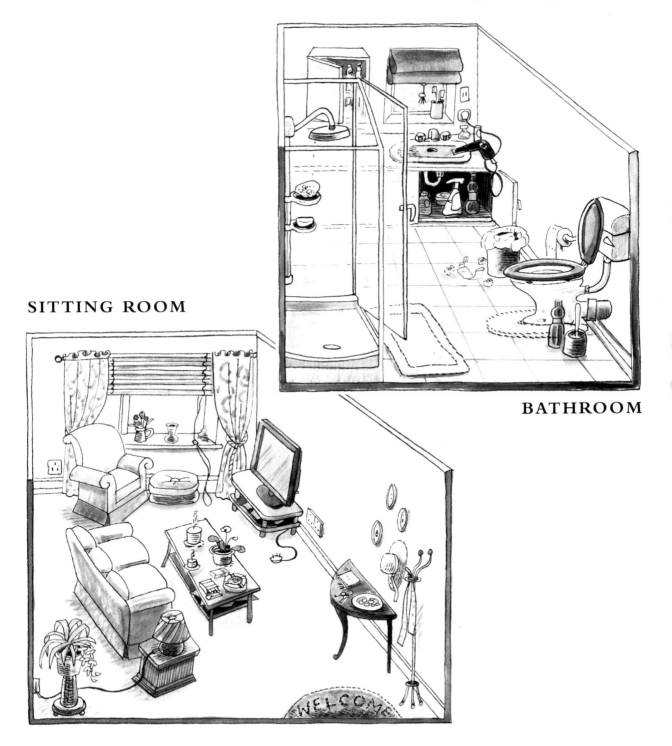

SITTING ROOM

BATHROOM

DANGERS IN HOUSEHOLD SAFETY

Kitchen: electrical sockets must be covered to prevent electrocution; bin needs lid and put where it can't be gotten; plastic bags, cleaning supplies, knives, and office supplies need to be stored in a locked, inaccessible place to avoid accidents; gaps need to be stuffed so child can't get wedged in; pots need handles turned sideways or backward to prevent burns; iron and ironing board should never be left out to prevent burns; cat litter and pet food needs to be in an inaccessible place to prevent choking and eating litter; tumble dryer door should be closed to prevent getting trapped inside.

Bedroom: cords on blind should be short to prevent strangulation; cot should be away from window to prevent falling out; sockets should be covered to prevent electrocution.

Sitting room: vases, ornaments, table lamps and plants (poisoning hazard) need to be placed out of harm's way; candles, lighter, matches and cigarettes should be inaccessible to prevent fires and burns; furniture should be away from windows so he can't climb up and fall out; wires should be in caddy to prevent tripping; sockets should be covered to prevent electrocution; coins should be inaccessible to prevent choking.

Bathroom: bin should have a lid and be in an inaccessible place; toiletries such as razors, lotions and hairspray should be placed in an inaccessible cupboard to prevent harm or poisoning; shower door should be closed and toilet lid down to prevent drowning; sockets should be covered and hair dryer put away to prevent electrocution.

> This quiz is meant to give you the basics on toddler proofing, however your home may have additional hazards that you must deal with – stairs, for instance, or open fireplaces. You need to assess and deal with the dangers of your particular situation.

COMMON HOUSEHOLD POISONS

Lock them all up:

- **dishwasher tablets, liquids and powders**
- **oven cleaners**
- **ammonia**
- **bleach**
- **toilet-bowl cleaners**
- **rubbing alcohol**
- **vitamins and prescription and over-the-counter drugs**
- **rust removers**
- **paint strippers**
- **spot removers**
- **glues**
- **fungicides**
- **insecticides and weed killers**
- **rat and mouse poisons**
- **antifreeze**

Become 'The Terminator'

Whether you are at home or at someone else's house, enter every room as if you're The Terminator: scan the safety issues straight away. The diagrams and quiz on pages 78–80 provides the basics of what you'll need to look for. Here are some other things to think about:

- Is there a fireplace? Are there matches around? Sharp fire pokers?

- Are there working smoke alarms in every room?

- Are there child safety devices – windows locks, safety catches on cupboards, corner protectors for sharp edges?

- Is there a porch, and can he get out onto the balcony?

- Are there stairs that he can tumble down?

- What other dangers might this room have?

Is it safety or control?

What's the difference between a lockdown for safety and a lockdown because parents want to make their lives easier? I once walked into a house with toddlers where everything was locked down. Every door, every drawer was locked. You don't need to go that far. You only need to lock the cupboards with all the chemicals and cleaning supplies, the medicine cabinet and the drawers that contain the sharp knives. It's OK to keep a drawer or cupboard that he can reach, filled with items he can play with. Toddlers need to be able to explore their environment.

Jo Jo No No: Toddlers underfoot while cooking

If you've got a little one in a kitchen, you need to teach him to watch you from a certain distance when you're at the stove. I've seen parents looking like a one-armed bandit, pots boiling over, with one hand stirring and one hand holding their child. That's dangerous. Use my tips for happy times with toddlers in the kitchen, below.

Toy safety

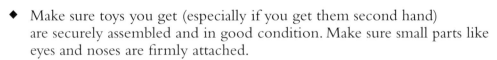

In Chapter 6, I go into detail about toys that are suitable for toddlers. In fact, in terms of toy safety, the biggest tip I can give is to choose toys that are appropriate for your child's age. That way they will not be a safety hazard. Check the label or the box, and bear in mind the following:

◆ Make sure toys you get (especially if you get them second hand) are securely assembled and in good condition. Make sure small parts like eyes and noses are firmly attached.

◆ Buy non-toxic art materials.

◆ The leading cause of toy-related death is choking, mostly on latex balloons. To reduce choking hazards, avoid letting a toddler have a balloon or any toy that is less than 4.4 centimetres (about 2 inches) in diameter. This includes marbles, small balls, plastic toys, etc. Watch also for small game pieces.

TODDLERS IN THE KITCHEN

◆ **You need a safety parameter – especially in an open-plan kitchen. If there is no natural line – such as where the carpet ends – it might help to create a masking-tape line and teach your toddler that he can't cross the line while you're cooking.**

◆ **Make sure there are plenty of things for him to do on 'his' side of the line, perhaps a low drawer of toys or Tupperware and wooden spoons. It will not only be safer than him being under foot, but you'll feel better having 'your' space, too!**

◆ When you purchase a new toy, check for the CE mark. This signifies that the toy has passed all the necessary compliance tests for toys imported into and manufactured in the EU. Another symbol you can look for alongside the CE Mark is the British Lion Mark, which is awarded by the British Toy and Hobby Association (BTHA).

◆ Over the past few years, there have been several major toy recalls due to unacceptable amounts of lead in the paint used on them. You can check recall websites (see page 333) if you have any questions about recent toy purchases. Try also to avoid older toys that have peeling paint, as ingesting lead paint, either through flakes or paint dust, can lead to lead poisoning.

LEAD POISONING

If you live in a building constructed before 1970, it may contain lead paint. Lead paint is particularly dangerous to children if it's flaking or peeling – allowing them to put it into their mouths or breathe in lead dust or fumes. Lead can also be found in old water pipes, soil in your garden, paint on old children's toys, children's beaded necklaces, and even old Christmas lights. For more information, contact the non-profit Lead Paint Safety Association (see page 333), which offers a free lead paint test for your house.

Water safety: inside and out

Water is dangerous for unsupervised toddlers. *Full stop!* Whether it's a pond, pool, river, bucket, puddle, toilet, sink or tub, never *ever* leave your toddler by herself, anywhere near water. A child can drown very quickly and silently in just half an inch of water. I can't overstress how important it is to be cautious around water. Consider the following:

◆   Never fill a tub and leave it − even if your toddler is in another room. In the blink of an eye, a toddler can get into the tub and the worst can happen. When she's just starting to walk, make sure the toilet seat is down.

◆   Store all electrical appliances, such as curling irons, electric toothbrushes, hair dryers, etc., away from tub and sink to prevent electrocution.

◆   Put a rubber suction mat on the bottom of the tub. This helps to stop her from slipping, falling and hitting her head. Never fill the tub higher than your child's waist while she's sitting down. And teach her to sit in the tub at all times. No standing!

◆   When she was a baby, you turned the hot water down to the lowest setting and made sure to test the water with your elbow before putting her in, to avoid burns. Now you have to think about a little one who can reach up and turn on the taps herself! When you run a bath, make sure to run the cold tap last. Not only does that prevent her from being scalded if she reaches up to turn on the taps, but any drips that come out after the tap has been turned off will be cold, not hot.

◆   Keep your hot-water heater set below 48°C/120°F to prevent scalding.

◆   Make sure the bathroom door can't be locked from the inside, trapping your toddler alone in the room.

◆   Swimming is a wonderful activity that can be loads of fun. If you're taking your toddler to the public pool or the beach, she needs to be supervised at all times. She'll want to run and jump off the ledges, blow bubbles and swim underwater, and it can be difficult to keep a close eye on her. But you must! Don't rely upon supervision from a lifeguard, whose job it is to oversee every swimmer at the pool. They can easily miss something happening to your child. Make sure you are 100 percent focused, as she can go under in the blink of an eye.

◆ No matter what age you start swimming lessons, begin teaching your toddler basic water-safety rules: 'What's the number-one rule at the pool? Always be with an adult!'. Done!

Developmentally, most kids aren't ready for formal swim lessons until age three or four. You can, however, take her to a parent-tot swimming class before this time, to get her used to holding her breath and blowing bubbles. Lessons should be no longer then 30 minutes, or she may become cold, and that could put her off the whole process.

BE PREPARED

Despite our best efforts, accidents do happen. Be prepared, remain calm and stay with your child. Bear in mind the following:

◆ **Take a CPR class and see the instructions on pages 298-299. These will act as a refresher if your first-aid knowledge is a little rusty. Don't rely on books in an emergency, though. It's much better to have the knowledge and know how to apply it than fiddle about at the last minute.**

◆ **Have a well-stocked first aid kit readily accessible (see page 302).**

◆ **Immediately call for help in any emergency. Programme the emergency numbers into your home and mobile phones, including your GP's number, 999 or 112, your local hospital and poison control centre, and the NHS Direct helpline (see page 332).**

◆ **Programme in the numbers of one or two close neighbours, who can be called to watch other children or help out with a problem situation.**

◆ **Keep a list of these numbers posted on the fridge for caregivers.**

Road safety

Once your child becomes mobile, she'll want to walk and run everywhere. You can't always keep her strapped in her pushchair – and nor should you. It's important for her to have lots of outdoor playtime, allowing her to run around and expend energy. Exercise is also important to develop her motor and coordination skills. Those little muscles need to be used! That's why you need to teach basic road safety, from the moment she starts toddling. Make it clear that *any time* you are near a road – or crossing the street – she must hold your hand. Rehearse what to do each time you come to a crossing: 'OK, look for cars. Look both ways. When the signal is red that means "Stop". When the signal is green, we can go.' You can even make it a question-and-answer game: 'What's the number-one rule when crossing the street? Look both ways before crossing the street.' This is something you should repeat every time you're out.

♦ **Energy**

♦ **Discipline**

♦ **Perseverance**

THE GREEN CROSS CODE

Remember the Green Cross Code? It's a great shorthand way to teach your little ones to cross safely. The wording has changed a bit over the years, but the 2005 version goes like this:

1 *THINK!* Find the safest place to cross, then stop.

2 *STOP!* Stand on the pavement near the kerb.

3 *USE YOUR EYES AND EARS!* Look all around for traffic, and listen.

4 *WAIT UNTIL IT'S SAFE TO CROSS!* If traffic is coming, let it pass.

5 *LOOK AND LISTEN!* When it's safe, walk straight across the road.

6 *ARRIVE ALIVE!* Keep looking and listening.

Outdoor safety check

If you have a garden or take your child to play at a playground, do a safety scan to make sure the area is safe. Your toddler will want to run and get into whatever she finds. Things to watch out for include:

- Exit gates: do you come in the same way you go out or is there another way out?

- Rope swings, jump ropes, pet leashes, clothes or other strangulation hazards within reach.

- Old equipment lying around.

- In the garden: fertilisers, poisons and other gardening equipment.

- Openings between ladder rungs that could trap a child's head.

- Poisonous plants and berries that can end up in little mouths. If you aren't familiar with common poisonous plants, see *www.horseweb-uk.com/features/plantmain.htm.*

- Swings with seats that are made with wood or metal (heavy material could injure kids walking by).

- Asphalt, concrete or grass under the playground set, which would not break your child's fall. Playgrounds should have wood chips, bark mulch or rubber mats underneath the equipment.

- Metal playground equipment. Metal slides can get incredibly hot and burn a child within seconds.

The 'Rolling' and 'Roaming' techniques for road safety

It's a fine balance: You want your toddler to have freedom and get exercise by walking, but you also want to ensure that she understands the dangers of running away. Here are two of my techniques to begin to teach your toddler independence in public, while keeping her safe.

You're out on a walk and your toddler doesn't want to be in the pushchair. It's time for the 'Rolling' technique (see following page), which teaches her to walk beside you. This technique works well when you have both a toddler and a baby.

THE ROLLING TECHNIQUE

◆ **Give a clear choice between two options: hold your hand and walk or hold onto the pushchair. What she *can't* do is walk by herself.**

◆ **If she refuses to listen, she has to be in the pushchair.**

The 'Roaming' technique takes this a step further, and involves teaching your toddler how to remain safe and stay near you, while giving her space to roam, as well as building trust between you both. It's really 'controlled freedom', where the independence you're giving can build her self-esteem and sense of responsibility (see below).

THE ROAMING TECHNIQUE

◆ **Practise in a quiet, car-free place, such as a park. You want the environment to be safe as he learns the basics.**

◆ **Explain that you are going to let him out of the pushchair, but that when you say 'Stop!' and hold up your hand, he needs to stop – wherever he is.**

◆ **Say, 'Now you can get out!' and help him out of the pushchair.**

◆ **For the first few times, encourage him walk just ahead of you and then say, 'Stop!' If he doesn't stop, ask him to hold your hand or the pushchair for a few minutes. If he does wait for you, praise him and then let him go again.**

◆ **When you say, 'Stop!', use a low, authoritative tone of voice.**

◆ **Work up to allowing him to run in the park for a little bit, explaining that Mummy or Daddy always need to see him, so he can't run off too far.**

◆ **As you build up trust and he shows he can listen, let him walk further ahead. Remember, trust is built on an invisible child rein.**

Troubleshooting the 'Rolling' and 'Roaming' techniques

If it's not working, ask yourself the following questions:

◆ Have I consistently placed his hand onto the handle of the pushchair and walked with him before letting him let go when it's safe?

◆ Have I found safe places for my child to roam rather than always having to hold onto the pushchair? Overusing the pushchair means that your child's going to run like a wild horse as soon as he's out.

◆ Have I allowed him to walk beside me again after running off, rather than being made to get back in the chair? If you don't follow through on the consequences, then this or any technique won't work.

Car safety

British law states that all children travelling in cars must use the correct child restraint until they are either 135cm in height, or the age of 12. This means that your toddler must be strapped into his car seat at all times when your car is moving. This is mandatory.

When buying any car or booster seats for your toddler, use the same standards you did when purchasing your baby's car seat. Never buy one that is used or has been in an accident, and make sure it conforms to the standard United Nations ECE Regulations R44.03 or R44.04, marked with a letter E in a circle and a number. As a reminder, the number for the UK is 11. Make sure you follow the manufacturer's instructions as well as your car's manual for proper installation. One of the most common errors people make with car seats is that they go by their child's age and not weight.

If your child weighs between 9 and 18kg (roughly 9 months to four years, again depending on weight), he needs to be in a car seat. Booster seats are for children from 15kg to 25kg (roughly four to six years), or, depending upon make and model, from 15kg up to 36kg. Only move your child to a booster seat once he has exceeded the maximum weight for the child seat, or the top of his head is higher than the top of the seat. When you go to the shop to buy your car seat, ask the staff to show you how to fit it properly. Bring your toddler along if it helps. He can try it out in person and, by engaging him in the process, you help him feel the importance of choosing 'his' car seat.

When driving, don't forget to turn on your child's door and window locks. It's too easy for little fingers to reach over the push buttons as you're moving. Part of keeping your child safe in the car is keeping him engaged and comfortable. He'll be less likely to act out or try to get out of his seat if he's happy. For this reason, make sure your car is not too hot or cold. Ditto for the car seat – especially the child restraint buckles. On a hot day, the metal can easily heat up. Keep the sun out of his eyes with a sun shade that attaches to his window, or roll down the window a bit, hang a towel over the top of the window, and then roll it up again. Putting towels on the seats keeps them cooler as well.

The biggest safety reminder is this: *Never leave your toddler in the car unattended.* One, for safety, and two because the inside temperature of a car can rise to fatal heights. Even if you just have to run into the shop for one second, take him with you.

> ## Is his car seat too tight?
>
> If you strap your child in and can't get two fingers under the strap, it's too tight.

Getting her into a car seat

Let's face it: not all toddlers are keen to be strapped into a seat – away from Mum and Dad, and unable to exercise their new mobility! The following tips can help to ease the process of getting her into – and keeping her happy in – her seat:

◆ Bring the car seat into the house and let her play with and become accustomed to it. Let her fiddle with the straps and climb in and out. Explain to her that everyone wears a seat belt. It keeps them safe so they don't get hurt. Practise buckling the belt with a cuddly toy in place.

◆ When in the car, distract her with a toy and, when her body is relaxed, buckle her in and go.

◆ Toddlers love to express their independence. If she wants to get into the seat herself, let her. But put a time limit on it. You can have a song you sing, letting her know that by the end of the song she has to be in the seat.

◆ Don't start the car until everyone has their seat belt on. You can even call out 'Safety check', and have each person in the car say 'Seat belt on'.

◆ If she takes off her belt when you're driving, pull over. Get the belt back on before you continue. Don't try to deal with it and drive at the same time.

◆ When all is said and done, safety is the priority. Strap her in and deal with the crying. Be consistent. Never give in and let her go 'just this once', without being strapped in. It will make it that much harder to enforce the rule next time and there should be no exceptions.

Sun safety

Running in the park, playing on the beach, having fun in the garden – these are all great outdoor activities for your toddler. However, whether it's hot or cold outside – or even cloudy – you need to make sure she's properly protected from the sun. Sunburns received in childhood increase the risk of skin cancer in later life. So sun protection can truly be a matter of life and death. Here are some sun safety precautions to better protect your toddler:

◆ Time your outings. The sun's rays are the strongest between 11am and 3pm, so if you are out during these times, take breaks in the shade. If you're at the beach, bring an umbrella. At the park, look for trees or awnings to sit under. Lead by example. If you sit in the shade, so will your child.

◆ Choose a waterproof sunscreen specifically designed for children. You're looking for an SPF of at least 30, which offers broad-spectrum protection. This means it protects against both ultraviolet B (UVB) and ultraviolet A (UVA) rays.

◆ Dress her for coverage. Protect her head with hats that have a peak or brim and tails. Dress in clothing with long sleeves. Make sure you apply sunscreen under clothes. UV sunglasses are also great to protect her eyes.

◆ Apply the sunscreen about 30 minutes before going outdoors. Then reapply it every two hours and after she gets wet.

◆ Make sure you are using enough sunscreen and covering her everywhere. If you find it hard to ensure even coverage with all the wriggling, you might want to invest in some coloured sunscreen, which shows you exactly where you've managed to apply it. As a general rule, you'll need to use about half an ounce of sunscreen (about two tablespoons) to cover her entire body.

◆ The areas that you don't think about can burn the worst. Pay special attention to the backs of knees, ears, neck, tops of feet and hands. Lips can burn too, so put on lip balm that has an SPF of 15. Remember, we're aiming for fun in the sun.

Safety with pets

If you don't already have a pet, it's best to wait until your toddler is older before bringing home a dog or a cat. You may be tempted because your four-year-old is begging for a puppy, but remember that puppies turn into dogs, and dogs require lots of work and plenty of your time. So, before you are tempted to get a pet, think twice. You're already focused – and extremely busy – dealing with your toddler, and adding in a dog or a cat can be a bit much! When your child is older – say eight or nine – you can consider it if he's mature enough to meet the responsibilities himself. Otherwise, you'll just be making work for yourself and I'm pretty sure you have enough of that!

Do you already have a family pet? The same rules that he had as a baby apply to your toddler now; in other words, never leave your toddler alone in a room with a pet. Toddlers love pulling tails, grabbing fur, and jumping on or chasing animals. You never know how your pet is going to react.

If your young toddler pulls the cat's or dog's tail, you need to say, 'Don't pull her tail. That hurt the dog/cat. Owie!' If he continues to do it, you need to work out if it's simply play or undertaken with intention to hurt. If he planned to hurt your pet, he needs to be disciplined in just the same way that he would if he'd hurt a person.

I once had a call from parents whose four-year-old pulled the dog's tail and jumped on him. They wanted to know if there was any reason to be concerned. There was. Toddlers who are intentionally rough-handed with animals can certainly dominate other kids, too. This bullyish behaviour needs to be nipped in the bud with consequences and discipline that drives home the point that we need to treat animals as well as people with kindness.

PET SAFETY TIPS

Keeping your toddler *and* your pet safe means being vigilant. Consider the following:

◆ **Keep your pet's food and water out of your child's reach. Both dog and cat food can be a choking hazard for little ones.**

◆ **Make sure your pet eats without being disturbed. Dogs in particular can become possessive about food.**

◆ **Keep the cat litter tray out of the way and teach your child to stay out of it.**

◆ **Teach your toddler never to take toys or bones from your dog's mouth. You can train your dog to 'Drop it', but your child should never grab anything away from them.**

◆ **Show your toddler how to pet dogs and cats gently. Approach them slowly and gently stroke their fur. He should not pull, tug, grab or poke. He should also understand that he must always ask an owner's permission before petting their dog or cat.**

◆ **Teach him to never approach a dog that is growling, barking or showing its teeth – or a cat that is hissing.**

◆ **Always wash your child's hands after touching any animal – whether you're at the park, your home or at the petting zoo.**

◆ **And because it's too much to ask a toddler to remember these rules, be sure there is *always* adult supervision around a dog or cat.**

Allergies

I can't do a chapter on safety without discussing allergy awareness. As a young child, I was prone to many allergies, so I am particularly sensitive to this issue. Even if you made it through the baby years without your toddler showing signs of an allergy, there's still time! As her immune system matures she can, at any time, show signs of developing allergic reactions to food and/or substances in the environment, also known as allergens. Neither of my parents was allergic, but there is often a strong genetic component. If you and your partner suffer from allergies, your child has a 75 percent chance of developing them as well.

Common allergic reactions include: diarrhoea, sneezing, runny nose, itchy eyes and ears, wheezing, coughing, sinus problems, or a rash and eczema. The worst-case scenario is an anaphylactic reaction.

•••

Anaphylaxis is a life-threatening allergic reaction. Symptoms can include:

- ◆   *generalised flushing of the skin*
- ◆   *nettle rash (hives) anywhere on the body*
- ◆   *sense of impending doom*
- ◆   *swelling of throat and mouth*
- ◆   *difficulty in swallowing or speaking*
- ◆   *alterations in heart rate*
- ◆   *severe asthma*
- ◆   *abdominal pain, nausea and vomiting*
- ◆   *sudden feeling of weakness (drop in blood pressure)*
- ◆   *collapse and unconsciousness*

If your child experiences some of these symptoms, call 999 immediately. If your child has an EpiPen or Anapen, it should be administered at once.

•••

Allergic reactions can occur from pollen (found in grasses, weeds and trees), moulds, house dust mites, pets such as cats, dogs and rabbits, insects (wasps and bees), industrial and household chemicals, medicines, latex (found in balloons, art materials and even stickers) and food. You'll find more details on food allergies in Chapter 9 (see page 204).

Not all of these substances are capable of causing life-threatening reactions, but they can make your child uncomfortable. The most potentially dangerous food allergies include peanuts, tree nuts (e.g. almonds, walnuts, cashews, Brazils), sesame seeds, fish, soya, shellfish, dairy products and eggs. In the non-food category are wasp or bee stings, latex, penicillin or any other drug or injection. A mild reaction on one occasion doesn't mean she has a 'mild' allergy. Any allergic response should be monitored and reported to your doctor, because subsequent contact can produce a much greater response.

In most cases, allergic children who are at risk of anaphylaxis will be prescribed an EpiPen or Anapen, which is an injection of adrenaline (epinephrine) that will constrict blood vessels, relax smooth muscles in the lungs to improve breathing, stimulate the heartbeat and help to stop swelling around the face and lips. If your child is prescribed an Epipen or Anapen then you will be trained to use it, but the box below contains a reminder of the basics.

ADMINISTERING ADRENALINE

Injectible adrenaline pens (Anapens or EpiPens) come with their own set of instructions, and you will need to familiarise yourself with them. You'll be given two pens, as a second may be required in the case of a serious reaction.

◆ **Take the grey end off your EpiPen.**

◆ **Grasp the pen around the centre, and do not put your fingers over either end.**

◆ **Push the 'needle' (grey cap) end of the pen firmly against your toddler's *outer* thigh, near the top. You don't need to remove his clothes to do this, unless they are very thick.**

◆ **Count slowly to 10 before withdrawing the needle.**

◆ **Call 999 and ask for an ambulance, explaining that your child has had an allergic reaction and you have used the EpiPen.**

If your child is unconscious:

◆ **Place him on his side.**

◆ **If your child does not improve within five minutes of administering adrenaline, then use the second EpiPen in the other leg, using the same procedure.**

◆ **Even if your child has recovered by the time the ambulance arrives, they *must* go to hospital to be assessed.**

Don't panic

It can be very frightening to have an allergic child – particularly if he is in danger of severe reactions – but try to stay calm. He'll react much better to the situation if he knows you are relaxed and confident about caring for him.

Serious reactions are not that common, and many children can outgrow them. If you have a history of allergies in your family, it's worth talking to your GP to get a referral to an allergy specialist, who can run some tests to see if your child will be affected.

Getting tested

If you notice that your child experiences mild allergic reactions, such as sneezing, itchy eyes or a constantly running nose, an antihistamine can help to reduce the symptoms. You should then contact your GP for a conversation about being in control of your child's allergies. They can run tests to establish the cause or refer you to an allergist who can do patch testing (skin-prick tests) and blood tests to determine the specific allergens.

Once you identify the type of allergy your child has (especially if it is severe), make sure everyone who takes care of him knows what it is, how to avoid problems, and how to treat symptoms. This includes co-carers, babysitters, childminders, day centres and nursery schools. You may need to supply them with medication such as inhalers for asthma, antihistamines and, in the case of severe allergies, two EpiPens. You'll need to keep them on hand at all times, too.

Other allergic conditions

It's great if your child doesn't have any symptoms of anaphylactic allergies, but what happens if she's been diagnosed with asthma or seems to react to indoor allergens such as dust mites or pet dander? That's when you need to get into action to clean your environment and remove the triggers causing problems. There is a host of allergic conditions that can affect your toddler, and these include asthma, eczema and hayfever.

Before you give your cat away or scrub down your house from top to bottom, take note. Research shows that kids who grow up in houses with pets are less likely to have allergies later in life. The same research also points out that dust and bacteria also help shape the immune system in a way that protects against allergies.

Asthma

With an increase in environmental toxins, asthma in children seems to be on the rise. If your child has been diagnosed with asthma you will need to limit flare-ups by decreasing exposure to any triggers. Keep your doors and windows closed during peak seasonal allergy times (you can check the pollen count on the Met Office website if you aren't sure; www.metoffice.gov.uk). Control indoor allergens by weekly cleaning and washing your house, especially your child's room and her bedding. Prevent or decrease the amount of mould by decreasing the moisture in the air with a dehumidifier. Plants can also carry mould or pollen, so limit houseplants.

One of the best things you can do for a toddler with asthma is not to avoid treating him as if he is sickly or weak. I've had asthma since I was five, but I'm not an asthma 'sufferer' – those are two words that don't belong together. It's the language we use that shapes the mentality and emotional health of our children. If you treat it as something that is terrible, your child will get that message. If you treat it positively, he'll feel that way, too. It's the difference between, 'You can't go to the party because it might trigger an attack', and 'Let's take your asthma medicine so you can go to the party'. The first makes him feel different in a bad way, the second shows him that he can be like everyone else.

REDUCING ALLERGENS AT HOME

Controlling indoor allergens means getting rid of dust mites and mould spores, protecting against pet dander, and controlling cockroaches. Here are some tips to stay on top of cleanliness:

- **Wash your child's bedding in hot water over 130°F (54°C) once a week. In other words, use your washing machine's highest temperature setting.**
- **Consider getting zippered, allergen-proof coverings for his duvet, pillowcases, mattress and divan.**
- **Vacuum his room once a week with a vacuum cleaner containing a HEPA filter. Shake rugs outside and sweep and then damp-mop floors at least once a week.**
- **Frequently dust all hard surfaces, such as blinds, fans and furniture with a damp cloth.**
- **Limit the number of cuddly toys he has in his room. If he has one or two favourites, wash them weekly in hot water.**

5

Discipline

Contrary to what some of you may think, kids are not born with social skills or an inbuilt understanding of right and wrong. *You* may understand what type of behaviour is acceptable in society, but they don't. This gives you a tremendous responsibility to teach your toddler the difference between right and wrong – and every single other thing that she'll need to know to become a responsible adult in the future. This may seem like a mammoth task, but once you get started, it's easy to guide her, so that she understands how to treat others kindly and with consideration.

Consider the consequences if you *don't* teach these things: What kind of human being are you raising if you accept bad behaviour? The long-term impact of your acceptance is huge. It's your responsibility to make your child more aware of other people's feelings, to teach him empathy and respect, and to take on your morals and values. This is important for your family life, his future relationships, and his ability to exist in society in a healthy, functional way. It will affect everything from his ability to learn and create and sustain healthy, happy relationships to his success in life in the future. So, even when he's young and it seems absurd to load him with information that you don't think he'll understand, it's important to be consistent with discipline, because this will provide the boundaries that form the foundation of the way he operates both now and in the future.

I can't emphasise enough how important a foundation of discipline is in the toddler years. These years are critical. It may be challenging to stick to your guns when he's having a tantrum, but it will save you decades of trouble. If you lay down the rules now, your toddler will learn very quickly. If you don't, you'll have to work twice as hard to fix bad behaviour later. By the time your child enters school, you want him to have a clear sense of how to behave. Teachers want to focus on educating your child, not have to teach him basic good behaviour. And you definitely don't want to deal with an out-of-control teenager!

Getting on the same page

Before we begin, take a moment and reflect upon how you were taught right from wrong. What about your partner? What would you do the same and differently with your child? Getting on the same page with your partner and becoming clear about how you will discipline is very important. Together you should come up with a list of rules upon which you agree and want as the basis of your home life. This is a very meaningful conversation as it solidifies what's important to you, both as individuals and parents. I'll give you my own suggestions, but they are only suggestions – your rules are yours.

Over the years, I've found that every family has different rules: eating on the sofa, going in certain rooms, touching certain things and, of course, general behaviour. The key is for you and your partner to decide together what's important to you. Of course, boundaries are also about safety, to keep your mobile toddler safe as he explores. To a great extent, however, you are establishing the conditions for living in your family and interacting with people in the outside world.

Anytime you make a rule, you are setting a boundary. You're establishing what's important to you as a family. To your toddler, you are making it clear that 'Mummy and Daddy are not going to budge on this, because this is important to us. These are our family values and this is how we expect you to behave.'

Rules and boundaries are not just there to teach your toddler good behaviour. You're setting parameters within which he can feel safe, because he knows that he can play in the space in between. Without that, life seems too confusing and overwhelming. Believe it or not, he wants you to lay down the rules! He'll feel *secure* when he knows where he stands.

Throughout this chapter, you'll find tips and proven techniques to help you to confidently introduce rules and discipline. I suggest that you read it together and agree on a course of action now.

Finding the right balance with rules

Let me ask you a question. If I say the word 'strict', how does it resonate with you? For some people, 'being strict' brings up memories of their own childhoods, where strict meant no compromise, no choices and no fairness. Or, even worse, corporal punishment. Of course you don't want to repeat that with your children. But you don't want to go in the other direction and have your toddler swinging from the chandeliers, either. Too many parents these days have become so frightened to discipline that they've gone to the other extreme and let their children run wild. You have to find a happy medium. In this book you'll learn to pull from both ends – firm but fair.

RULES CHECKLIST

What are the basic rules you should be teaching your child during these years?

◆ **Be kind to one another.**

◆ **Listen and do what you are told.**

◆ **No name-calling.**

◆ **No throwing food or toys.**

◆ **No jumping on furniture.**

Add to this list your own family rules.

It's a good idea to post the rules, even though your toddler can't read, because – to be honest with you – it's an important reminder to you and your partner about staying on the same page and being consistent. If you say one thing one day, and then disregard it the next, you're sending mixed messages to your toddler. So if one of you says 'No' and the other 'Yes', the list can help you stand firm together.

Introducing the rules

The toddler years are all about exploration and learning. I call toddlers my little Curious Georges, because they are curious in such a lovely, innocent way. They drop the spoon down the toilet to see whether it can float in the water. Or, they watch a cartoon where the characters are on a treasure island, then go and dig up something from the garden and make a big mess.

When I think of the toddler years, I don't think of little kids being all clean and pristine. I think of a toddler eating spaghetti, sauce all over her face, or playing up to her neck in mud and paint. Everything's new. She's learning so much and has a wonderful enthusiasm about the world from her tiny perspective.

Understanding that much of what toddlers do stems from curiosity and learning – and not an intentional attempt to do something wrong or naughty – will help you to keep *Perspective*. Parents complain about things like: 'She just started drawing on the wall'; however, from your child's perspective, she was simply drawing on paper and wondered: 'Does it work on the walls as well?' She didn't go out of her way to mess up the walls. She just didn't know she wasn't supposed to do it because she hadn't been told. And told again: 'We sit at the table or we stand at an easel and we draw only on paper.' It really is that simple.

- ◆ **Confidence**
- ◆ **Patience**
- ◆ **Discipline**
- ◆ **Perseverance**
- ◆ **Energy**
- ◆ **Commitment**
- ◆ **Plan Ahead**
- ◆ **Perspective**
- ◆ **Humour**

You'll actually need all of the tools in your backpack as you create the foundation of good behaviour with your toddler: *Confidence*, to believe in what you're doing so you don't waver; *Discipline* to tackle it; *Patience*, *Perseverance* and *Energy* and *Commitment* to do it over and over; *Perspective*, because you may need to remind yourself *why* you are doing it; *Plan Ahead* to avoid meltdowns; and, of course, *Humour*, to laugh inside at the lengths to which your toddler will go to get his own way.

TIPS FOR SETTING RULES

- ◆ **Teach your toddler there is a rule in place by being firm, repetitive and consistent.**

- ◆ **When you say 'No', explain why. Many times! But, remember, these little ones can't reason, so don't go into a long explanation. Something simple like: 'We don't draw on the walls, we colour on paper' or 'We don't pull the dog's tail because it hurts him' is what's needed.**

- ◆ **Eventually she'll learn what type of behaviour you don't want, and she'll accept it and cohere to it. She's learning from you how to do it properly, which, in turn, makes it the right way.**

It takes as long as it takes

Here is something important to understand: your toddler will not learn your rules overnight and if she's already developed bad habits, it will take even longer.

Parents are always asking me, 'How long will it take?' The answer is this: It takes as long as it takes you to follow through and be consistent with it. So I throw the question back: Parents, how long will it take?

It's through repetition and conditioning that children learn the difference between acceptable and unacceptable behaviour. Parents often ask why they have to explain things over and over again, and the simple answer is because repetition is how *anyone* learns. You get better at a sport if you practise it. It's the same with your toddler and her behaviour. She gets better the more she practises. She's not going to learn the first time you say something. Not only is she trying to understand what you're teaching her, but she's learning language at the same time. She's just starting to put sentences together and grasp concepts.

Some parents don't believe this, insisting, 'This is just the way my child is.' That is simply not the case. She just hasn't been taught properly. *You* shape your toddler's behaviour by your standards and expectations, and your reinforcement of them.

Remember, just as repetition works in teaching your child good behaviour, it also works in teaching bad behaviour. If you're teaching the wrong thing over and over again, it becomes so much harder to change. The reason is that the behaviour you *don't* want has already been ingrained. Take heart: it's not impossible to change poor behaviour, it just takes longer. That's why it is so important to teach your toddler good behaviour and immediately re-train when you notice bad behaviour. And be sure to follow through – this is where the teaching begins.

When to start teaching the rules?

When your toddler is younger than two, tone of voice and facial expressions are used to let him know when he's doing something he shouldn't do. By two or two-and-a-half, most toddlers have the mental capacity to *begin* to understand the difference between 'good' and 'bad' behaviour. It's at this age that I suggest you start using what are commonly known as 'Time-out' strategies, such as the 'Naughty Step' technique on page 108–10, or the 'Toy Confiscation' technique on page 113. Soon enough he'll begin to understand that there is a consequence for his behaviour.

The rules are fundamentally the same, whether your toddler is two, three, or four. 'No hitting' is no hitting. It's just that the older your child becomes, the more he's able to understand and remember what's expected of him. While the rules remain the same, your expectations need to be realistic and age appropriate. Remember: it's only through breaking the rules and having consequences again and again that a toddler understands what to do and why.

> ## Tip: Rule role-playing
>
> ◆ **One way you can begin to teach rules is through role-play. I think of it as 'mini-world', where you can have Teddy throwing his food on the floor at the restaurant.**
>
> ◆ **Role-play what Teddy should do.**

Testing, testing

When you first teach the rules to your toddler, you are informing her about what is right and wrong. You don't use a discipline technique because she didn't actually know that she'd done anything wrong. However, once you've given the explanations and explained the consequences for continuing the behaviour, she has some choices! What if she keeps doing it?

You shouldn't put a technique in place the first time you introduce a rule. He should not be disciplined because he hasn't yet been told not to do something. Only after you've explained and he then does it intentionally do you start the steps of discipline.

Parents ask me how they'll know whether or not she actually *understands* she's doing something wrong. Actually, it's pretty simple. You'll know she understands when you tell her not to do something, and she looks at you and goes back to do it again. Often she might even laugh. That's her way of clearly defying what you're saying and wondering if you're going to hold firm in stopping her.

Sometimes you see kind of a crabwalk. She shuffles sideway and puts her finger out, as if to touch something. She's waiting for a reaction – testing the boundaries: 'Are you really saying this is a line I can never cross or is this something that you're just saying for now?' as you shout out, 'I mean it!' To mean it is to follow through.

There are so many things going on at this toddler age that you have to decipher. Is it a power play because she wants to overrule what you're saying? Or, is it because she doesn't understand? You have to work it out so that you know when to discipline and when to step back. Your motivation is also important. You need to create boundaries with valid reasons behind them. It's not about wanting perfection or worrying about your toddler making a mess. It's about safety and what you feel is right.

Don't be angry the first time your child breaks a rule – the only reason she *knows* that it's a rule is by breaking it.

BEYOND 'NO'

Do you find yourself saying '*No, no, no*' all day long? Communicating with toddlers is almost like learning a new language. Here are some tips on ways to let her know what to do without actually using the word:

◆ **Get down on her level and make direct eye contact.**

◆ **Keep your statements simple and short.**

◆ **Use words that convey what she would feel. Touching the hot stove would be: 'Ouch, hot. Owie.'**

◆ **See if you can rephrase your request in a positive way. Instead of 'No, don't pull the cat's tail', say 'Pat the cat gently, like this' and demonstrate.**

Issue a warning first

A warning establishes that you're being serious about what you're asking your toddler to do – or not to do.

Toddlers are primarily right brained. The right hemisphere of the brain is where non-verbal facial expressions and body language is perceived, while the left hemisphere is where language and logical thinking occur. The left hemisphere does not strongly come on line until school age. Because of the dominance of the right hemisphere, your facial expression and tone of voice catch a toddler's attention much more than the words you're saying. That's why, when you issue a warning, you do it with a slow, low tone of voice and a firm face. It reinforces your message.

I also suggest getting down to his level, and holding his hands to keep him at arm's length. This doesn't mean grabbing his arm or being aggressive (that's a sign of a loss of control and anger), but gently holding his hands down as you connect eye-to-eye and issue the warning (see below). The gestures that you make are just as important as the tone of your voice when you give warnings or discipline your child. If you're explaining in a firm voice why she has to stop throwing, but you have body language that's apologetic, that's confusing. Or, if you're angry and clenching your jaw, your body language speaks far more than anything that you could ever say.

> **WARNING TECHNIQUE**
>
> ◆ **Get down to his level.**
> ◆ **Take his hands.**
> ◆ **Look him directly in the eye.**
> ◆ **Use a low tone.**
> ◆ **Have a serious look on your face.**

Changing your voice tone and body language can be effective when disciplining, but not if you are using your 'warning voice' all the time. If it becomes your normal tone of voice, then when you do have to issue a warning it won't work. It's like the boy who cried wolf too many times. Another thing I see parents do is to allow their toddlers to hug them as they are issuing a warning. This sends a mixed message that confuses him – is he doing something wrong or not? Also, you need to be able to see his face and make eye contact so you know if you are getting through to him.

Asking or telling? Get clear!

When disciplining, parents get into trouble in many ways. The most major problem lies in the way they are communicating their expectations. Are they asking or *telling* their child something? There's a big distinction. If I ask you, I give you a choice. If I tell you, there's no negotiation. When you are making a boundary or teaching a rule, be sure that you tell, not ask. I see parents make this mistake all the time: 'You don't want to hit your friend, do you?' rather than 'No hitting'. Say what you mean.

Stay calmly in control

Using a slow, low tone also helps you to feel more in control than if you shout and yell. If he shouts at you, use your slow, low voice to tell him not to speak to you like that. Don't join in! Shouting and yelling come from a place of anger and frustration. When you're in an emotional state, you're losing control and it's not effective. Your child becomes afraid and you can end up doing or saying something you'll regret later.

If you feel like you are becoming short-tempered with your child and feel you want to shout or hit in frustration, take a breather. Calm down before doing anything else. Take yourself into another room. You do not want to lose control; it's unhealthy. Lock yourself in the bathroom and slowly count to ten, breathing in through your nose and out through your mouth. This breathing exercise will regulate the tension you are feeling, so your whole body will calm down and feel more relaxed. If ten isn't enough to calm you down, do 20 ... as many as you need to have a clear head.

Smacking

This is as controversial today as it ever was, and it's something that all parents need to avoid. What exactly does this physical act support? Certainly not a healthy relationship – or positive role modelling or effective discipline – but, rather, more of what I would classify as fear. If teaching your child the importance of doing something morally correct involves injecting fear that she may be hurt as a consequence, then what is she actually learning?

No parent ever gave their child a smack when they were feeling OK. It always comes from a place of frustration and anger. We know healthy communication cannot flow if anger is present. Smacking creates a breakdown in communication. It can't replace what needs to be said. Don't hit your child.

Many parents have lost it once with their toddler and thought: 'What did I just do?' That realisation may help you to understand what is not working – and then you can change it. If you have lashed out in frustration, you need to take responsibility, and take steps to discover what is causing you to feel helpless and out of control. From here, you'll need to take the necessary actions to discipline without resorting to violence. And, as you are a role model, and teaching your child the importance of good behaviour, you should also, without question, apologise: 'It's wrong to hit and I am sorry. Mummy lost control and that's not right.'

The toddler years are not just about your child's journey, but your own. You are tested every day. It's not an easy road, but it is also not an impossible one. When you realise that you've made a mistake, you can self-correct.

Discipline techniques

As you read this section, you will see that I have not offered 101 ways to discipline. That's because having too many options pretty much guarantees not doing any of them properly. Why? Because the mind won't focus and sustain what's necessary. While it is true that children have different temperaments and personalities, no child escapes the developmental stages of the toddler years. From working with hundreds of parents and toddlers, I've found that the results have been more successful when parents master one technique and use it effectively, rather than having loads of options to consider.

The Naughty Step

Known by millions of you who've seen me on my shows; however, not always implemented correctly!

The 'Naughty Step' technique is a form of timeout. It is a very effective and efficient way to teach a child that some behaviour is not acceptable. For young toddlers, it's about calming down and realising what happens when they behave a certain way. But, for a mature four-year-old, it's also about thinking about his behaviour with remorse. He learns that if he misbehaves, the consequence will be sitting there for a length of time and he'll be missing out on the good time he could be having.

Because I deal with different ages, I decided that the length of time on the Naughty Step should be one minute per year of a child's life. So, for a four-year-old, that's four minutes. Half an hour would be unrealistic. You can't get a toddler to sit at a table for 20 minutes, so how would you get him to sit in timeout for 30?

NAUGHTY STEP TECHNIQUE

1. Low-toned authoritative warning. Use eye contact.

2. Take child to step and explain.

3. Walk away. Set timer for one minute per year of age.

4. Replace child in timeout without talking. Reset timer.

5. Explain for the second time.

6. Apologies.

7. Hugs and kisses.

8. Move on.

THE NAUGHTY STEP TECHNIQUE

◆ **Before you need it, designate a spot in your house.**

◆ **When she misbehaves, give a warning. This gives her a chance to self-correct.**

◆ **If she continues to misbehave, take her to the step and explain why she's there: 'You have to sit here because we don't hit.' Tell her how long she's going to be on the step, this lets her know what's expected.**

◆ **Walk away, and set the timer for one minute per year of age. You walk away so that *you* remain composed and so that there can be no conversation or power play on her part and so that she realises that actions equals consequences.**

◆ **She'll mostly likely try to get up, at least at first. If she gets up, you put her back and reset the timer without talking. If necessary, do this again and again, until she can sit still for the length of time you've set.**

◆ **Consistently putting her back sends a very strong message that you mean what you say and are following through. Your job is to stay calm and consistent, no matter how many times you have to put her on the spot. What's most important is that you are in control. You know that if she gets off, you are going to put her back. She feels your Commitment and Perseverance, and that goes a long way towards making this work.**

◆ **Your child may get off the step and look to play what I call 'cat & mouse', waiting for you to run and place her back over again. If she runs back to the spot when you approach, ignore it. She's already put herself back.**

◆ **When the timer goes off, go back and say, 'OK, time's up.' Explain again why she was there because when she's very young, she may not remember. You may also have placed her back for so long that you may *both* be struggling to remember why she's on the step. Repeat the message: 'You hit and that's not OK.'**

◆ **Ask her to apologise. The apology is very important, as it helps your child take responsibility for her actions and helps her start to learn how to redeem herself when she does something inappropriate.**

◆ **Once she's apologised, give hugs and kisses, which show that you're not withholding any affection or love from your child, but teaching the concept of consequences.**

◆ **Give yourself a slient thumbs up for being calm, consistent and following through. A lesson taught is a lesson learnt.**

When I was developing the technique, I also knew that at the same time you're teaching right from wrong, your child is at an age where she is experiencing intense separation anxiety. That's why I use a step or spot where your toddler can see you. Step, chair, mat – it really doesn't matter what you choose, as long as it's a safe spot and one where you can see what he's doing. Usually it's somewhere near the kitchen or play area.

Having spent two decades teaching the Naughty Step technique, I am still faced with the same two questions. The first is: 'Why won't he stay when I put him there?' The answer is that he feels he doesn't have to until you reinforce – through repetition – that you're in charge. Would a man stay in prison if he wasn't forced to? I'm also constantly asked: 'Why is it taking so long? I thought he would get it faster.' What's the answer to that one? It's because the steps aren't being done properly. Let me take you through it, step-by-step, and explain why each step is important.

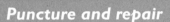

- ◆ **Persistence**
- ◆ **Patience**
- ◆ **Perseverance**

Puncture and repair

Why is this technique so important from a relationship standpoint? You are teaching your child what psychologists call 'rupture and repair'. I like to call it 'puncture and repair'. Through the Naughty Step technique, your toddler is learning that when he does something that's not OK, a puncture between him and another person has been created, and it needs to be fixed. Apologising is the repair. Think of it like a puncture on a bike, which you have to repair before you can get back on again. Of course your toddler won't understand this intellectually, but he's learning a critical relationship skill.

As a parent, it's important to occupy yourself with something else while implementing discipline. You don't want to be like a prison guard standing over your child. Know within yourself that you're going to follow through on the steps, and after you place her on the step, show her that you're going about your own business. Wipe a few plates, load the dishwasher, or engage with your other children – this shows her that being on the Naughty Step is not stopping everything else.

Remember, it's not the magic of the prop, it's the magic you are going to bring out of yourself to sustain the process. Have patience and persevere. It doesn't matter how many times it takes. If you stick to it, eventually she will learn. I've seen parents go from putting a child back 40 times to eight to nothing. The key is to *follow the steps consistently and not to give in.*

Your child's temperament may influence how strictly you keep her on the Naughty Step. If a strong-willed child gets off the step and is sitting near to it, I would put her back. With a generally easy-going toddler, I'd let her sit next to it, rather than directly upon it. You'll know your child well enough to decide how precise you need to be for her to get the point.

Troubleshooting the Naughty Step technique

If it's not working, ask yourself the following questions:

◆ What if she talks to me and calls me names on the step? Simple answer is you ignore her. She wants to reel you in to take away the control.

◆ She laughs, she thinks it's a game. She laughs to diffuse you being in charge. If you give her all the power and control then you will feel disempowered and it will seem like a game to you.

◆ She puts herself in timeout. It has no effect. A timeout is not a timeout unless it's coming from the disciplinarian in the family. Any other time than that, it's an ordinary step or an ordinary chair.

◆ Am I using it for everything, like not sharing and crying, rather than only when a rule is broken?

◆ Do I put my child back *every* time she runs off, no matter how many times?

◆ Am I doing every step as outlined above? There's no such thing as the technique failing. You fail the technique. For example, it's important to have the second explanation because you're reminding her why she's there. A lot of parents are so exasperated after spending an hour placing their child back that they're not even worried about whether they get an apology or not. Or parents will place their child on the step and, when the time is up, shout out from afar, 'You can get off your step now!' rather than coming back and finishing properly. Each and every step, taken in sequence, is important.

- Am I keeping time? A lot of parents say that they don't wear a watch. Well, then, put a stopwatch around your neck or go to the microwave or a timer.

- Am I doing it for every child who needs it? Sometimes parents say that they can't do two or three children at the same time. So, if you've got multiples, do one – then do the other.

- If you don't remember the steps, copy them out and stick them on the fridge or above the spot (or step) you've chosen to do the technique.

One strike and you're out

This is another form of discipline that can be used when your child has a lot of angry behaviour that needs to be diffused – or you have a child with poor listening skills or oppositional behaviour. You'll find that as you help him diffuse his anger and his listening skills improve, you can then go on to use the Naughty Step. Because of the separation-anxiety issues with two-year-olds, I primarily use this technique with three-and-half- and four-year-olds.

I recently used this solution on a little four-year-old boy with whom I was working. He'd throw things when he got angry. He'd seen his older brother act the same way, so it was natural for him to copy. The 'One Strike and You're Out' technique quickly taught him to control his anger. Here's how to do it.

THE ONE STRIKE AND YOU'RE OUT TECHNIQUE

- **This technique has no warning and no time limit.**
- **Remove him from your personal space and let him know why.**
- **If he manoeuvres himself back, remove him again without saying anything. Each time he challenges you, put him back.**
- **When putting him back, don't pay attention to him, avoid eye contact, and use your low, stern tone of voice. The key is to stay calm and not give him any attention at all.**
- **His temper will peak at some stage and then he'll begin to calm down. That's when he'll ask to come back.**
- **Let him know that he can come into your personal space when he apologises.**
- **When he does apologise, praise him and let him back into the room with everyone.**

Troubleshooting the One Strike and You're Out technique

If it's not working, ask yourself the following questions:

- Do I allow my child to come back without apologising for his behaviour?

- Do I allow the behaviour to go on for far too long before saying, 'You're going to go to One Strike and You're Out'? One Strike and You're Out means one strike. Not two, not three. It means you're nipping the behaviour in the bud. It's as simple as that.

The Toy Confiscation technique

Another discipline technique I've found effective for older toddlers is the removal of toys. This is most useful if the problem *involves* toys. For example, I was working with a three-year-old boy who threw his toys every time he got angry. I'd take his toys, put them into a box, and keep them for two days. He'd be so upset and say, 'I want my toys back!' But I'd hold firm for two days, saying, 'Respect your toys or you will lose them.' Pretty soon, he stopped throwing.

THE TOY CONFISCATION TECHNIQUE

If your toddler is fighting over toys or throwing them or otherwise acting out with his toys, take them away.

The length of time you keep the toys away depends upon your toddler's age – and what he's done. I would give a very mature four-year-old two days to make the point; however, this technique doesn't really work with younger tots, as they don't have a long enough attention span or the ability to understand the concept of bargaining that's involved.

If you use this technique, don't buy him a new toy for good behaviour. That just sends the message that no matter how many toys you confiscate, he's always going to get more.

Helping toddlers deal with feelings

A toddler can't tell you how she feels. Instead, she shows her emotions through facial expressions and sounds: '*Grrrrh!*', '*Whrrrr!*' or '*Eeeeee*'. Part of your job is to help her to put language to those things: 'Oh, you're angry', 'I see you're sad' and 'Oh, you're frustrated'.

What you shouldn't do with the emotion is try to control it. It's OK for your toddler to feel the way she does, as long as her secondary behaviour is not destructive. I don't think it's unhealthy to be angry, jealous or frustrated. These are natural emotions. But I see parents all the time try to get their toddler *not* to feel those emotions. We need to teach that all feelings are healthy, as long as they don't result in harmful behaviour. Even tantrums should just be ignored, rather than controlled. It's only the lashing out in aggression that is not acceptable.

We're becoming a society of parents who don't want their kids to feel anything that we've decided is 'negative'; however, I believe that every emotion should be felt and allowed to breathe. When we start to control, emotions become buried – particularly if you think, 'No, they can't feel that way'. From this, children learn that they can't express outwardly what they are feeling. So where does it go? It sits there and it comes out when they're older.

PROBLEM PARENTS

Do you recognise any of these characters in yourself?

- **The Negotiator: 'If you do this, I'll give you this.'**
- **The It's-OKer: 'You just weed on the rug, but that's OK.'**
- **The Procrastinator: 'We'll get to it … in a minute.' And the minute stretches on and on …**
- **The Too-Many-Choices-Giver: 'What do you want to wear today? What do you want to eat? What do you want to play?'**

Each of these behaviours sends a confusing message to your toddler. Be straightforward, firm but loving, and follow through.

Tantrums

It's no longer just known as the 'terrible twos', but the terrible threes and sometimes even fours as well. It even might start as early as 15 months. I'm talking about the melt-down into a screaming mass that we call tantrums. No matter who your child is, chances are that at some point in the toddler years she will erupt into rage and frustration.

Tantrums shock parents more than anything else. How can this screaming, unreasonable person be my sweet child? You feel helpless and, if it occurs in public, embarrassed. Don't. That's what she's hoping for.

Tantrums are a perfectly normal way for your child to express herself. She's overwhelmed, tired, angry and doesn't know how to express herself any other way. Most of all she's frustrated. She wants to do something and either *she* doesn't have the skills or *you're* setting limits. Whatever you do, don't give in. If you give her what she wants, you're setting the scene for future tantrums. See my 'Tantrum' tips on the next page for help.

Tantrums happen with toddlers. You can be observant and minimise her tiredness or hunger to avoid them in certain situations. You can divert her attention or distract her when she's very young. But there are times when, no matter what you do, tantrums will occur – they are part of how toddlers develop and learn how to regulate feelings. They won't last forever!

Make no mistake, however. Some of these behaviours are taught – for example, when your child screams because she wants you to pick her up and you do; when your child throws food on the floor and she avoids having to eat her dinner; when your child lays down in the park and therefore doesn't have to get into the pushchair; or when she causes such a scene that giving in seems better than the embarrassment of being seen by the entire neighbourhood.

HELPING A CHILD CALM DOWN

When you say, 'Calm down', how can your toddler know what you are talking about?

◆ **When I tell a child to calm down, I say, 'You're angry. I don't want you throwing things and feeling really angry. Calm down. This behaviour is not calming down.'**

◆ **For younger kids who might not get the concept, you can create an emotional wheel. Little lollipop faces showing different emotions help her to learn about feelings. Tell her to point to the face that she's 'feeling'. While she can't put words to her feelings, over time you are helping her to learn to label emotions.**

◆ **If you know what upset her, help her tell the story of what is going on: 'So you saw the big dog coming towards you and that scared you?' This will help her to calm down because she doesn't feel alone in her feeling, which can be scary.**

Outside the house

If your child has a tantrum away from the house, take her outside or off scene to deal with it. If there is no place or time to do a Naughty Step, give a warning: 'If you don't stop, when you get home, you will go on the Naughty Step.' If she doesn't stop, then be sure to follow through when you get home. This is crucial because if there is no follow through, she will soon not believe your words.

Heading Tantrums Off at the Pass

If you know your child has trouble with things like leaving a friend's house, turning the telly off, or not wanting to go somewhere, head tantrums off by being what I call a 'Speaking Clock':

◆ Soften the blow by giving a warning: 'In 5 minutes you have to turn the telly off (or leave Chris's house).' Oftentimes that is enough to prevent a meltdown.

◆ If that doesn't stop him from reacting, then you have to take the bull by the horns. Give him a choice if possible: 'Remember, I told you that we were going to have to turn it off. Do you want to do it or shall I?' 'Do you want to put your coat on by yourself or shall I do it?'

◆ Two to five year olds love to get into power plays with you and so might well get up and do it to 'win'. If not, you do it. Following through on your word is crucial.

Troubleshooting tantrums

If your child's tantrums are getting worse or more frequent, ask yourself the following questions:

◆ Am I making this a bigger deal than it is? Tantrums are part of toddler behaviour.

◆ Am I giving in to what she wants to avoid a scene? This only reinforces it.

◆ Do I have one standard at home and another when in public? Again, it encourages her to do it more.

◆ Am I interacting with him, apart from simply making sure he doesn't hurt himself? Interaction is attention, and that's what he's looking for.

> ## TANTRUM TIPS
>
> - ◆ **Look around to make sure that there's nothing nearby that could hurt her.**
>
> - ◆ **Ignore her behaviour. Giving a tantrum attention reinforces the idea that if she acts this way she'll get what she wants.**
>
> - ◆ **Some children will come out of a tantrum faster if they are held. For others this only intensifies it. Experiment to see which works better.**
>
> - ◆ **Don't get angry yourself. If you feel like you're going to lose your temper, leave the room. Getting mad will only make the situation worse.**
>
> - ◆ **Don't try to talk to or reason with her. She not an adult, and she won't get it. Simply wait until the tantrum burns itself out. Then re-engage.**
>
> - ◆ **And, please, there will be no videotapes or photos of this performance**

Acting out

In addition to tantrums, toddler frustration and their regular testing of the boundaries can manifest itself in different ways, depending on their age and the activity in which they're engaged. You may see biting, hitting, throwing and even weeing on the floor. These are all forms of acting out. If any of these happen, it's good to remind yourself it's not personal. But, yes, it's intentional and it's impulsive. She's frustrated. She's saying, 'Pay attention to me and give me what I want now.'

Many parents feel horrified when their child bites another child – or refuses to share her toys, hits or throws things. In Chapter 12, I'll go into details about the best ways to teach toddlers to share and acquire other social skills. Here, however, we're going to look at understanding the naughty behaviour and learning how to curb it.

First of all, ask yourself: Is this behaviour a one-off thing or is it recurring? Try to look at the underlying cause, so you can make a plan to solve the real problem. If your child gets away with aggressive behaviour at home, it leads to being disrespectful and hostile to other kids at school and beyond. When behaviour of any sort becomes destructive, it needs to be disciplined using the Naughty Step or One Strike and You're Out techniques. Full stop.

Hitting and Biting

For some reason, parents seem to think biting is worse than hitting because it leaves a mark. But both come under the category of unacceptable behavior and must be dealt with. If it is your child who is hitting or biting on a playdate, here are the steps:

- If your child is under two, say, 'Owie, no, that hurts. Say you're sorry' (or have him give a hug). Give praise with your tone of voice, 'yes, that's what we like. Be nice.' Put him on the sidelines with you so he has to watch the play rather than participate for a few minutes.

- If he's over two, follow the same steps as in the bullet above, but then institute the naughty chair (or spot if you are outside) for an amount of time equal to the child's age.

- If your child is the one who is bitten, console him and hope that the other parent will deal with it. You can ask the parent to teach her child that it's inappropriate, but you can't make it happen. If she's not willing, remove your child and yourself from the situation. You don't want to end up in a fight as well.

- In some circumstances, when a group of parents are minding kids together and everyone has the authority to put discipline in place, you may end up being the one to teach another child by using the steps above.

Bullying

Bullying behaviour begins in the toddler stages, when you start to see little ones using their bodies to intimidate or take something away from a more docile child, name-calling or being aggressive to animals. As a parent, it is your job to recognise that this behaviour is unacceptable and nip it in the bud straightaway. If left uncurbed, you will see more and more bullying behaviour as he gets older.

If you don't teach your child not to behave in an antisocial manner at home, there will undoubtedly be more complications for you and for him down the line. Unfortunately, there are toddlers at this age who are being expelled from nursery schools because of this type of behaviour, which distracts other children from participating in a happy nursery environment. So what can you do now? Here are my top tips:

- Stop it as soon as you see it, using the Naughty Step or Sideline techniques (see p109 and p123).

- Encourage his social behaviour by setting up one-on-one play dates. Role-play how to join in and interact positively beforehand. Once he can do one-on-one, encourage him to join up with larger groups.

- When he's about four, teach him the importance of having empathy. Ask him to think about how the other person feels: 'How do you think that person felt when you hit her? Do you think she was sad when you did that? Do you think you would be sad if somebody did that? How would you feel?'

SIGNS THAT YOUR TODDLER NEEDS MORE CONSISTENT DISCIPLINE

- **Everything becomes troublesome.**
- **He doesn't listen or take direction.**
- **He's obstinate on every level – you say 'black' and he says 'white'.**
- **You feel like there is no pleasing him. Even when you give him what he wants, he changes his mind.**

Dealing with defiance

If you are dealing with defiance, you most likely have a child with a very feisty, strong-willed temperament. There are no two ways about it: you're going to be even more challenged on the discipline front. But knowing and expecting this means that you can take a deep breath in and think: 'OK, we're here. It's hard, but I know what's going on.' He will resist discipline; he doesn't want it, but he needs it. Otherwise he feels he's in control and that's terrifying for him. He'll continue to push in order to get you to assert control. You *have* to set limitations and say: 'This is it and I'm not backing down.'

When you are met with defiance, it's the first time that you're being tested as a parent. You either have to stand up and raise him with your core values, or you're going to back down and teach him that what you believe doesn't have any clout. This sets the stage for disaster and your lives will only get harder by the day. Mark my words. It's easy to shift the goalposts to avoid a fight, but the consequences in the long run can be disastrous.

You have to step up and show him that you're the authority figure – the one who's in charge. When you do that calmly and consistently, he will follow your lead and understand that you can't be overruled on certain things. Without being fearful of you, he knows what he can and can't do, and what the consequences are if he breaks a rule. This creates a sense of both safety and respect.

If you're seeing super-defiant behaviour over and over again, there is a problem. And the problem is not him. It's you. Chances are you are trying to control too many aspects of your child's life. With a strong-willed child, it's important to work out when you need to be in control and when you can let it go. You don't need a power play on everything. You can't fight every battle. You've got to work alongside him to let him have control over the things that don't matter – such as whether he wears the green jumper or the red – but stay firmly in control over the important things, like holding hands while crossing the road. If you get into a power play, and he won't answer, say: 'Either you make a decision now or I will do it for you.' And then do it. He'll learn to speak out next time.

Believe me it's hard; I know it's hard. If it was easy, nobody would have a problem disciplining toddlers. Which is why I'm here to offer you tips and techniques to pull you through. Every child will up the ante when you step up and take charge. What's your breaking point? Your child may reintroduce you to yourself. People say to me that when I have children, they will be well-behaved; but I always reply that my children will have tantrums because *all* toddlers do, and they will most likely be strong-willed because I am. But I won't fail to show you how to deal with it.

Discipline with multiples or siblings close in age

When there is a problem between children, getting down to their level and listening to both sides is important because even if they can't fully explain exactly what happened, you can grasp a majority of the story. Look at both sides as much as you can. If you weren't present at the outset, you may have to piece it together as best you can.

Don't assume if one child comes in holding her head, crying that her brother hit her that she is the innocent one. Kids are clever! Don't assume anything. Get a bigger picture of what went on and *then* make a decision about how you're going to deal with it.

At the end of the day, you have to make a decision whether they both end up being given a warning – or one ends up in discipline, or they both do. If you decide both need to go on the Naughty Step, you can take turns disciplining one at a time or do them both together; it's entirely your choice. Whatever is easier for you. If you do discipline at the same time, choose spots away from one another so they can't interact. And if you find they try the divide and conquer on the Naughty Step – both running off at the same time, do it one at a time.

It's important to give each child eye contact when you're listening or issuing a warning. When you look at or talk to only one child, the other won't feel that she's being heard, and that feels unfair. Parents tend to favour eye contact with the child who is more verbal, because they can get a response back. So be very wary of this when you are in the midst of a conflict between multiples or children close in age.

Above all, don't ignore fights between toddlers. They are not old enough to work things out on their own. That will come later in life. Right now, you do need to intervene. I know it may feel like you're the WWE ref every 15 minutes – which is probably roughly how often you will be dealing with things, every 15 or 20 minutes – but they do need a referee at this stage.

Discipline outside the house

You're out and about and your child is acting up. Disciplining your child in public puts you on the spot because you feel that people are judging you. And, in fact, they may well be! But if you're not consistent, you actually create greater problems for yourself. Your toddler is very observant! She'll notice the difference and will act up accordingly. Why wouldn't she throw a fit at the shop when you give in so easily? Changing the way you discipline just because you're out in public can lead to uncontrollable behaviour. Because if it's OK to be inconsistent and let things slide when you're out of the house, soon that behaviour will take place when you are at home, too.

Your toddler *will* test you outside the house. She'll wonder whether your rules will apply outside, too. Take a deep breath and conserve your energy and focus to deal with the issue at hand, rather than focusing on who is in your surroundings, however embarrassed you may be. Don't worry about what people think. You've set the rules and boundaries. That's your standard and if those are broken – whether you're at home or out in public – you have to hold the line. Plain and simple.

Depending on their age and level of understanding, adapt the technique to the situation, always ignoring tantrums apart from ensuring that she won't get hurt. The Naughty Step can, for example, be adapted to a spot like a bench, a patch of grass or a car seat. A two-year-old who is fighting needs to be picked up and taken off scene, with a simple explanation: 'No throwing. It hurts! Owie!' Give her something else to do in a different spot.

You can certainly discipline three- and four-year-olds when you return home as well. It's up to you. Give her the warning to stop the behaviour. If she continues, tell her that when you get home she's going on the Naughty Step. Then, follow-through is a must. With younger toddlers it's more effective to do it straightaway.

If your child has a meltdown when you're driving, your main concern should be keeping your eyes on the road to drive safely. Can you block it out until you get to where you're going? If not, or if she's trying to get out of her car seat, pull over to the side of the road so that you can give her your full attention and deal with the situation.

Don't try to drive with one hand and reach back – and don't shout. I know many parents wish that their arms could stretch out like the character from *The Invincibles*, but they can't. These are the same parents who are constantly turning around to look at their child as they're driving. *If you can't control the situation while looking ahead, then pull over.*

Once you pull over, look at what triggered the meltdown. Why is she screaming? Does she keep on dropping a toy or something she's playing with on the floor? Is it, 'Why don't you pick me up?' Talk to her and try to distract her, put music on, and sing songs. Calm her down so that you can safely get to where you're going. Make it clear that you are not happy with this behaviour because you need to drive safely. Implement warnings freely and be aware that your focus will become better as you practise concentrating on what's in front of you as mayhem takes place in the back. By now I could put an entire orchestra in the back of a Mini and still drive.

THE SIDELINE TECHNIQUE

Sometimes your child is not misbehaving – meaning he's not being aggressive towards another child – but he's just not interacting well. He's picked up three or four toys rather than just one, for example, or not playing fairly. This doesn't warrant a Naughty Step. Instead, I'd use the Sideline technique:

- ◆ **Remind him to share what he has.**
- ◆ **If he doesn't, pick him up and place him on the sideline of the activity so he can see everybody else getting along and having fun.**
- ◆ **Say, 'You know what? You didn't play fairly, so now you've got to sit out for a little while and then you can go back and join in.'**
- ◆ **There's no set time limit for this. Don't overdo it, or you'll end up wasting their playtime. It's just a couple of minutes to drive home the point, 'This is what we want to see so that we can play fairly.'**

Troubleshooting the Sideline technique

If it isn't working, ask yourself the following questions:

- ◆ Am I allowing the sideline to become a part of the playing field? He has to sit just outside the space where the play is happening.

- ◆ Do I let him creep back in and join in with the play? The point of this technique is to be excluded so he learns that he has to behave in order to have fun.

- ◆ Do I give him something else to do while he's excluded? If he's playing, he's not excluded.

Whining

There's no doubt about it, most parents find whining highly annoying. It often shows up around three or four years of age. What exactly is it? It's when a child communicates with you using a regressed voice in a tone that's highly strung until she gets what she wants. It's the sister pest to the chant and if you are a parent who is highly stressed, then you need whining like a hole in the head.

Parents often relent in order for the noise to stop, which, of course, only guarantees that it will happen more often. The quickest way to stop it is not to say 'stop whining', but to mirror it back. When I am with a three- or four-year-old who whines, I say, 'Ask properly. Use your proper voice, not like this …' – and then I caricature back to her how she sounds in a humorous way with an exaggerated face. She'll look at my face all screwed up and think it's funny, but she'll begin to get it. Have her repeat her message in her proper voice so she shows you that she understands. Be sure not to respond to her request until she uses the right tone or you will reinforce whining as a way for her to get what she wants.

There is, however, a difference between your toddler making whining demands and coming up to you right after she's been hurt or upset and asking for something in a high-pitched tone because she needs soothing. It's important to recognise the difference and respond to your hurt child's needs.

Troubleshooting whining

If it's not working, ask yourself the following questions:

◆ Have I given in to whining? Whining continues when you give your child what she's whining for. It stops when you refuse to respond unless spoken to in a normal voice.

◆ Am I locked into a battle of wills? There's no toddler who does not know how to ask for something in a normal tone. She may refuse to ask properly because she's been so used to getting what she wants that way that she feels you'll give in. But, believe me, if she wants something badly enough and you stick to your guns, she *will* eventually give in.

◆ Am I consistently insisting she speak in a proper voice? Or are you only doing it sometimes? Every time you give in to whining, you reinforce the idea that it's OK to whine, so it will take longer to curb.

Talking toddler

When you're disciplining your toddler, he's not going to like it. He may shout, scream, throw a fit and, as he gets more verbal, say the most hurtful things. Don't take it personally. Parents so easily feel guilty and insecure – especially when this child they love so much is so upset. Have confidence that you're doing the right thing. To help you persist, here are some translations from common toddler language:

◆ 'I hate you!' means 'I'm angry right now.'

◆ 'I don't love you!' means 'I don't like what you're doing right now.'

◆ 'Go away from me!' means 'I don't want to hear what you're saying.'

◆ 'I don't like corn!' means 'I don't want it today.'

Really, all toddlers are saying in these circumstances is: 'I don't like that you're making up these rules! I don't like that I'm not in control. I don't like that you don't like what I want to do.' You've got to take their comments with a pinch of salt. When you take things personally, your child knows he's getting to you and that's what he wants. If it does hit a raw nerve, know that he doesn't comprehend the power of his words at this age.

'I Hate Granny'

You may be upset or even shocked by some of what your toddler says. Children use language differently from adults. Too often parents give such statements as 'I hate Daddy' or 'Grandpa stinks' power by focusing on them: 'Oh no you don't.' Instead:

◆ **Don't take such comments personally.**

◆ **Disarm the situation by ignoring it. Change the subject.**

Watching your own behaviour

Say what you mean

It's easy to get your language turned around and say 'no' when you mean 'yes'. 'Mummy, can we go to the park after dinner?' 'No, eat your dinner. We're going after dinner.' That's really 'Yes. We'll go to the park as soon as you eat dinner.' Don't say 'no', when you mean 'yes'. It's confusing to a toddler. Mean what you say and think about that before you say it: 'Mummy, we're going out to the park now?' 'Yes, we are going to the park, but we all need to take toilet trips first.'

Don't give toddlers too many choices

Do you remember when you were preparing for the arrival of your first baby? You went to the shop and were probably immediately overwhelmed with all the choices. What kind of pushchair? What brand of nappies? Now that you've entered the toddler years, the choices don't end, but the problems definitely start when you begin to give your little one too many choices – from what he wears to what he wants to eat.

We've become this consumer world where there are so many brands, so many choices. And, thanks to the Internet, we can research everything. Suddenly we're not just deciding between two things at the shop, but researching ten different items from different countries, reading reviews – and making ourselves crazy.

So, if we're overwhelmed, imagine how your toddler feels. I once saw a father asking his four-year-old what flavour of ice cream he wanted. The little boy said, 'Ummm …'. Faced with 15 different ice creams, he couldn't make a decision. His Dad was getting impatient and it was making the little boy anxious.

Look at it from the four-year-old's perspective. For him to choose an ice cream, he has to look at the colour of the ice cream, which has the most desirable wrapper, which is the biggest, and which comes with something extra special. That takes a long time. Toddlers simply lack the analytic capacity to analyse multiple choices. Simple solution – don't offer the whole menu! Do the eliminating yourself. Don't ask what kind of ice cream he wants. Say, 'Between chocolate and vanilla, which would you like?' Doing this sort of thing actually enables him to begin to learn how to make decisions.

When a toddler is between about 18 months and two years old, it's OK when he makes a choice and then changes his mind. He's just learning what he likes. By the time you get to three or four, he knows. So I say, make an older toddler stick with his decision. It will help him learn to live with the consequences of his choices.

Bargaining is as bad as too many choices

When you say to your child, 'You can have a treat if you eat five more bites,' you are setting yourself up for a contest of wills that will, when he gets older, eventually result in living with a mini-lawyer, negotiating over *everything*. Even at this young age it's not healthy. Because what happens? You throw out your five bites bargain, he eats one and then wants the treat. So you lower your request to three and he refuses. Pretty soon you're begging him to have just one more, he screams and you give in. He's won this skirmish and you're set up for future battles because you've just taught him that the rules are changeable.

Jo Jo No Nos: What *not* to say

You're in the midst of a toddler meltdown and are trying to get your toddler to calm down. Suddenly the most outrageous things come out of your mouth. Here's what some of my readers posted on my website that they've said in a moment of despair with their toddlers. This is where I thought you could do with some Humour from your backpack.

- **'If you don't listen, we will call up Santa and tell him to ignore you this year.'**

- **'If you two don't stop fighting, I'm going to put one of you in the boot and the other on the roof of the car.'**

- **'Annie loves *Willy Wonka and the Chocolate Factory*. When she starts acting up, I say, 'I guess it's a good thing we aren't in a chocolate factory. You might end up as a blueberry or a bad egg and then the Oompa Loompas would have to sing about you.'**

- **'When my boys were going through a period of taking delight in shocking everyone with their nudity, by running bare through the house several times each day, I told them they'd better be careful because the dog was going to 'bite it off!''**

No 'Wait until your father gets home'

Did you hear that when you were a child? It's hard when you're at your wits' end not to be tempted to use a threat, such as: 'Watch out or the monsters will take you away' or 'Daddy will deal with this when he gets home'. I've been told that the modern-day threat for some parents is: 'I'm ringing Supernanny *now*.' Great! Loving that one. I've now become the new bogeyman. My hope is that if you use the solutions I've talked about in this chapter, you won't need to resort to threats. If you take control and stay calm, you won't need to call *me* – you can just call yourself.

Praise for positive behaviour

I can't end a chapter about discipline without also talking about praising positive behaviour. So many people, when they've been dealing with a troublesome tot, tend to recognise all the things that are going wrong rather than what is going well. I really encourage you to find a balance. It's not all bad. If you can look through spectacles that see the good, then you have a ledge on which to start building.

You may be focused on disciplining him for not listening or throwing sand. But he also needs be encouraged and praised. Because, at this age, he's watching how you react to different situations and what you say. When communication is positive and encouraging, it starts to create a different kind of energy. It helps him to know what he's doing well and helps you to look at the brighter side of where you are with your child. Positive communication is an open door.

Encouraging and praising your child is the most effective way to reinforce good behaviour. Now, I'm not saying give blanket praise for everything. What's more important is to be specific and praise the effort and choices he's made: 'You remembered to say thank-you. Well done!' Then he'll know what he needs to do to create success again.

> ### Tip: The voice of praise
>
> ◆ Just as you want to use a low, firm voice when you're disciplining, you want to do the opposite with praise. Your voice should be higher and full of enthusiasm – 'Good job!'
>
> ◆ Include a hug, squeeze, high five, cheer, clap or whoop for more emphasis.

Praise is important because it makes your toddler's brain emit a feel-good chemical called dopamine. It gives him a little lift. So your child is now going to want to work hard to please you and get that feel-good blast again. If all you've been seeing is a downhill slide of negative behaviour, try to create opportunities for him to do something right. Praise his attempts to do small things right, even when they're not perfect. It's so important to avoid saying, 'No, no, no!' all the time, or 'To the Naughty Chair!' Praise his effort: 'Wow! You just had the whole afternoon and you didn't have to go to that Naughty Chair one time!'

By the age of three, you can start using reward charts in addition to praise. It's a way to visually record positive behaviour that is immensely effective for children this young because it is tangible. Five stars in a row and he gets a small treat. But don't go overboard and reward your child excessively for good behaviour. If he comes to expect a toy for things he should be doing anyway, you'll quickly be manipulated.

The hugs, the praise, the 'I love you' – all of these verbal and non-verbal affirmations are so important to your child. Above all else he wants to please you. And there is no such thing as too much positive attention. You don't spoil your child this way. A spoiled child is one who is allowed to disregard all the rules. One who has no boundaries.

REWARD CHARTS

- **Once he turns three, let him design his own chart with his favourite stickers and colours. He'll love the chance to be creative and you can give him a reward when he's finished to start the ball rolling.**

- **You can personalise the chart to fit your child. For example, perhaps he collects silver coins to go into his pirate chest. Or you draw a train track that goes over ten tunnels before it reaches home. Or a fairy jumps onto flower petals before it reaches the nectar. With a little bit of imagination, you can make a reward chart truly special for your child.**

- **Once a behaviour has been well learned, take it off the chart and add something new. You don't want to be giving stars for going to bed well for years when you could work on improving something else.**

6

The importance of play and stimulation

Coming out of the baby years, you've been focused on meeting your child's basic needs. As your little one enters his toddler years, it's now important to prioritise time for stimulation, too. Daily stimulation – both mental and physical – is critical to your child's brain and body development.

But this is not the age for structured lessons. It is through play and exploration that toddlers learn and develop. That's why you create a routine that does not just include set times for sleep, meals and snacks, but one that incorporates different types of play – pretend play, managed play with games, puzzles, books and outdoor activities. In this chapter, I'll share with you the different kinds of stimulation that your toddler needs, good activities, games and toys for each age, and my tips for engaging your child in ways that are fun for both of you.

Types of stimulation

There are four areas of human development where you can help support your toddler to grow:

◆ *Auditory*, listening and speaking, which is necessary for following directions and expressing oneself;

◆ *Visual*, seeing and recalling, which is necessary for sequencing and getting ready to read;

◆ *Motor*, using the large muscles of the body and being able to balance and be aware of left and right sides of body, as well as the body in space (spatial relations). This is important for physical activity;

◆ *Fine motor*, using the muscles of the hands and fingers, important for mastering tasks such as buttoning, doing up poppers, and holding a pencil.

Through specific activities, you can stimulate these areas and help your child develop mentally and physically, getting him ready for more academic tasks once he enters school.

These four categories are not necessarily separate. With toddlers, we do a lot of showing (visual) and telling (auditory). For example, you might ask your two-year-old, 'Where are your toes?' Or ask a three-year-old, 'Which one is the blue one?' You are helping them learn by pairing a sound with a sight. Similarly, 'Pick up the green sock and bring it to me' encourages him to use motor, auditory and visual skills. But it is good to understand what simple activities you can do with your toddler in each area.

◆ **Plan Ahead**
◆ **Commitment**
◆ **Perseverance**
◆ **Energy**

Don't worry – you don't need a degree in early childhood education to give your child the stimulation he needs! The common activities, toys and games toddlers love are the very ones that help them to develop. But you do need some tools from your backpack to make sure you plan the right kinds of activities – and put in the time necessary to foster brain and body development.

Auditory stimulation

You can help your toddler's speaking and listening by narrating what you're doing: 'Now we're washing up the pans' and 'Let's brush your hair'. Yes, your mouth will feel like sandpaper from so much talking but, believe me, it really helps a child to learn language! Chattering stimulates them on so many levels, and encourages an interest in their world.

At 18 months, you can help your child learn to follow instructions by giving her simple tasks to do. Make them very easy at first: 'Please pick up the socks and bring them to me' while she's in the same room with you. As she gets older, you can work up to multiple items and different rooms, so that, by the time she's four, you can say: 'Pick up your socks and knickers, put them into the laundry basket in the bathroom, and then come into the kitchen.'

There are also listening games you can buy that have your toddler identify all sorts of sounds from bumblebees and dogs barking to water running or a siren. I like those very much. But you don't have to spend any money on a shop-bought game. Instead you can simply gather together a number of common household items, such as keys, a timer, beans or rice in a jar, a bell or dish of water in which you can put your fingers and splash. Have your toddler close her eyes and see if she can identify the sounds. Or go out into the garden or park and see how many sounds you can hear. You can also play 'What does a cow say?' going through all of the farm-animal noises. Books with sounds also work for this.

See me, hear me

I loved to play this game with my little charges. It helps pair a sound with a visual. I collect sounds on tape (you can also use a DVD or download them from the Internet), such as a dog barking, a siren blaring, a bird tweeting and a baby crying. Then you paste pictures of these things on a board (draw them, cut them from a magazine or download them from the Internet). The game involves playing the sound, and encouraging your toddler to point to the correct picture. It's great for two- and three-year-olds.

Tapes or CDs of songs and stories written specifically for toddlers are also great for language development. And don't forget musical instruments, from maracas to triangles and tambourines, and little drums to castanets and jingle bells. It's so core for me to have a lot of music for toddlers, because it's happy and fun, while promoting listening, language and movement.

Don't be afraid to sing with her. I never sang so much as when I took care of toddlers. 'Row, Row Row Your Boat', 'The Grand Old Duke of York', 'Mary had a Little Lamb', 'Twinkle, Twinkle' and so many others. You can mix it up by having her sing them loudly and then softly. Add silly words, too, to help her spot the odd ones out!

It's also the time for reciting lots of nursery rhymes. The pairing of words with rhythm aids the learning of language. So does the pairing of words with hand actions. You probably started when she was a baby with 'This Little Piggy', by wiggling her toes, and 'Pat-a-Cake', clapping her hands together. As she gets older, she'll graduate to 'Incy Wincy Spider' and other more complicated rhymes. By three she can say and do them with you, as repetition has taught her how.

How could I write this book and not give you a few? You can find some of my favourites in the Appendix (see page 284), to get you started.

Visual stimulation

Visual stimulation is about seeing and remembering. It helps her to become 'reading ready'. Games like 'I Spy With My Little Eye' can be played anywhere. You say 'I spy with my little eye, something (red or round or whatever quality to describe the object you're seeing)' and she has to find it. You can do this inside or outside the house – or in the car, choosing objects inside the car (outside things move too fast). You can also play 'Find a blue car' or 'Find a white truck' when you are on the road.

Once she's around three years old, I like to stimulate a toddler visually by playing memory games. I put three items on a tray or piece of paper and then take them away. She has to remember what they were. As time goes on and she gets good at this, you can increase the number of items. As she turns four, you can make this more complicated by adding sequence. You put the three items on a tray or table in a particular order, have her look, then jumble up the items and have her reproduce the order.

Games like matching the top and tail of an animal, colour-matching games and Snap – where you find two of a kind of animals, numbers or the letters of the alphabet – are also wonderful.

Of course, there is no more important visual stimulation than reading to your toddler. Research shows that the best way to raise a reader is to read to her from babyhood. There are so many fabulous books for this age group, including lots with things to do – lift tabs, pull levers, pop up, push fingers through, touch and feel.

I like first books that are about recognising where a particular object is on the page or naming a particular animal. It helps with both language and visual recall. Sticker books are also fun because they are interactive – your child can stick while you read. Typically you begin with board books that can be wiped off and then graduate to the soft- or hardcover varieties. You can't really go wrong with these established brands for children's books: Lion, Usbourne, Dorling Kindersley, Ladybird and Campbell. Some of my favourites for each age group can be found at the end of the book (see page 293). There are also many fun books that highlight the stages that a toddler is going through – a new baby, potty-training, staying in bed, etc. – and you can use these to support what he's experiencing. I could go on and on about the positive messages that books establish, but I think you get where I am coming from.

Motor stimulation

To help your child's large muscles develop, you need to provide a lot of chances to run, jump, skip and hop. It's great to get him out into the garden or park, for swings and slides and climbing equipment, or even join a toddler gym class. Push-and-pull toys of all kinds, as well as riding toys that he pushes or pedals, are great, too. And what about chasing and jumping after bubbles you blow? Toddlers love that!

When the weather is bad, you don't have to go without motor stimulation. You can also make up games, like 'Pretend Animals': 'Hop like a bunny. Jump like a kangaroo. Gallop like a horse. Crawl on your belly like a snake.' Or 'Over and Under', where you set up an obstacle course using furniture and pillows or large boxes, and then give instructions: 'Go under the table, over the couch, on top of the pillows.' And don't forget dancing! When you put on music, toddlers naturally start moving – especially if you join in. To help with body awareness in space, as well as language, have him stand on a chair (or other sturdy object), and then in front of it, behind it, beside it and under it.

With older toddlers – say, three-and-a-half to four – I like to play movement games like hopscotch, 'Red Light, Green Light', and 'Simon Says'. These can be played outside or in, as long as you have a long hallway. 'Follow the Leader' is great, especially if you incorporate lots of different movements, such as shaking, twisting, and bending. Younger ones love 'Ring-A-Ring O'Roses'. Or put a hula-hoop on the floor and have him jump in and out. Hold a hand if he can't quite do it yet. Or hold both hands and jump together. You can also teach opposites like big and small, under and over, using his body – make your body big, now small.

Balls are also great ways to promote motor development – balls to kick, balls to roll and balls to throw. Start with rolling and go from there. By four, he can progress to a large plastic bat and ball.

Make or buy bean bags and create a tossing game where you have to hit a certain mark or line, and graduate to large baskets. You can also use clothes pegs and large containers. I recently worked with a family and we invented a throwing game using small balls and the washing basket.

Just because he's small, don't be tempted to purchase a bike that you push with a long handle. It can become nothing more than a novelty pushchair, with you doing all the work. If it has pedals, he should be using them! Start with a small wooden bike that he pushes with his feet, move on to a tricycle with pedals, and then, around the age of four, graduate to a big bike with stabilisers.

Fine motor stimulation

Fine motor activities prime your child to do many life skills, such as button, tie shoes, and brush teeth thoroughly, to name but a few. They also prepare him to hold a pencil and write. Here are my favourite fine motor activities:

Puzzles

Start off with knob puzzles. These are ones that have big knobs sticking out of each puzzle piece. Then move onto pincer puzzles that require a thumb and forefinger grip. Begin with very simple, four-piece puzzles, then go onto eight, 12, 24, and so on. I like the ones where you have to put a shape into the correct space.

Building blocks

These should be big to begin with and, as your child gets older, become increasingly smaller. The smaller the blocks, the more hand control your toddler must have. Beware of the building sets with tiny pieces for older kids – they can be a choking hazard.

Drawing and painting

Give him lots of opportunities to scribble and paint. You don't even have to buy paper. Use the backs of envelopes and letters, cereal packets and cardboard packaging from parcels. Name the colours as he uses them, to encourage learning. With painting, start him off with a large brush and gradually move him to smaller, finer brushes that require more control. As he gets older, have him try painting with cotton swabs. This helps to develop his pincer grip, which is needed to write in school. You can add a bit of washing liquid as well as water to powder paint to make it less runny and easier to use. Finger paints are fun, too.

Playdough

What toddler doesn't love playdough? Add rollers and cookie cutters and you'll increase the fine motor stimulation. Be prepared for all the colours to be mixed together and be sure to pack it back in the containers and put the lids on tightly if you want it to stay pliable.

Cutting

Get some child-friendly scissors (blunt and made of plastic) and some old magazines and let him go for it.

Threading and lacing

Buy big threading beads or lacing buttons and string. Encourage him to make his own creations, or, as he gets older, follow a sequence to create a pattern. Choose smaller beads as his fingers become more nimble.

Cupboard crafts

As a nanny, there were many times that I would simply look in the cupboard and see what there was to create an activity. Here are some of the ideas that I came up with:

◆ Thread big pasta noodles on a string, then paint and throw glitter on top. When dry, you can wear as a necklace.

◆ Lentil pictures: with a glue stick, make a shape on a piece of paper. Then throw lentils or other small grains or pulses on top, and pick up the paper. The loose grains fall off and you have a lentil picture. Make sure you supervise this closely – as you should be doing with every activity – to make sure your toddler doesn't put the lentils in his mouth and choke.

◆ Don't have any playdough? Make *oobleck*. It's a fun, squishy substance first named in a Dr Seuss book. When pushed together it seems dry and solid, when you let go, it flows like a liquid. Take 1½ mugs of corn flour, add a mug of water and a few drops of food colouring, if desired. Mix together, and it's ready for action.

◆ What about papier mâché? Just mix together 1 part flour to 2 parts water, to create a substance with the consistency of thick glue. Add more water or flour as necessary. Mix well to remove any lumps. To use, create a mould or use a balloon. Tear, don't cut, newspaper into strips. Dip one strip at a time into the gluey paste. Squeeze off the excess, and press the strip over the balloon or other form. Continue until it's completely covered with overlapping strips. Let it dry for 24 hours and make another layer, if desired. Three layers are best. After it's completely dry, paint and decorate.

◆ Make a collage with 'found' objects, such as dry pasta, popcorn, leaves, feathers, small stones, acorns and anything else that you and your toddler can find together. All you need is glue and a clean Styrofoam meat tray or shoe-box lid. Let your toddler glue objects. You can even hang it, once it's dry.

◆ Make oatmeal clay beads. Mix together 1 mug of porridge oats, ⅔ of a mug of plain flour, ½ a mug of water and food colouring in a large bowl, adding more flour if necessary, until the dough forms a lump. Knead it on a floured surface, adding flour as needed, until it is smooth and not too sticky. Form into beads. Take a large needle or skewer, and poke a hole through so they can be strung later. (You do this part of course.) Air-dry overnight. Leftover clay can be refrigerated in an airtight container for up to three days.

◆ Create 'cereal-sand' pictures by crushing any kind of breakfast cereal with a rolling pin. Your toddler will want to help with this step! Put glue in patterns on a piece of paper and sprinkle on the 'sand'. Shake off the excess and display.

TIP: USE RECYCLED OBJECTS

You don't have to spend a lot of money on arts-and-crafts supplies. In a day and age when we're very conscious of recycling, you can re-use all sorts of things for your toddler's entertainment and fine motor development. At the age of three or four, with a child's imagination and a few of these raw materials, you can make something fabulous. Many a time, I've made a space rocket out of some old felt, a cardboard box and some old silver foil. Here are some things to keep on hand:

◆ **toilet rolls and paper-towel (kitchen-roll) holders**

◆ **leftover silver foil and cans**

◆ **egg cartons and boxes of all sizes**

◆ **old buttons**

◆ **scraps of fabric**

◆ **leftover wrapping paper**

Providing enough stimulation

If you're having discipline issues, your toddler might be acting out because he's not stimulated enough. Boredom leads to bad behaviour and it's not good for your child's brain, which is unable to make the new connections that will enable him to learn more. I often see this in families where the stay-at-home parent doesn't understand the importance of stimulation for toddlers.

For example, I worked with a family who were very focused on their little boy's misbehaviour. He was very bright and it was clear to me that he just wanted to explore and discover how things work, which led him into trouble. His mum didn't have a sufficient routine in place to create the proper stimulation and socialisation with other children that he needed.

She continually felt exhausted and run down as a result of dealing with a child who she called 'hyperactive'. And, yet, he wasn't hyperactive at all. He was a lively toddler who got into things and that, for her, was a problem because it meant that she had to be on her feet 24/7, wondering what he was up to. All I needed to do was help her recognise what he needed to be stimulated on a mental and creative level and create a safe environment for him to play on his own.

I had her break down her day, which helped her to understand his body clock. After having 12 hours of sleep, he was lively and alert in the morning, and eager to soak up everything like a sponge. And so her mornings became about providing the kind of early-learning stimulation I suggest in this chapter. She started to do things with him and saw he was engaged. She'd never seen him engage in anything before.

She had felt that his attention span was minimal, because he never wanted to play with his toys. But when I looked at the toys, I realised that he'd outgrown them by about two years. He didn't want to play because he was bored. We got new things and he became more engaged. She recycled things as well – lids and tops, jars and buttons – and he was able to be more creative. She also became more active. She was a Mum who just thought that all you had to do was give a child some toys, and he'd entertain himself all day long. She now realised that she needed to become more active with him. Together they went on walks and nature trails, and went out on bikes.

She actually started to enjoy her son more, and to enjoy motherhood, when she'd previously been bored by the whole process. There's nothing worse for a toddler than to be looking up at a parent who doesn't want to be with you. They both flourished.

As this story shows, if you don't provide something for your toddler to do, he'll probably find something to do himself. And that may not be the 'something' that you want. He has this curiosity ready to be channelled, so he'll come up with something. Adults call that being mischievous, when he's probably absolutely bored. You've probably seen me go into many homes and declare that the trouble-making toddlers are under-stimulated and the truth is that many toddlers are.

SIGNS THAT YOUR TODDLER IS UNDERSTIMULATED

◆ **She only has toys she's already conquered very easily.**

◆ **She wants *you* as the toy all the time at the age of three and four, when she's able to play competently alone for a while.**

◆ **She's not spending enough time engaged in an activity, when you know she has an adequate attention span.**

◆ **She's generally well-behaved, but is being mischievous or naughty.**

◆ **At playgroup or nursery school, there are no problems with behaviour.**

◆ **When you see any of these, it's important to move her onto the next level. The box may say 'Age three', and your child's three, but if she's nailing a puzzle very, very quickly, then buy the next stage up.**

Providing a variety of experiences in different environments minimises boredom. Look at the day and create a structure for different activity options. Is it going to be an active morning and a creative afternoon, where we read and do puzzles? Have a structure in your mind to work out what you're going to do with the playtime. But within that structure, don't dictate the play itself.

For example, an art session with your three-year-old doesn't mean that you have to say, 'We're going to make planes today. And this is what we're going to do.' Instead, say, 'Here's the paper, the glue stick, the sequins. Get messy!'

When your child is two or three, he will be happy to find what's around in the room and start playing. Everything's the 'first time' for him. He's always excited by almost anything, because it just seems new. As he gets older, he'll definitely voice an opinion about what he wants to do. For all ages, your job is to observe, guide and balance out the right amount of activity, as well as create a *variety* of activities within each day. Again, you don't have to be fanatical about making sure that you get the amount of visual, auditory, motor and fine motor stimulation *exactly* equal every day. Just try to include them all.

But don't push too hard

On the other side of the spectrum, you don't want to overdo it by pushing your child too hard. You have to find the balance between providing enough stimulation for her development and not too much to shut her down.

Take it in moderation and don't stay with one activity for too long. Know how much time is reasonable for your child to spend on an activity. If you get 20 minutes, you're on a roll. If your child has repeatedly lost her concentration, think about switching to another task or taking a break. There's a saying: 'She whispers before she shouts.' If your child has had enough, she can be triggered into a meltdown. Or she'll just shut down and refuse to participate.

Signs that it's time to move on

- It becomes hard work.
- She's rubbing her eyes, playing with her ears, or yawning.
- She's sitting down, not as lively as she was ten minutes ago.
- She becomes crabby, irritable or whiny.

Your roles in play

Your number-one job is to enjoy playing with your toddler. Let loose and have fun! Kids feed off your energy. If you're excited and engaged, they will be, too. If it's not a good experience for both of you, then it's no good. Besides having fun, you have a few roles to play during activities with your toddler:

The game salesman

I've heard parents say, 'Oh, my child doesn't want to sit down and do any of the little picture puzzles I've bought.' OK, here's the thing: You can't just put a toddler in a room and say, 'Play' – especially when you are first introducing an activity or a toy. Be proactive, use your energy to sell it to him as if you were the game salesman. Talk about how great it's going to be. Then start doing it yourself. If he sits down and does it with you, you've just won your commission.

The coach

OK, we've established that you can't just hand a toddler a toy, game or puzzle, and say, 'Play!'. You have to show her how to do it. I always think of myself as the coach. If she gets stuck, I'll offer suggestions, but look to her to find the solution. If she still can't do it, I'll show her how. I'm always looking for ways in which I can nurture a child's potential. I want to help her so she can feel good about what she's learning. When she succeeds in doing something, she feels good and wants to do it again. Anytime she wants to do something again and again – reading books, assembling puzzles, playing Snakes & Ladders – it's because she's enjoying the experience. This is a great thing to foster.

The attention-span stretcher

Children are just not born with long attention spans. You have to train a child to develop his attention span. I can see pretty quickly whether a parent has given her child that time – or whether she's not.

You help to stretch attention when you encourage him to stick with things. If he's not engaged enough in the activity he might just walk away. You need to coax him back, with a: 'Come on, we're not finished, look!' Then you may have to show him: 'You could put that piece there. You can do it! Look at that!'

Parents often tell me they're too busy to do this. But when you put in the time to help him understand how to do something and stick to it, it's actually a win-win. He'll learn to enjoy what he's doing and want to play it over again.

And when he's happily engaged, that's when you can go and do something else. The longer his attention span, the more you can get your work done. It will also help him when it comes time for school.

The energy-watcher

You can't be militant about play. It's all got to flow freely. If you have your antennae out and feel the moment, you'll be able to assess when the energy is high and you can get her to engage longer with a toy. Then the energy goes flat and it's time to switch activities or have a snack.

I do this energy-watching when I'm helping a family. I say, 'We need to do this, this, this and that.' And they'll say, 'In what order?' I reply, 'I don't know yet. We got to feel it.' And you do, too. Become adept at subtly adjusting your routine and your play schedule according to how your toddler is feeling.

THE PLAY MINDSET

Adults are so used to 'doing'. We're used to working or getting stuff done around the house, filling every moment with activity. When it comes to play, it's important to switch your mindset. Playing with your toddler is a time to let your hair down, be silly and have fun. Play is not about achieving an end goal; it's about being interactive, using your imagination, getting down to your toddler's level and enjoying being together.

Letters, numbers and other 'academic' building blocks

I like to encourage toddlers to start understanding numbers by learning their age. At first, she holds up her little fingers. Later she can say it. Counting games and rhymes like 'One, Two, Buckle My Shoe' are also good for learning these concepts. By the age of four, I have her tracing numbers, and learning shapes and letters.

When you read the same books over and over to her, at some point you may find that she can 'read', meaning she's memorised what's there. Such activities are all building blocks for your child's academic success. I think parents who are proactive in giving their toddler the basics are doing their job: colours, numbers, shape and letter recognition … These are all things we can do at home.

You can't force the timing or speed of brain development, but you certainly can encourage it. I've actually heard parents say: 'You're not going to eat until you can count to ten!' And the child doesn't even know how to ask for a cup!

Allow your child to go at her own pace with you encouraging her alongside. When you encourage, you make her eager to carry on learning. That's when you hear: 'Again, again!'. If you truly pay attention to who she is and get your expectations of who she should be out of the way, you can follow her lead to determine how fast she wants – and is able – to go. That means you've got to check the kind of parent you are, right?

In all, your toddler has four years before she'll be coming home with satchels as big as her body. This should be the time for fun. If it's fun for her to race ahead academically, well then, that's fine by me. But don't kid yourself that rote learning all day long is fun when it isn't. She'll learn more through games and play than she will any other way.

IMAGINARY FRIENDS

So, suddenly your toddler has an imaginary friend – something that up to half of all toddlers do, say researchers. You may find yourself having to save a place, provide food and even set up extensive birthday parties for this 'friend', who you clearly cannot see! Frankly, I believe there's no harm in playing along – you're not going to damage your child's sense of reality, let's face it. As long as it is pretend. I wouldn't, for example, provide real food. Some children also use their dolls or soft toys to talk in the third person about the things they feel, which can be particularly helpful in sensitive situations. Have patience about this short phase in your child's life when this is his truth.

Do look out for blaming the imaginary friend for mischief that your little one causes! Or saying that it was the imaginary friend who said they should get out of bed. Even here there are boundaries. Most children grow out of this stage by six or seven, when they understand the difference between fact and fiction.

The importance of pretend play

Did you know that pretend play actually helps with reading skills? It's because playing pretend requires the ability to symbolise – to allow one thing to stand for another, which is a key ability in reading. So when a child pretends a blanket is a super cape, she's allowing one thing to stand in for another, which will help her ability to understand that words on a page stand for thoughts and ideas. When two- and three-year-olds pretend without any materials, they're remembering images they've seen in books or in the world around them. When we pretend with toddlers, that's why we use things they've seen. Pretend play also helps with socialisation, as she acts out roles like 'Mummy' and situations like 'house'. I like to call this mini-world.

Pretend play starts with a young toddler making the '*vroom, vroom, vroom*' noise when pushing a car, and continues until, by age four, she's created whole worlds and stories. You can encourage pretend play with this easy guideline: *The more a toy encourages a toddler to use her imagination, the better.* In addition to the recycled materials I suggested you collect on page 138, here are some further suggestions to encourage pretend play:

- Play versions of common objects, such as a cash register, plastic food, doll house, fire station, etc.

- Blocks, Lego and construction sets

- Cars and trucks, big and small

- Dress-up clothes, shoes and jewellery – the shinier, the better

- Costumes, such as superheroes, firemen, fairies, etc.

- Face paint and non-toxic makeup

- Dolls and action figures

- Finger puppets

Note, this is where you get to loosen up and have some fun. Just because you're an adult doesn't mean you can't act like a child. Dress up along with your kids and play pretend. I bet you'll like it. You can add a storytelling aspect for even more fun and creativity: 'We're all in the circus. What happens next?' Toddlers love it when we do creative play with them. I once worked with a single Dad who wanted to learn how better to relate to his toddler daughter. He also had a son, with whom he was comfortable, but he didn't know how to connect to his little girl. Once I found out that he was interested in drama, I encouraged him to play dress-up with her and he did – including hat and feather boa! I'll never forget how his daughter's face lit up when she realised they were going to have a tea party.

They sat down at a table with a tablecloth and little mini-tea set and I served them as if I was the waitress. I took the order, bashed pots around the kitchen, and then came out to do it after I left.

MAGIC BOXES

It's another rainy day and you and your toddler have cabin fever. It's time for Magic Boxes.

- **All you do is take a toy and put it in a box and wrap it like a present. It could be some arts-and-crafts materials or a game. It doesn't even have to be something new. It's the magic of the ritual and your excitement that makes this work.**

- **Make two more.**

- **With a great deal of drama, declare that it's 'Magic Boxes' day.**

- **Bring them out with great fanfare and allow her to choose a box.**

- **She can now play with whatever's inside. You'll soon have her begging for Magic Box day every day!**

Buying toys

In general, look for toys at or slightly above your child's skill level. It is important for him to have toys that he can manage as well as those that challenge him. Challenges should be fun and stimulating, not frustrating. Don't be tempted to get out toys that are too advanced. Save them for the right time – and ditto for all the toys he gets on his birthday. Put some away for a rainy day.

TOP TEN TOYS FOR EVERY AGE GROUP

1–2 YEARS

- push toys, like a bubble mower, corn popper or shopping cart
- simple, four-part, big-knob shape puzzle boards
- board books
- big building blocks
- stacking cups and other nesting toys
- activity sets for pushing, pulling and turning a toy
- workbench for pounding
- a drum and or xylophone
- pull toys
- a soft, medium-sized ball

2–3 YEARS

- farm sets, train sets and car garages
- sandboxes, buckets, spades, cups and dump trucks
- musical instruments, like maracas, bells and child flutes, etc.
- giant beads to pop together and apart
- a large ball for rolling and tossing
- plastic cars and trucks to sit on and push or drive
- toys for water play – pouring, mixing
- shape-sorters
- pincer puzzles (see page 136)
- dolls

3–4 YEARS

- smaller blocks and Duplo (not complete sets, but those designed for imaginative, unstructured play)
- sets for imitating adult activities, such as cooking and shopping
- a doctor or nurse's kit, or a carpenter's kit, etc.
- tricycles and scooters
- dollhouse and playhouses
- floor puzzles
- board games (see page 148)
- a Slinky spring
- an easel
- alphabet games

4–5 YEARS

- a junior ball and bat for cricket or rounders, and a small football
- fancier building sets, such as cubes or gears that fit together, Meccano and building logs that snap together
- see and spell puzzles, either board or electronic
- snap circuits, to create things like flying saucers and strobe lights
- maze books
- beading kits
- hand puppets
- card games, such as 'Snap', 'Go Fish' and 'Old Maid'

Great games for toddlers

Games encourage thinking and good sportsmanship. Don't be surprised if you get a strong reaction when your toddler first loses – or if she tries to cheat. She needs to be taught good game behaviour.

2 and over

- Elefun
- Mr Potato Head
- Pop it in the Post
- Red Dog, Blue Dog
- Old MacDonald Lotto Game

3 and over

- Incy Wincy Spider
- Gator Golf
- Monkey Madness
- Snakes & Ladders
- Mr Men: My First Scrabble

4 and over

- Hungry Hippo
- Jenga
- Buckaroo
- Scaredy Cat
- Four in a Row

ELECTRONIC LEARNING TOYS

There are many electronic learning toys that are absolutely wonderful. After all, we live in the 21st century. We're hardly waiting for Henry VIII's carpenter to carve us a spinning top. However, my main concern is that you continue to talk and play with your toddler, and not let these talking, beeping, flashing toys become babysitters. Like all toys, you'll need to show your child how to use them, play alongside, and ensure that he's appropriately stimulated and interested. In other words, you need to be there.

Playing alone

Many parents make a rod for their own back because they think they have to play with their toddler all day long. As much as it is important to interact with your child and to stimulate him on every level, it's also incredibly important – as part of his learning curve – that he becomes comfortable playing on his own. This is when he uses his own imagination and creativity. Of course, even when a toddler is playing on his own, he is being supervised. To help him learn to do this, use the 'Play and Stay, Play Away' technique on page 157.

Alternatively, however, I've seen too many parents dump a toy on the floor and say, 'Go off and play.' It's OK to do that occasionally, as long as you also spend a good part of your time being interactive with your child. It's a matter of balance. If all you're doing is housework and you're not meeting the needs of your child on the levels I've discussed, that's a problem.

How to tell if your child's outgrown a toy

Your toddler will outgrow toys at her own pace. The age guidelines on a toy are based upon estimates of when children *typically* reach a certain development stage. Your child may be ahead or behind that.

I make a distinction between learning toys and playing toys. For learning toys: if she can master, in real life, the skill that the toy was helping to develop, it's time to move on. Why? Because she's not learning anymore. For example, pincer puzzles are designed to help your toddler's pincer grip. Once she's good at that, she should be moved on to puzzles without knobs.

Toys for play, especially the ones I include in the section above on pretend play, tend to last a lot longer because they are not designed to encourage a specific skill. You'll know they need to go when your child is bored of them. If you decide to keep a few of these around, it will be because they have emotional value. When a child rediscovers that toy again, she'll want to play because she remembers it fondly – kind of like us playing Twister as adults.

> **Time it!**
>
> To make sure you share your time equally, set a timer for 20 minutes of one-on-one time with each child. You don't have to do each child every day. You can spread one-on-one time throughout the week.

Dealing with multiples and siblings close in age

Of course you can do many activities all together, but you also need some one-on-one playtime with each child. One of the great blessings of multiples or close siblings is that they learn patience from the beginning. Even as babies, they learn to wait their turn to be changed, fed or picked up. This continues into their toddler years, as they learn to sit back and wait their turn.

So here is what you do: If you have triplets, for example, get two involved in an activity that you know they like to do and *can* do on their own, so that they won't need you to engage with them. Then concentrate on the other. Why? Because, through the repetition of circulating among them, each will have the reassurance that she'll get her share of your undivided attention.

When you're doing a stimulating activity all together, make sure that one child doesn't dominate. It's really important to let the quieter one(s) also get their turn.

TV or no TV?

The current recommendation from medical doctors is *no* TV viewing for toddlers. The reason is the same as the one I wrote about earlier. In a nutshell, it is through the interactions with humans and experiences he has that a child's brain wires up properly. (No, TV watching is not an experience. Experiences are about doing something.) There are also studies showing that toddlers exposed to more TV are prone to aggressive behaviour, higher weight gain and less activity.

Because I am a realist, have spent 20 years inside of people's homes, and have also put the television on myself for 30 minutes or so to entertain a toddler, I know that at some stage you're going to do the same. So I ask you this: Be selective about what he's watching and limit the time to 30 minutes a day. Make sure the shows are age-appropriate and don't rely on the TV as a babysitter, or a crutch for a whole morning or afternoon. You and I both know that a three- or four-year-old's attention span can't be sustained for 60 or 90 minutes. There are plenty of other forms of entertainment that can be used to engage him, such as puppet shows, children's pantomime, singing and dancing. As children's TV changes so rapidly, making recommendations would not be helpful. Be conscious of the content and if you want to be more in control of your child's viewing, you can buy age-appropriate DVDs. You can choose to watch with your child or not, it's up to you. Sometimes it can be a nice breather.

Video games and computers

It is of no benefit for toddlers to be spending time on the computer or playing video games as recreation. Doing so nurtures bad habits and these toddlers turn into tweens who show signs of poor concentration and focus, lack of physical exercise, addiction to video games, and a withdrawal from the family. If you don't believe me, I suggest you watch 'Jo Frost's Extreme Parental Guidance'. Some of you may have toddlers who use computers at school, but this time will be limited, designed for their age group, and supervised. There is absolutely no point in introducing them at home.

ATTENTION TO WHAT?

If your four-year-old can sit through a 90-minute film, think of all the other wonderful things he could be doing: swimming with the family, taking a bike ride along the river walk, going to a children's theatre show, running around and playing with other children in the park, making papier mâché masks, enjoying a family meal out together, 'reading' to his baby sister on a lazy afternoon, ticking off a life skill on his 'I Can Do' list or lining up his cars for a race.

7

Positive transitions

In this chapter, I'll help you deal with all kinds of transitions – from a simple hand-over of your toddler to a caregiver, to introducing a new baby and handling life changes like divorce, deaths in the family and remarriage. Transitions of all types can be very tricky, as they need to be dealt with sensitively – particularly because they run parallel to challenging developmental stages that your child may be going through. For example, one- and two-year-olds dealing with separation anxiety is a tough gig for parents who are divorcing. For three- and four-year-olds, these big changes can be hard because they are more consciously aware of the impact that such an event has on their lives.

Coping with separation anxiety

At some point you've probably noticed that your baby – who was comfortable being passed around to all the relatives – has turned into a clinging monkey, who cries if he's separated from you. This is actually a sign of healthy development, as it shows his attachment to you – he feels that you are the centre of the universe, and the one to whom he looks to understand what's going on in life. Separation anxiety, which generally begins at around nine months, and recurs around 18 months, is a stage of development. It can also be triggered later on by life events, such as moving, a new baby, divorce, a new childminder, and more.

Separation anxiety can be intense for you and your toddler because it's hard to walk away from a child who is screaming for you – and being prised off your neck. You can make it easier for both of you with the suggestions for positive transitions that I'll outline in this chapter.

Tips for dealing with separation anxiety

◆ Accept that it is a stage that will pass.

◆ Reassure the parent who is not favoured that he's done nothing wrong and that your toddler loves him. Let him know what he can do to help you.

◆ If you can, time your first going away from your toddler when he's not ill or tired. He can become even clingier then.

◆ Take a deep breath and calm down when you feel yourself getting stressed.

◆ When you leave a room that he's in for a short time, talk to your toddler so that he knows you are still there.

◆ Play peek-a-boo games, which will help him learn that what he can't see is still there – use a towel or get under the covers on the bed. You probably did this when he was a baby, but young toddlers love it, too.

◆ Pretend to be Paul Daniels and get two cups and a small ball and make the ball disappear and then reappear under the cup. It helps him to learn about things being there even when you can't see them.

◆ Never leave without saying goodbye. This only creates more anxiety.

THE OFF-THE-HIP TECHNIQUE

When a toddler has separation anxiety and keeps raising up her arms and crying, parents tend to pick her up and hold her on their hip. The following technique will help you to get her off that hip, and down to the ground, for both safety and healthy-detachment reasons.

◆ **When she cries to be picked up, come down to her level, and hold her at arm's length.**

◆ **Tell her you're not going to pick her up – and what you *are* going to be doing, such as, 'I'm making the dinner now.'**

◆ **If she follows you, still crying (and she will), crouch back down and, at arm's length again, say, 'No, Daddy's busy doing this. You can go and play with your toys. Then we can get back to having some fun in a moment.'**

Troubleshooting the Off-the-Hip technique

If it's not working, ask yourself the following questions:

◆ Am I continuing to pick my child up whenever he asks?

◆ Do I know the difference between picking him up to show affection and trying to cook dinner with one arm?

◆ Have I become somebody who does everything with my child attached to me?

◆ Do I have any space for myself?

Goodbye, hello again

◆ **Confidence**

◆ **Perspective**

The time when your child is experiencing separation anxiety is when you really need your backpack filled with *Confidence* that it's OK to leave – and *Perspective* to know that he'll adjust and won't always be so clingy. This is definitely only a phase. Reassurance develops when he's able to see that every time you leave, you come back. It is far smarter to confidently tell your child where you are going and to see you come back than to sneak out of the house and leave him wondering. Needless to say, it can be still taxing – on the one who is left *and* the one who goes.

I now fondly remember – although I didn't at the time – the turmoil that occurred 30 minutes before one of the mothers for whom I used to work as a nanny would go to work, leaving behind her two-year-old son. She would start to panic and become nervous, knowing that he was going to cling on to her clothes and I would have to prise him off. I would tell her that as soon as she left, he was absolutely fine. But she needed reassurance that this was true, because each day she walked out of the door with him in absolute sheds of tears.

The house was set up with windows to the side. So, one day I suggested that she go out as usual and take a look through the windows. After the door shut with him in tears as usual, I very enthusiastically suggested that we go and play some game. He jumped up from crying hysterically and decided that this was a great idea. I looked at the mother in the window – who had an expression of 'Is that all he gave me? Two minutes of crying!' – and then she went happily off to work.

It was a funny moment – but dramatic at the same time – because she'd realised that it was actually just a melodrama before she left, and that he was perfectly fine and happy while she was gone.

Jo's transition formula

Your child's individual personality and temperament will affect how difficult or easy transitions will be. Some toddlers take Mummy leaving in their stride; others, like my former charge, carry on like an Oscar-winning actor. That's why I've created this formula:

When you observe how your child behaves with change, and offer the guidance your toddler needs, things will go more smoothly – whether it's a pass-off to a caregiver or dealing with a blended family.

The key is to be able to read your child and understand how she's likely to respond. Then you'll know how much guidance to give. Do you need to plan extra time for the transition because she's the type that needs more reassuring? Should you introduce the new sitter a few times while you're still there? Or does she take change in her stride and therefore need only a one-time intro? Does she need you to give her one of your possessions to keep her company – and reassure her you will return? A child who is more independent in her life skills is more likely to be content to be engaged in her world and so deal with transitions more smoothly. The more you know your child, the more you'll be able to work these things out.

Don't assume it will be difficult

Be careful that you don't place your own feelings of worry or sadness onto her. Don't let it rub off. She may be more comfortable with the new situation than you are! She may be thrilled about the new baby or her new room. But if this transition is becoming difficult for you emotionally, then who's doing the pacifying? If you're taking your child off to school for the first day and admiring her school uniform, but feeling sad that she's not your baby anymore, hide behind the camera while taking those first-day photos. Cheese!

Getting your toddler used to being away from you

To ease the transition to other carers and new places, I encourage parents to start getting their young toddler used to bits of time away from them with the 'Play and Stay, Play Away' technique. Practising this technique will make it easier to transition when you have to go to work full-time or have decided to have your toddler go to daycare or nursery part-time. It's also useful if you want to exercise for an hour and leave your child in the crèche.

THE PLAY AND STAY, PLAY AWAY TECHNIQUE

◆ **Play with your toddler for a bit and then say, 'Mummy's going to go to the kitchen, I'll be back in a minute.' You want her to be engaged before you go, so that's why you start off by playing with her – for example, stacking blocks, doing easy puzzles or placing rings on the stick.**

◆ **Walk out of the room and then quickly come back. You don't want to leave your child unattended for a long period of time. This is just to show her that you may go into another room, but you always come back.**

◆ **Do this at various times and in various places so that she'll learn through the repetition that you always return.**

Time away from you

Even if you are at home full-time after your child is two, there are a lot of benefits to having him do something without you – at least an hour or two, a couple of days a week. Getting into the routine of going somewhere else and being with other people helps him begin to develop a healthy detachment from you. He starts to see that it's OK to play and enjoy himself without you because you'll come back. It also helps him to develop relationships with other people.

Consider starting with a family member – or taking turns with a friend. She can watch your child for an hour and you can watch hers later in the week. These are familiar faces, so your child can ease into not being with you. An hour a week could be a good start and you can build from there. This can help you to schedule appointments, knowing you can have that hour to exercise or do something else for yourself.

Another option is to put your child into a morning programme for an hour or two. You get a bit of a break and your child eases into the transition she'll eventually make full-time when she goes to school. It's a lot easier to go from two hours, two mornings a week, to afternoons, five days a week, to full-time school. It's a nice gradual process in which you get your toddler nicely weaned onto enjoying herself without you having to be a part of that enjoyment. Don't feel guilty. Remember that fostering a healthy detachment from you is all part of your child's development – and yours.

INTRODUCING A BABYSITTER

+ **When hiring a babysitter for the first time, have her over for an hour or two to watch your toddler while you do chores around the house.**

+ **Arrange something fun for them to do together, so it's an enjoyable experience. It will help to make your child feel more comfortable when you leave him.**

+ **If your child comes to you, take him back to the babysitter and confidently say, 'She's here to play with you.' Go back to doing what you were doing.**

If you are a parent who has chosen to be at home with your kids before they go to school, I still strongly suggest that you create consistent opportunities for your child to be in other people's company. He needs to be able to learn to engage in activities where he is away from you, even if you're looking on from the sidelines. This helps to develop healthy boundaries, and you will be grateful for the adult company. It will make the transition to school much less traumatic for the both of you!

Easing the transition to childcare

◆ Talk about what's happening to prepare your child. Be excited, and explain what's going on: 'Mummy's going to work because that's the thing that Mummy does during the day. And you're going to go to a place to play. You're going to have so much fun.'

◆ Visit the place ahead of time and walk your toddler around, pointing out all the exciting activities he's going to do and the people he'll play with: 'This is Miss So-And-So and here are all these other little boys and girls – and look at the slide. You love to slide ...'

◆ When the day comes, you can give him something of yours, such as a scarf, and say, 'Hold onto that for Mummy because Mummy will be back to pick that up.' That can reassure him that you will return.

◆ Walk him in, give a big kiss and hug, promise him you'll pick him up, and be excited and happy. And then *leave*! Waiting around is not going to change the fact that your child does not want you to go. Of course he wants you there. You're just postponing the agony.

◆ Of course for many it will be gut wrenching! But try to leave your tears, sadness or worry out of sight of your toddler. The first day is the hardest, I know, but it will get easier over time – believe me. No matter how much he's carrying on, he will recover and get involved in an activity. The professionals you're leaving him with have been through this hundreds of times and know how to distract him. With change come exciting new adventures.

'I Don't Want to Go!'

If, after a period of time for the transition, your child continues to say that she doesn't want to go, it can be very disheartening. You *know* she's in a good environment, so why isn't this experience generating the happiness it should be? What's going on?

What I've noticed in this situation in many cases are younger children with poor social skills, who struggle to interact with other children. Try some play dates with one of the children from the same centre or nursery so she gets used to building a friendship. That will increase her self-esteem and give her more confidence – making going a more enjoyable experience.

Another factor may be an immaturity in her emotional development – or if she's regressed – and this could be certainly the case if there's a new baby in the family or another life transition is going on. When she's used to you doing things for her and she's suddenly thrust into a place where she has to do more for herself, it's more of a challenge, which is why you might get resistance. This can be resolved by having her do handy tasks at home and become more independent with those life skills. These will better enable her to be part of the structure of school and more able to learn and enjoy.

Changing carers

Follow my advice for easing the transition to childcare (see page 159), adapting it to this circumstance: 'You're now going to be with Mrs So-and-So and new friends. It's going to be great!' If you can tell a very simple story about why things are changing, do it! For example, 'You aren't going to Mrs X's anymore because she's going to have a baby of her own!' What you don't want to do is get into long explanations about how you disagree with her previous minder's approach – or talk about how he's going to be sad. Focus on the positives and be as casual about the change as possible.

> ## Supporting a positive attitude about childcare
>
> If your child says, 'I don't want to go today', *don't* say, 'I know you don't want to go. I know it's going to be difficult. I wish you didn't have to go.'
>
> *Do* say, 'You'll have a really good time. I know you feel like you don't want to go, but you're going to really enjoy yourself.'

Visits from birth parents in open adoptions

As I said in *Confident Baby Care,* and I'll say again here, the most important thing in an open adoption is having a good, healthy relationship between all the adults concerned. Hopefully you had a professional to help with the legalities of this very sensitive situation at the beginning and you have clear guidelines about supervised visits – how often and how long.

If the birth mother is having trouble separating – she's asking to see your child more than was agreed upon or she gets upset when leaving – it's really important that she seek professional help, and you can gently encourage her to do that: 'I'm noticing you are crying when you leave. Maybe you should see someone to help you with these feelings.' It's really important that any kind of inner or outer conflict not be conveyed to your toddler.

As far as your toddler is concerned, she's having periodic visits from one or both of her birth parents, but you are her Mummy and Daddy, who she sees every day. So you need to establish an identity for this other person. A toddler is not able to understand the difference between a birth parent and an adoptive parent. You wouldn't sit down and say to a three-year-old, 'Well, this is the lady who gave birth to you. And we're the ones who look after you.' I would stick to something like, 'A best friend of our family is coming to visit.' Later, at six and seven, if the visitations are successful, you can then talk to your child in more

TALKING ABOUT ADOPTION

- Toddlers don't understand what adoption is. However, just as you would tell a three- or four-year-old birth child the story of the day she was born, and show her pictures, you can start talking to your adoptive child about the day you met her, show photos of where you went to get her, and so on.
- Treat the issue of adoption casually and naturally so that when she gets older, she'll feel comfortable talking about it and you can go into more detail.
- Two great books to read to four-year-olds are *The Day We Met You* by Phoebe Kohler and *I Wished for You* by Marianne Richmond.

detail about who this person is. As the child's parent, your job is to protect her well-being. If the birth parent is sporadic in her visits, promises to come and doesn't show, or has on-going emotional issues, then you need to go and revisit your legal arrangement.

Introducing a new baby

I've heard some parents tell their toddler during the third trimester that there's a baby coming and others who get the child involved from the beginning. There's no single right way. That's your choice. But if you're contemplating telling him right away, remember that nine months is a long time for a toddler to wait. At this stage he really has no concept of time. (Remember that car journey when he asked you 200 times when were you going to get there?)

The big adjustment comes, of course, when the baby is born. How your toddler reacts depends on many things – his age, temperament, and how you help him to adjust. I've seen toddlers who straightaway exhibit serious love and a desire to help with the baby, and others who want to know, 'When's this baby going back?'

It's an adjustment

No matter how he responds, your toddler is adjusting to the new family configuration just as you are. You know now that your heart is big enough for two (or three or however many), but didn't you worry about that at least a little bit before the second one came? You and your partner weren't sure that was true until you experienced it.

Your toddler is trying to figure out the same thing. She can't ask you to sit down and have a conversation about her adjustment to the baby: 'Well Mummy, I'm feeling a bit insecure here. I wonder if you still love me. I used to be the apple of your eye and now I'm feeling like I'm not.' That would be quite funny, actually. Read between the lines and give her some time to get used to the change.

Tips for a smoother transition

Encourage your toddler to accept the new family configuration. Here are my tips for making this transition as smooth as possible.

Keep your toddler's routine the same

If possible, don't make any other changes – to your childminder, your home or schedule. His routine gives him a great sense of security and stability – there may be a new baby to share my parents with but the rest of my life is the same.

Don't be afraid to get help

You're now meeting the intense needs and demands of a baby, as well as caring for a toddler (and perhaps older children, too). You may need your partner to step up more or get a relative to assist.

Celebrate his becoming a big brother

There are even cards that say, 'You've just become a big brother'. This helps him to become excited about his new position in the family. I've also seen families where the baby gives his big brother a gift.

Buy a doll for your toddler

This can be a gift from the baby, if you want. It really works to have him do with his baby what you're doing with the real baby. It helps him not feel left out.

Involve him in helping with the baby

Have him become active in caring for the baby by allowing him to give suggestions: 'Should I put the baby in this or should we put the baby in that? What would you want to put the baby in?' Or 'What song shall we play?' Again, he feels a part and so hopefully won't be so jealous. If he's old enough, he can even do things like put on your baby's bootees.

Make sure you have alone time with him

This one's obvious, but not always easy to achieve, particularly with a newborn. But you really need to make sure you and your partner are spending alone time with your toddler. Take some time to spend with him when your baby's sleeping, or when you partner has taken the baby for a walk.

Give him a little prop

Toddlers love make-believe and dress-up. Tell him that you're going to give him a sheriff's badge for helping with certain duties during the day. You're going to do these things with or without the badge. He'll get excited about the badge, so the day goes more smoothly. It doesn't have to be a sheriff's badge – it can follow any theme in which your toddler is interested – fireman, police officer, Mummy's helper or big sister. You can make it out of paper and pin it on with a safety pin.

I remember working with a family who were worried about how their little boy would receive the new baby that was about to be born. I felt it was really important that they recognise that this event was a celebration, and not a threat for that little boy. I made sure he felt included from the start. We went to the hospital to see his sister, and he helped me make a card and put up decorations for the homecoming.

His routine was maintained so his life didn't change from the way it was before the baby arrived. He had time with his Mum alone. And he had time with his Mum and his sister as well. I helped him to understand what was going on: 'Do you know why she's crying right now? Because she's hungry. She can't eat with a fork like you! This is the way she talks. She cries to let us know.' Sometimes he'd say, 'Oh, stop! Stop!' when his new sister cried, and I'd say, 'Yeah, if only she would! But she won't right now.' There was a lot of humour and nurturing, so the transition was easy.

When I think about the times when this hasn't been the case, it's generally because parents have found it difficult to keep a toddler in his routine while caring for the new baby's needs. Fine-tuning that is something you have to master for a smoother transition.

Dealing with regression

Regression occurs when your toddler unconsciously thinks, 'Mummy and Daddy love the baby, so if I'm a baby they'll love me.' Suddenly she can't do things for herself anymore. She's been feeding or dressing herself for six months and suddenly she doesn't want to.

This can be frustrating for parents. Just when you need her to be more independent because you've got an infant who needs you, she goes on toddler strike! Time to take out the backpack and fill it with *Patience* and *Perspective*. Know that if you deal with it appropriately, regression is a short phase – I'd say about a month. If you get angry or impatient, your toddler understands that she can get a reaction from you and then it can become a power struggle that lasts longer. So stay as calm and neutral as possible. Meet her halfway. If she won't feed herself, have her do one spoonful and then you do one. Then say, 'Now you do two and I'll do one … Now you do three and I'll do one.' Don't go backwards and do it all, or you'll be stuck doing everything. And have her put her sock on or do her spoonful first before you do yours. Otherwise, you'll do your one and she won't do the other. If she's been potty-trained and you're seeing accidents again, I'd stay firm but non-emotional: 'We don't do that in our pants. You go to the potty because you're the big girl.'

◆ **Patience**

◆ **Perspective**

If your toddler is very young, her regression may last a little bit longer. She may have temper tantrums when she doesn't want to wait for your attention; she may want to sit on your lap when you're breastfeeding, and she may not be interested being read to while the other one's there. Calmly and firmly hold your ground. You need to meet the needs of your baby and toddler: 'We are going to do this. You can sit here but I will feed the baby, too.'

THE BIG SIBLING TECHNIQUE

When your four-year-old starts to behave like a two-year-old, it's time for the 'Big Sibling' technique. Here's how it works:

◆ **What are the things that you can allow him to do so he feels like the big sibling? Because you want him to think that's the best thing to be.**

◆ **Think in terms of responsibilities and privileges: 'You can go with Daddy to the museum because you're a big boy, the baby can't', or 'You can put your shoes on by yourself because you're a big boy, the baby can't.'**

Aggression

Some toddlers will hit the baby to get attention. If he's old enough to know better – and he's learned about not hitting – then it's a warning and the Naughty Step technique if he doesn't listen. This really needs to be nipped in the bud. At this stage you are fully aware that your child is trying to get your attention through negative behaviour.

For the young toddler, under two, you shouldn't discipline. Use your low, slow voice and very firmly say, 'Sit here with Mummy. No naughty behaviour, or else you have to get down from the sofa.' Show the behaviour you want through action. He is encouraged to sit on your lap, but if he isn't nice to the baby, he has to get down. You may have to use your spare arm to protect the baby from any sudden movements by your toddler when he's in your lap. Your job is to make sure your baby is protected at all times.

> ### Protect your baby
>
> Even if your toddler is ecstatic about the baby, never, ever leave them unattended together. Babies can be injured by too-eager hugs as well as acts of aggression. You can't expect your toddler to know how to support your baby's neck – or not to shake her.

Keeping your baby safe

It's all about safety with a newborn. Toddlers are very rambunctious, and even if they're not intentionally aggressive, they are constantly experimenting with cause and effect: If I do this, what will happen? A toddler is just not aware that what she does has repercussions. So you have to be very careful. You have to think differently than when you had your first one – like leaving your baby in a place that may seem OK because he can't roll. All of a sudden, he *can* roll because big sister's hand can reach out and roll him for you. Or she takes away the bolster you were using. You also have to make sure that she doesn't climb into the cot and accidentally squash the baby. *You* must *supervise their interaction at all times.*

Teaching your toddler how to treat your baby

At some point you're probably going to hear, 'I want to hold, I want to hold.' It's great to encourage the connection between your toddler and your baby, but I would not allow a toddler to hold a newborn. She's just too tiny. When your baby is six or eight weeks old, you can have your toddler sit down and hold her under supervision (see box opposite). Sometimes the baby will cry. When that happens, I

> ## BABY CUDDLE TIME
>
> - ◆ **Have your toddler sit on the sofa in the corner and put his arm on the arm of the sofa so that you create a sturdy right angle.**
> - ◆ **Sit next to him and lay the baby down so that her head is nestled in the crook of his supported arm.**
> - ◆ **You are there to supervise. He must understand that he is never to hold the baby on his own.**

always say, 'Oh, she's not crying because of you! You haven't made the baby cry. Babies just want to know where Mummy is.'

To avoid the big squeeze, teach your toddler to give some love to the baby by kissing her gently on the forehead. Demonstrate first on him because a toddler can't naturally gauge the right amount of pressure. You have to teach him by showing, rather than just saying 'gently' or 'softly'.

Dealing with big life changes

Just because you have a toddler doesn't mean that you might not have to face a challenging life change – the death of a loved one, for instance, or the breakup of your relationship. Not only will you have your own reaction, but you have to parent your toddler through such times. Here I offer my tips on helping your young one cope with these upheavals.

The death of a loved one

The most important thing for parents to understand is that whether it's a family member who has passed away or a pet that has been put to sleep, toddlers experience a loss when someone they have had a relationship with dies. The more time he has spent with this person or pet, the more connection there is. Emotionally, it is a difficult circumstance for all.

However, a toddler doesn't understand the finality of death and is largely impacted by the emotions of grief that blanket the rest of the family during bereavement. This means that a toddler can have a hard time trying to feel grounded when surrounded by adults who are mourning. It's frightening for him to see you upset, although he knows it's not threatening.

Routine can change and so can environment when a death occurs. So you may see some regression or acting out because of insecurity. My suggestions on dealing with regression when there's a new baby apply here, too. If he's around four, you may see him experiencing sadness one minute and laughter the next. It's important to understand that this response is not disrespectful – or an indication of being uncaring. Young children do not mourn the same way that we do. It doesn't mean he's not sad. It doesn't mean he doesn't remember. He just doesn't understand death the way that we do. So he can be easily distracted. Take his behaviour in your stride.

Even though toddlers don't understand death, what they do quickly realise is that if they bring up the name of the person who has passed away, it causes us to react – perhaps to cry. And they think that may be not a good thing. So it stops them from talking about the person. For this reason, it's important to mention to your child that you're happy to talk about your loved one, even though it makes you sad, and that even though you feel sad right now, things will get better. Because kids are full of questions.

HELPING TODDLERS COPE WITH DEATH

A toddler won't generally talk to you about how she feels, but there are things that you can do to help her with her feelings:

♦ **Create photo albums, especially including pictures of her with the person or pet she's lost. I once worked with a two-year-old whose Dad had passed away. She remembered him and loved to look at the album we made with pictures of her and her Dad.**

♦ **If they lose a family member, a lot of parents say to me, 'I'm scared that my toddler is going to forget.' I always say that you can keep your loved one's spirit alive by talking about your memories and experiences.**

♦ **If it's one of your parents, talk about the things that you used to do with them when you were your toddler's age.**

♦ **Of course, if you're a family that has a particular religious belief, I'm sure you'll talk to her about that also.**

THE CHEST TECHNIQUE

♦ **The grandad in a family I was working with passed away and the little kids, because they saw their mother's sadness, felt they couldn't mention him because they were afraid it would upset her. So I bought a little chest for them.**

♦ **As a family, they put little things in the chest that reminded them of grandad. Whenever they wanted, they could go to the chest, take out something and talk about him.**

♦ **You can use this same technique for any significant loss.**

Children are also very observant. A friend of mine was very sad at the passing of her grandfather. Her toddler niece very confidently came up to her, hugged her and said, 'Don't be sad, Auntie. Granddad's in heaven and he's looking at us all.' And she smiled.

Divorce

If you and your partner have decided that you really can't live together, I hope you have realised the importance of remaining committed to your child's welfare and coming together to make the decisions that are best for her. Above all, know that this is not a game of chess, and that using your child as a pawn against your partner is just wrong. Unfortunately, I felt the need to mention this because I've been the mediator between too many adults, where anger towards one another has led to negative behaviour. This is so harmful to your child on every level of her well-being. If you're behaving this way, you're thinking only of yourself – and not her.

Your job is to create a positive transition for her, so get the help you need to do that. A child should never feel torn between her parents. *Never.* Remember: any time you throw verbal poison darts at your spouse, it goes *through* your child first, because in between you is your child. A toddler is so young. She can't really understand what's going on except to sense that she has lost the family stability she had. If there is tension, if there is sadness, she can feel it. And she has her own sense of loss to deal with, without having the language or awareness to do so.

As with the death of a loved one, you may see regression or acting out. See my suggestions earlier in this chapter for handling regression. The better that you both handle the situation, the easier it will be for her. I've seen plenty of divorces where both parents have accepted the situation, which allows them to open the doors to healthy communication and remain committed to the foundation their toddler needs.

If your toddler is around four, you may get a lot of questions, because that's what four-year-olds do. Prepare for this by coming up with answers that are not are fuelled by anger: 'Daddy and I decided we would be happier living apart.'

If you're not in that place emotionally, then the most important thing is to recognise that it's never OK to share your feelings with your toddler or act out against your ex. This means that you've got to grow up and be mature. Stay focused on your responsibilities as a parent and make sure that you have outside support. You're an adult – you can push through this and you will. I once worked with a family where the parents were divorcing. They asked for my help because they wanted to focus on giving the kids what they needed rather than getting stuck in their own feelings.

The father had his own place, but he hadn't shown his kids. So I helped him to decorate so it would have a homely feeling, and to introduce the place to his little ones. He said, 'This is where Daddy is going to be living. You live in your house with Mummy and you're going to live here sometimes with Daddy, on the weekends and during the week.'

The room where the young ones were going to sleep had flowers and stencils of footballs. It was warm and cosy, and felt like another home where they could be safe. He'd put photos up on the fridge with magnets that they could decorate to make it more their own. And I had them each bring one of their blankies to Daddy's to keep there so they had something cuddly and familiar.

It wasn't easy, but they were able to get on with creating a routine that would remain the same no matter where the kids were living. They also agreed to produce a schedule where each of them would have a break for a little 'me' time. It didn't make the split any easier for the kids, but it certainly gave them the stability of knowing that there was still a safe roof over their heads.

While both parents had an emotional journey to endure, they were able to learn to communicate with one another in a healthy way in front of the children. They are now in such a good place that they are able every now and then to spend time together as a family, even though they're not together as a couple.

JO'S TOP TIPS FOR DIVORCING PARENTS

- ◆ **Remember your commitment to your child and her healthy development. Keep the lines of communication open between you and your ex, if possible.**

- ◆ **Find adult support and share your feelings with them.**

- ◆ **Know that you will go through ups and downs emotionally. Don't let that affect your ability to parent. Stress can create less patience, for example, but if you are aware of this, you can take steps to rectify it.**

Living arrangements in divorce

Keep things consistent in your child's life and avoid changing his routine as much as possible. It's up to you and your partner to decide how to do that. One way is to keep the primary home, and then create with the non-custodial parent a home that has familiar surroundings for the toddler to visit.

If you decide on joint custody or care – three days with one parent, four days with the other, for example – then your toddler has two homes and the transition is from one to the other. In this situation, I strongly suggest that, if possible, the two of you agree on the same boundaries, rules and routines. Then, only the sleeping arrangements change. If that's not possible, remember that a toddler is resilient and will adapt if you give her time. Only when I see animosity and immaturity on the part of parents do I see on-going problems with a toddler.

Whatever living or visiting arrangement you agree to, be consistent. Be honourable with the times you've agreed to pick up and drop off, and stick to dates you've agreed together. Know that what you reap is ultimately what you sow. If you say you'll see her tomorrow at 9am, and then don't show up, you'll be creating a very difficult situation for your little one. She's all revved up to see you. Don't put your child through that. Keep your word.

As far as toys are concerned, unless it's too big to lug around, I'd let your toddler bring anything she chooses back and forth. It gives a sense of continuity.

THE IN-BETWEEN CASE

- ◆ **Your toddler will want to take his favourite teddy and blankie – and other special toys – when he goes to his other parent's house.**

- ◆ **Set aside a special little suitcase that goes with him every time. I like those old-fashioned little cases that are becoming popular now, but it can be anything that can take the wear and tear of being carried back and forth.**

- ◆ **Tape a checklist on the front. That way you'll make sure he doesn't forget anything.**

Remarriage and blended families

You've fallen in love again and have decided to come together into a new family configuration. How do you make this a smooth transition for your toddler? The first priority is to get on the same page with your partner. You have your way of doing things, and your partner has his. I hope that in making the commitment to marry one another, you've discussed everything from household management and money to how you're going to raise the children. It's as simple as that. The more you know about where you stand, the easier it will be. If you haven't already had those conversations, please do so right away. If you are united that will give your toddler a greater sense of security.

As for your toddler, hopefully she will have met this person already and had some positive experiences with him and his kids – if he has any. Make sure she has chances to bond with him *without you*, too, with some fun trips to the park or zoo. A child this age needs to learn to depend on the other parent. If you're not present, she *has* to rely on him and so quickly gets over the hump of connecting.

Young toddlers don't understand what marriage is, so talk more about how you are all going to live together and how much fun that will be. This allows her to see that she's a part of this bigger picture. Older three- and four-year-olds understand weddings and should be involved in the event as much as possible, as a flower girl or ring-bearer, for example. Their focus is all about the ceremony.

If you both have children, talk to your toddler about how Mummy is marrying Daddy (or whatever name you've decided on for him) and she is going to have new brothers and sisters, and become one big family. It's so wonderful!

Helping children to connect

Blending a family is usually easy with toddlers. They don't come with the emotional baggage that some older kids might have about divorce, remarriage or step-siblings. All you need to do is nurture the relationship between them and emphasise that 'We're all one family now'. Have them do assignments together, such putting all the shoes in the bucket or setting the table. The more you hold the mindset that you're one family, the easier it will be. When you say to a toddler, 'This is what it is', he thinks, 'Oh, this is what it is!' Love one, love all.

> ## THE MAKE, TEACH, DO TECHNIQUE
>
> If you're bringing together new siblings with a wide age span, what can the older sibling make, teach or do with your toddler? It should be something that comes out of her expertise, talents or interests, rather than a chore.

If there's a need for shared bedrooms and you have a choice, consider your kids before you pair them off. Who is well suited to whom? Who would be a positive influence on whom? Who would be a deadly combination? Two obstinate toddlers – fireworks! Can you split them up?

There are advantages to having a larger family. Toddlers learn to share more quickly – and learn more quickly, full stop. If an older sibling knows how to climb, your toddler will want to do it, too! If a sister or brother says, 'I can do this', then you can bet your toddler will believe he can as well.

If you have an older child in your blended family, who is learning to accept your toddler, it's important to treat the older one in ways that show respect to his age and stage. He will need time to adjust to the fact that he's got a toddler in his life. Make sure he has time and space to do age-appropriate activities – and don't turn him into your live-in childminder. He needs time alone with his own parent, so that he doesn't feel threatened by you coming along. What's more, create times for the two of you to be alone, so that he realises you are his parent now, too.

I once worked with a family who had a teenager named Amanda. She felt that she had lost special time with her Mum, who had remarried a man with a young daughter. There was a gap of ten years between the two step-siblings. I encouraged this teenager to see herself as a very positive role model for her younger sister. I told her she had to teach something to her new sibling. She was a gymnast, so she taught her younger sister how to do a somersault.

This was a way to bring together new siblings with such a large age gap. It allowed Amanda to realise the positive influence that she has on her younger sister, and to recognise how rewarding this situation could be for both of them.

Moving house

Toddlers are not generally affected by moving house in the same way that older children can be, because their world is so focused on you. They remember the old house, but *also* quickly get used to the new one.

The key is to set up his room and the play area first (as well as the rooms of any other children) and allow him to play there during the day so that he becomes familiar with it. Make sure you unpack the comfort items first, too – familiar blankie and toys. You may find he has trouble going to sleep or staying in bed at first. If that happens, a few days of the 'Sleep Separation' technique (see page 273) should do the trick.

Beyond that, it's important to look at the resources in your new area, and point them out to your toddler. So the playground that was once there is now the playground that is *here*. It reassures a child to know that what you used to do when you lived at the old place can be done here, too.

Preparing your child for school

If you have been following the advice in this book on stimulation and life skills – as well as providing your toddler with opportunities to have fun without you, a few hours or days per week – he should be ready to make the transition to school at age five. Opposite, you'll find a box with a list of the things that he should be able to do – and where you can find out how to do them, if you need to swing into action.

In addition to this, it's important to take him to the school's 'open day', so that he can see what his new classroom is like, check out the playground apparatus and meet other children. Help your child begin to build friendships with his soon-to-be schoolmates. Meet up in the park after open day, and invite them over to play. If he has a few friends when he starts, he'll find the progression that much easier.

This also provides you with the opportunity to build friendships with other parents. They may not be the friends that you see on a Saturday night with your husband, but it's good to become friendly with your child's friends. It can help with childcare, brainstorming solutions to problems that arise, and generally being in the know about what's going on in your child's class. It also makes it easier to set up regular play dates, which can help to get your child's budding social life on its feet.

As the time draws closer, talk to your child about what he'll be doing in school – and all the fun he'll have. Don't dwell on the negatives – such as, 'I'll miss you and you'll be gone all day and it's a big adjustment for us all ...' Instead, focus on how much fun it will be for him – and how it shows what a big boy he is now. Keep any of your sad feelings to yourself.

IS YOUR CHILD READY FOR SCHOOL?

Your child will need to have some key life skills, and be able to manage a few things on her own, before she attends school for the first time. It will make the beginning of her academic life – and the transition to school – that much easier if you help to ensure that she's ready. She'll need to be:

- **potty-trained (see Chapter 8)**
- **able to be happily away from you for several hours (see page 154)**
- **able to take her shoes on and off (see Chapter 12)**
- **able to take her clothes on and off, including jumpers (see Chapter 12)**
- **able to sit still for periods of time (which is developed through the activities suggested in Chapter 6, including play and stimulation, as well as the play suggestions in Chapter 12)**
- **able to listen (which is developed through the auditory-stimulation suggestions in Chapter 6)**
- **able to count to ten (the same goes here)**
- **able to recognise her name in writing (which is developed through the visual-stimulation suggestions in Chapter 6)**

8

Potty-training in a week

Potty-training in a week? Yes, it can be done and I am going to show you how in this chapter.

Potty-training can be one of the very stressful times for a parent, but the good news is that once it's done, it's done. You've got to find humour to persevere with the one-week 'Potty-training' technique, but we British have a good sense of humour when it comes to potty issues. How big is the poo? What colour? Texture? We're not afraid to laugh about it. So keep your sense of humour about you.

♦ **Commitment**

♦ **Perseverance**

♦ **Humour**

There is a specific sequence to potty-training and I'm going to take you through it step-by-step, so you can do it confidently. Once you start, don't be tempted to give up after a few days. You need to stick with it until he's got it.

Timing is everything

Every parent wants to know *when* they should potty-train their child. With many activities and preschools requiring that your child be potty-trained to attend, the pressure is on. But, put that pressure aside. The number-one rule is that *your child* must be ready. She must have the ability to control her bladder and bowels *and* understand and communicate when she has to go. Too many people try before their toddler can do both of these things, and that's why they have trouble. This is nature and it can't be forced.

A toddler's bladder and bowel control begins to mature at around 18 months. When her bladder fills up, her brain get the signal and her nervous system tells her she needs to go. Furthermore, between the ages of one and two, she's developing the cognitive skills of memory and understanding to picture a goal – go potty – and follow through. Between the ages of two and three her concentration, as well as her short- and long-term memory, improve. Hand-eye coordination becomes more agile and her language skills are developing. This means that she can focus better and not become side-tracked on her way to the toilet, she can pull her clothes up and down easily, and she can understand and communicate with you about the process.

The key is to observe your child closely and look for the signs that her cognitive and verbal skills are developed and her body has matured enough for you to train her effectively. You will see these signs between two to two-and-a-half, and that's when you can start. If, for some reason, you've missed the signs, and your child is now three or three-and-a-half, and ready for nursery school, that will be your key motivation for potty-training. For most parents, this pressure will create a sense of severe panic. So I would advise you to look for the signs beforehand, so you don't get caught with your pants down.

Start off with a little 'show and tell'. Leave the door open when you go to the loo, and explain what you're doing. A good thing to bear in mind is the fact that you're not just training her to go to the potty, you are also teaching the importance of keeping clean. So make sure you demo the full routine – potty, wipe, wash hands and dry.

Signs that your toddler is ready

Here are the signs I look for to begin potty-training:

◆ When I put him down for an afternoon nap, I start noticing that his nappy is getting drier and lighter. It's not sodden with wee, which means he has control over his bladder.

◆ I start tracking how much he has to drink before his nap. How much did he drink? A 200ml glass of juice? He then went down for a nap, so he's holding his bladder for an hour, an hour and a half.

◆ I then start hearing about it: 'Wee-wee … I've gone wee-wee.' That tells me there's an awareness of what's going on. He'll also tell me before he goes poo – or when he goes poo – because after that he wants his nappy changed. A child who can ask for things tells me he has the communication skills necessary to do the training.

Choose an uninterrupted week

When the signs are all there, I choose a time when I know I can focus on training for seven straight days. I've seen parents declare, 'We're training her now', and two months later it's still going on. Something is not right! If you give this your *undivided*, 100 percent focus, you really can do it in one week.

When I say focus, I mean it. It must become your number-one priority – and your partner's and your nanny's or childminder's number-one priority. Clear your schedule. When any commitments come up, tell people, 'Sorry, we can't. This week we're potty-training.' It's just a week, so it can be done.

Knowing that the focus of the week is training is important because you're going to need to be extra observant. When is she drinking fluids? How much? You've observed the patterns and know the signs that she has to go. Now you're going to have to watch like a hawk to prompt your child to sit on the potty. But first: the proper equipment.

Equipment

I'm a fan of basic potties for training. I'm not a huge believer in those that play music or sing every time she wees. This is not playtime. You're teaching her a basic function – go, clean up, leave and get back to playing.

Some kids will insist on sitting on the big 'potty'. She's seen Mum and Dad do it, so she wants to do it too. In that case, you can buy a ring that sits on the top of the toilet seat so that she won't fall in. Either way is fine. All that matters is that she feels as comfortable as possible, so she'll relax and be able to go. If she sits down on the toilet without support, it feels like a big gaping hole that she could fall into. Her natural reaction will be to tense up her muscles, instead of relaxing and releasing. You can hold her there, but it will be easier and feel more natural if she can sit by herself.

I also highly recommend getting a travel potty. I love them! I take it in the car or even to the park during the training week. Although not necessary, baby wipes are also great when you're first starting out because it's easier to wipe with a wet wipe rather than dry paper.

In terms of clothing, I believe strongly in starting with knickers straightaway. Training nappies can work at night-time, but it's confusing if you use them during the day. Think of it this way: for the past two-and-a-half years your child has had a nappy on day and night. She's heard all about nappies: 'Let's change your nappy, darling; take the nappy off, and put the nappy in the bin.' She knows what a nappy looks like. She knows what a nappy *feels* like. She probably takes her nappies off, and sometimes wants to put her nappy on, right? She's used to poo-ing and weeing in a nappy.

Then you turn around and put her in knickers. It feels different: thinner, less bulky. It helps her get the point that things are different now. When she wets her knickers, it's uncomfortable – she's wet and she notices she's wet. And that's part of the learning. Training nappies, on the other hand, are built to go up and down (like knickers) but absorb all the wee (like nappies), so she doesn't feel uncomfortable. It's confusing for the child.

Buy lots of knickers and *expect* that there are going to be accidents. Unless it's poo, I'm not a firm believer in rushing to change a toddler as soon as she's had an accident. You want her to learn that wetting her pants is uncomfortable and should be avoided. It helps her to think about being conscious of the feeling that she needs to go – and what happens if she doesn't make it to the potty.

I'm not saying you should leave her in dirty knickers as a punishment – simply wait until she registers the uncomfortable feeling. When a toddler has wet her knickers and tells me, 'I've gone wee-wee, Jo Jo,' I say, 'Really? We don't do wee-wee in our pants. This is when we go to the potty, don't we?' Then I'd take her over to show her the potty and only then would I change her.

TO REWARD OR NOT TO REWARD? THAT'S THE QUESTION

I'm not one for the 'poo for an M&M' philosophy. I don't want to set up the expectation that he'll get a treat every time he goes, which leads to the situation that he won't go unless he gets a treat! So I don't believe in rewards or stickers. He should go because he's supposed to go. You're teaching a life skill that's part of being a human being. Verbal praise works just fine. However, rewards are good to encourage a child to go if he's regressed. Use it for the first ten times or so, and then you can drop the chart.

The PT week routine

You've seen the signs, picked the week, purchased the equipment – now it's PT week. Here are the basics, to follow every day for seven days:

- First thing in the morning, put on her knickers. Then, choose clothes that are easy to pull up and down quickly – anything with an elastic waistband, rather than zips or poppers.

- Explain to her what it feels like when she needs to go. I press on her bladder below her belly button and say, 'When you need to go wee-wee, you can feel it in here.' I'm trying to help her understand the signal. If she's got the cognitive skills to be able to train, she'll get it.

- Throughout the day, monitor the amount of fluid that you're giving her to drink. If your child has had more than 100ml of liquids, you know that she's going to need to wee within the hour.

- It's the same with working out when she'll have a bowel movement. You've made sure that she's having regular mealtimes, which lead to regular bowel habits. You'll see a pattern emerge and start to realise that your child goes 'number two' maybe twice a day – and work out roughly when.

◆ When you think the time is getting close, prompt her, 'Do you need to go potty?' Chances are she'll say 'no', because she's engaged in what she's doing. Be firm: 'Time to go.'

◆ Be *very* casual about it. This is one of the only things she can control in her life. You need to get it done, but you don't want to draw too much attention to it, which can lead to a power struggle.

◆ Sit her on the potty, saying, 'OK, go wee-wee now.' Sometimes I turn the faucet on to help stimulate the flow. But, whatever you do, look away. Staring can make her hold in her urine. Again, it's all about encouraging natural relaxation so the muscles can release and let go. (By four, you may actually be told, 'Can you go?' She may want privacy. That's fine; I always say, 'Call me when you're finished then.')

◆ 'Go poo poo?' With bowel movements, I'll imitate straining my face.

◆ Have her sit there for about three minutes. If nothing happens, ask, 'Are you going to go wee-wee?' She may say, 'No, nothing' or 'Yeah', because maybe she's trying to go poo. If there's nothing, pull her knickers back up and wait a little bit longer.

◆ Ask again. Be patient, you might be asking many, many times a day. Look for the signs – holding her privates – and ask if she has to go: 'Do you need to wee-wee?'

◆ If she has an accident, don't change her right away: 'Went wee-wee.' 'Aw, that's not good! We go on the potty! It really feels yucky, right?' My facial expressions are very animated. You're firm, but you're not scolding or shaming.

◆ Talk firmly with an expectation, 'We don't do that here, we go in the potty.' Kids at this stage want to meet your expectations. Some parents say, 'OK, don't worry. That's OK, next time.' OK, next time … that's confusing. Help her understand that it's not OK without shaming.

◆ Once she goes, praise her for her efforts, but don't gush. You don't want her to get the idea that she can control you with her toilet behaviour.

◆ Wipe. If she wants to try wiping, just finish the job after. Flush the toilet and then wash your hands and hers.

◆ Repeat this process every day for the full week. Don't expect her to get it in a day. She needs the focus, consistency, repetition and practice of the whole week.

Potty-training do's and don'ts

◆ Do keep the potty close by. If you've got a house where the loo is far away, put it closer to where you're spending your time.

◆ Do offer encouragement and praise when she goes, but in a casual way: 'Good job!'

◆ Don't only rely on her to tell you when she needs to go. Prompt her repeatedly and always have her go to the loo before you go out or leave somewhere.

◆ Do give privacy – some children are shy and need to be alone to perform.

◆ Don't switch back to nappies for long car journeys or travel. This is confusing and sends the wrong message. Instead, take a travel potty and plan for stops along the way.

◆ Don't give her a book to read. The potty serves a purpose – purely for poo and for wee. It should not become a throne or seat. You don't want to offer anything that will distract her from her job.

◆ Don't go backwards and put her back in a nappy when a new baby arrives. Once you start training stick with it.

PRACTISE IN DIFFERENT SITUATIONS

During training week, get out of the house. You want to keep to your routine because he has to learn to experience going to the loo in different situations. Once, I was taking care of twins and we were in the midst of potty-training. I took them to the park with potty in hand – in the middle of winter I'll have you know. And did I care what people thought of me? Of course not! I was in training mode. I also brought a nappy bag full of wipes, a bottle of water for rinsing, and hand sanitiser to clean our hands after. I know you're dying to know – did they wee in the park? What do you think?

Training boys

When training boys, I recommend starting them *sitting* for both weeing and poo-ing, because it's easier. Aiming is a task that comes later. What I want him to learn before being allowed to stand is how to completely empty his bladder, without spraying everywhere like the Bellagio.

The first week of training, be sure to get him to sit back and tilt his pelvis. It makes it easier for the bladder to release. Sometimes little boys will wee and not finish the job. They'll rush through, when they need to empty their entire bladder. This can lead to accidents or even infections. Sitting back prevents this.

If he starts out standing because he's insisting on copying his Dad or older brother, have him sit down and back, every now and then, so he feels the sensation of completely emptying his bladder. Once you decide that he's old enough to stand, get him a little step stool so he'll be at the right level in front of the toilet – in this way, you'll reduce the likelihood of wee going everywhere. Have him watch Dad. But, again, if he's learned how to wee sitting down first, he'll have a greater sense of control and this will be less of a problem.

Bottom-wiping

For the first week, show her how to wipe herself. As you wipe, explain what you're doing, and then progress to letting her wipe first – supervising and finishing the job afterwards. With girls, it's important to teach them to wipe from back to front when weeing – and from front to back when poo-ing, to reduce the chance of infection.

Eventually you do want her to wipe herself without assistance. You might have to encourage her, by suggesting: 'Well, you can do it yourself. Mummy doesn't have to do it for you anymore.' By four, your child should be able to do the whole sequence – potty, wipe, wash and dry – without help.

Battle for control

I worked with a little boy who was more than ready to be potty-trained, but he was very controlling. His parents had been too passive. He would have an absolute fit when asked to wear big-boy pants. So his parents just gave in and gave him a nappy. By the time I came along, he was very set in having things his way. I put the nappies away and said to him, 'It's either this pair of pants or these ones. You choose which ones you want to wear.' Not surprisingly he refused. I said, 'You're putting one of those on. Otherwise, you can't come out and play with the rest of us.'

It took him at least a half hour, but eventually he chose which pair to wear. The next battle for control was about sitting on the toilet. But, again, I insisted and eventually he did it. Each time, it helped to have something fun lined up, which encouraged him to do what I asked.

Troubleshooting potty-training

If it's not working, ask yourself the following questions:

◆ Am I consistently following the steps with no exceptions? The biggest problems I see occur when you decide during potty-training week that you're going take a quick trip to your Mum's and you put a nappy on your child. Anything that sends a mixed message will make this harder and take longer.

◆ Am I taking the time it takes? Remember my story about the little boy – 30 minutes for him to get his pants on!

◆ Are you locked in a battle of wills? If so, you have to win.

◆ If you have trouble remembering the steps, copy them and post them by the potty.

> ### Aim for the Cheerios
>
> If he really sprays when he wees, try putting a few Cheerios in the toilet to give him something to aim for.

Training multiples

At the beginning of the book, I stressed the importance of recognising that each child develops at her own pace. In potty-training multiples, it's important to keep that in mind. It's likely that one will be ready before the other. If they are ready at once, I suggest training one during one week – and then the other the next. Don't think you need to do everyone at once. It's too hard to pay such close attention to more than one child at a time.

Of course, when you do go through the training, your other toddlers will be watching and learning. Make sure to get each child his own potty, so there's never any competition or problem if they have to go at the same time.

Poo and wee problems

I've heard many parents say that their toddlers will wee in the potty, but they won't poo. The reality is that some kids can be scared of taking a poo. If you've had a child who has been constipated and then gone poo, it can be very painful. It can also be the reverse – they'll poo but not wee. In either case, what I do is tell the toddler firmly – and *with* expectation – that he has to go in the loo. Usually that's enough.

> ### *Pooper check*
>
> While training, be cautious of your child going back to safety places to poo or wee. Some hide under tables or in rooms.

Once, however, I was potty-training a little boy who could wee in the potty – and he was very pleased with himself – but when it came to doing a poo, he was really scared of actually doing the deed. He would hold it until he had his nappy on for night-time.

I needed him to understand that it wasn't as frightening as he imagined. So I gave him breakfast food that was softer in consistency, which meant that it wouldn't bind him. Then we went off to a restaurant with friends for lunch, where he again ate food that was runnier than usual. As he was playing, he was so focused on having fun with his friends that when he realised he needed to go poo, it just came out.

It was a bit of a nightmare – as he ran up to me with poo all down his leg. We did clear the restaurant pretty quickly! We went into the loo, where I cleaned him all up and put on fresh pants. From then on, he had no trouble in that department again.

Anxiety over pooing can sometimes lead to constipation. If this is going on, try a warm bath, as it relaxes your toddler's muscles. If it becomes a regular problem, make sure your child is getting enough fresh fruits and veggies, and plenty of water. Avoid bananas, as they can be binding.

Potty-training at night

Almost all kids are potty-trained in the day long before they are at night. They simply lack the bladder control to hold wee for between nine and eleven hours at night. So you need to have nappies for the night until your child is able to remain dry.

Around four or five, you will see the signs that your child is ready to be night-trained. If he is ready before then, way to go! Once I see the signs, I use something called the 'Elevenish Get Up To Pee' technique, to help with the transition.

THE ELEVENISH GET UP TO PEE TECHNIQUE

◆ **Around 10 or 11pm (depending upon when he went to bed), get him up and take him to the loo.**

◆ **Wake him up enough so he's conscious and aware of what's happening.**

◆ **Don't carry him; he should be moving by himself.**

◆ **Escort him to the loo and let him pull down his pants and go.**

◆ **Take him back to bed.**

◆ **Eventually, you won't have to get him up – he'll do it himself.**

'I want to wear nappies like the baby'

That's like your toddler saying, 'I want to go on the baby swing.' You wouldn't do that because you know it's not age-appropriate. It's your job as a parent to make decisions for your child. You certainly don't want to encourage arrested development. Having a toddler who is already potty-trained regress to nappies is a huge step backwards.

As I said in Chapter 2, I've spent endless time telling people: 'Your child doesn't need to be sucking on a bottle anymore. She can have a cup with handles' or 'Your child can pick up a fork and spoon and feed himself.' You constantly need to think about how you can encourage your child along to the next stage of appropriate development. You certainly never want to halt his development simply because it's convenient, or because it prevents him from whining or begging.

SIGNS THAT YOUR CHILD IS READY FOR NIGHT-TRAINING

◆ **Good consistency of *unprompted* bathroom behaviour.**

◆ **Bowel movements have become regulated to morning and night.**

◆ **Wakens up dry several mornings in a row.**

I've seen some parents give in to such requests for nappies because they don't want to deal with the temper tantrum – or they feel bad because he's feeling left out because of the baby. The answer is simply to pay more attention to him as a big boy – not give in to the nappy. His sudden desire for a nappy may not mean that he needs you to spend more quality time with him – he may simply need you to recognise that he's still adjusting to the new situation. He may even be asking to see what happens.

Just say: Say, 'Nope. You're a big boy. Nappies are for babies.' Then explain all the things he can do that his baby brother or sister can't. Don't give in.

NIGHT-TIME TRAINING TIPS

◆ **Put a waterproof undersheet on the bed, to protect the mattress.**

◆ **Cut down on the amount of fluids he has leading up to bedtime.**

◆ **Make sure he goes to the loo right before bed.**

◆ **Use a reward chart to reward him for dry nights.**

9

Establishing
healthy eating habits

The toddler years are an important time when it comes to eating for the simple reason that you are establishing healthy eating patterns for the first time. When you establish a healthy diet, you can help to eliminate all sorts of future problems. With extreme eating issues such as obesity, type 2 diabetes, and eating disorders epidemic in today's society, it is increasingly important for parents to lay down a healthy foundation that will last into adulthood. That's why it's so important for me to educate you on eating healthily, because you're going to teach your young ones lifelong habits.

I'm passionate about this topic because parents and carers really are in the driving seat here, and have some major responsibilities. We are the ones who go to the supermarket, buy the food, put it in the pantry, freezer and fridge, cook it and put it in our toddlers' mouths. If you choose to put a doughnut in your mouth or drink two cans of fizzy drinks, that's your choice as an adult. But your toddler is solely dependent on you for the food that you give her – and what she drinks. How fair is that if you don't do right by your child? It's not! We have to make sure that we change how *we* think about food so that we don't continue the health problems we're seeing now. We are responsible for what we put in our children's mouths, and how we educate them about food, and we must take that job seriously.

The right equipment

Booster seat

Throughout his first year, your baby was eating in his high chair. As soon as he starts climbing up into the high chair, he's ready for a booster seat. This is an important transition, as the booster brings your child closer to being a full part of the dining experience with you at the table. It's also a signal that it's time for her to begin to learn to feed herself consistently – and to eat what and when you're eating. By the time your child is two, you should make the transition from high chair to booster.

Dishes and utensils

Set his place at the table with his plate or bowl – half the size of yours – and the appropriate utensils. Beginning at two, start to encourage his fine motor skills and move from finger foods to eating first with a spoon and then with a fork. You'll know that he's ready to make the transition to a spoon when he is able to pick things up easily with his fingers. Once he masters the spoon, move on to the fork. It will be easy – he'll see you using one and want to do the same. Toddlers' meals normally consist of food for which they'll use cutlery and something that I like to call 'picnic food', which they eat with their hands. If I serve food that is not picnic food, I encourage them to use the cutlery. Monkey see, monkey do.

In the beginning you can start with plastic – even if they don't work that well – and then graduate up to stainless steel. Smaller metal utensils work well, too. Giving a knife to a toddler is too dangerous; at this point you're still cutting his food into bite-sized bits for him to eat.

The right-sized plate

Your child's dinner plate should approximately 6 to 7 inches (15 to 18cm) in diameter, which is a little bit bigger than a side plate.

Bottles to cups

Between the ages of one and three, there are some transitions that should be taking place; in particular, your little one needs to move from a bottle to a beaker, then from a beaker to a cup with handles, and finally to a normal cup without a lid. What you're doing is moving her from the sucking reflex with a bottle to learning how to swallow, first from a beaker, and finally from a regular cup. I've seen too many parents move too slowly from bottle to beaker ('my baby loves her bottle') and then beaker to cup ('she won't spill and can walk around with it').

But you need to get your toddler to a regular cup by two-and-a-half to three for two important reasons:

1   It's bad for her teeth. With a beaker, the fluid is brought directly to the top of her front teeth. If she's drinking anything with sugar in it (that's milk or juice included), this can promote tooth decay.

2   If you keep treating your child like a baby, she'll remain a baby emotionally. It's important to get her to the next step.

> ## THE BEAKER BE GONE TECHNIQUE
>
> ◆ **If it's time to say bye-bye to the beaker, buy a plastic drinking cup, paint and stickers.**
>
> ◆ **Sit down with your toddler and help her to decorate her new drinking glass.**
>
> ◆ **She'll be so excited to use the new cup, she'll forget the other ones ever existed.**

There are two types of beaker spouts – soft and hard. The soft one feels like a bottle teat, so begin there first. Then, between 18 months and two years, introduce the harder spout. Between about two and three, take off the lid. Now she's drinking from a cup with two handles. Then transition her to one handle, and then no handles. If your four-year-old wants a cup that you can take out and about, consider using a metal bottle with a plastic straw inserted, or try a mini gym bottle.

The right quantities of the right foods

You need to establish healthy eating habits early on. It's much easier to set good habits than it is to break bad ones. You start by giving your toddler healthy food choices and eating together as a family as often as you can.

The key with any meal with your toddler is PVP: *Presentation, Variety and Proportion.* This is basically a balance of nutritional choices and not too much on the plate. You're setting up good expectations of what your toddler should eat – and how much. Most toddlers naturally know when they're full, so they'll stop eating. Some may refuse to eat because they want to play. You want to get your proportions right, so you'll know when to worry (or not) about how much he's eating.

Toddlers have small tummies and small appetites. Filling their plates with too much can be overwhelming. See the box below for suggested portion sizes of common foods.

PROPER PORTIONS FOR TODDLERS

Nutritionists suggest toddlers age two to four have daily servings of:

PROTEIN: 2 ounces, which is 2 servings per day of the following: 2 tablespoons ground or two 1-inch cubes meat or fish; 1 egg; ¼ cup tofu or cooked beans; 1 tablespoon smooth peanut butter; 2 slices of deli-sliced turkey breast.

MILK AND DAIRY: 2 cups, which is 4 servings of the following: ½ cup whole milk; ½ cup yogurt; 1 slice cheese; ½ cup cottage cheese.

VEGETABLES: 1 cup per day, which is 4 servings of the following: ¼ cup cooked squash or sweet potato; ¼ cup green peas, green beans, courgettes or other vegetables.

GRAINS: 3 ounces, with as many from whole grain sources as possible, which is 6 servings of the following: ½ slice of bread; ¼ cup cooked rice; ½ cup cereal; ¼ cup cooked pasta.

FRUIT: 1 cup per day, which is 4 servings of the following: ¼ cup applesauce; 1 banana no longer than 3 inches; ¼ cup juice; ¼ cup cut up berries, pears, apples, oranges.

Generally, toddlers eat three meals a day, with two to three snacks in between. Healthy two-, three-, and four-year-olds should be consuming between 1000 and 1400 calories per day. As calories are the fuel they need for growth and development, you want to make sure those calories come from foods packed with nutrients.

Instead of counting calories, I recommend you concentrate on the *types* of food that you're offering. It's not about getting your toddler to eat everything on the plate but, rather, making sure he's eating nutritious, balanced meals. As long as everything on his plate is fresh and healthy, and there is plenty of variety, you can be sure that your child is eating well.

You can set a really good example if you sit down at the table and share mealtimes with him. This can be difficult for some parents during the week, so make the most of the weekends. If you're not ready to eat when he is, you can have a snack to show him the importance of eating properly. If you don't eat during the day, and your toddler never sees you eating, why would he feel it is important?

Organic or not, make it healthy

Whether you choose to buy organic or not, buying fresh or frozen produce will bring you closer to eating foods without so much fat or processed sugar. Frozen foods do not have to be ready-made meals or junk; you can cook and freeze your own healthy meals for up to three months. If you made your child's baby food, you'll be aware of this.

SMALL CHANGES

Make one healthy switch today – choose wholegrain spaghetti, rice or bread over traditional white varieties and you'll be one step closer to adding important nutrients and fibre to your toddler's diet.

Food guidelines

Here are some general good food guidelines to bear in mind when preparing your toddler's meals:

Look for foods that are rich in:

◆ *Calcium*: Milk, cheese, yoghurt, broccoli, sweet potatoes, wholegrain bread, fortified orange juice, kidney beans, soya products and leafy green vegetables. Why? Calcium is necessary for the development of strong bones and teeth (800 to 1000mg recommended daily).

◆ *Iron*: Broccoli and other leafy green vegetables, sweet potatoes, squash, beef, chicken, pork, spinach, eggs, raisins, apricots, tofu, brown rice, iron-fortified cereals and tuna. Why? Iron is needed to make red blood cells, which carry oxygen throughout the body (12mg recommended daily).

◆ *Fibre*: Wholegrain breads and cereals, vegetables, fruit and pulses. Why? Fibre helps your child's digestion, keeps her from getting constipated, and makes her feel full longer (19g recommended daily).

Important vitamins for these years include:

◆ *Vitamin A*: Carrots, avocados, spinach, yellow and orange fruits and vegetables, leafy green vegetables, kiwis, prunes, papaya, eggs, milk and yoghurt. Why? Vitamin A promotes a healthy immune system, keeps skin healthy, helps prevent eye problems, and is essential for the growth and development of cells (300mcg recommended daily).

◆ *Vitamin C*: Red peppers, green peppers, avocados, cabbage, kale, turnip greens, collards, bananas, kiwis, broccoli, tomatoes, mangos, lemons, oranges, cantaloupe, strawberries; in fact, all fruit and vegetables contain vitamin C. Why? It helps build up your child's immune system so he can fight off bacteria and viruses, is necessary for the body to absorb iron and calcium, is essential for healthy bones, teeth, gums, and blood vessels, aids in wound healing, and contributes to brain function (40mg recommended daily).

◆ *Vitamin D*: Fortified milk and milk products, egg yolks, salmon, sardines, herring, tuna, meat and wheatgerm. Why? It helps the body to absorb calcium, strengthening teeth and bones (5mcg or 200iu recommended daily).

◆ *Vitamin B-complex*: Breakfast cereals, lentils, chickpeas, black beans, kidney beans, lima beans, asparagus, spinach, Brussels sprouts, broccoli, oranges and wholegrains. Why? It helps with metabolism, skin and muscle tone, immune function and nervous function, and can help to prevent some types of anaemia (150mcg recommended daily).

◆ *Zinc*: Mushrooms, wheatgerm, soybeans, pumpkin seeds, sunflower seeds, shellfish, meat, herring and eggs. Why? Zinc is essential for your child's normal growth and development (10mg recommended daily).

Also remember:

◆ Every meal should contain a balance of protein (meat, fish, tofu or dairy), healthy carbohydrates (wholegrains), fruit and veg (also a good source of carbohydrates and fibre), and healthy fats. It may surprise you that toddlers need fat, but it's very important for brain and nervous system function and development. For this reason, they shouldn't be given low-fat products until the age of five. Essential fatty acids (EFAs or 'omega oils') are the most important and these can be found in seeds, nut butters, oily fish and flaxseed.

◆ Salt and sugar are additives that toddlers don't need.

◆ Butter is fine for toddlers, as they do need some saturated fat in their diets and it's full of calcium, protein and vitamin D, too!

◆ The best way for your toddler to get the daily nutrients he needs is by eating a balanced diet and not through vitamin supplements. If you're worried about your child's diet, talk to your GP, who will help you to understand the nutritional value of foods. If there is a shortfall, vitamin drops or tablets may be prescribed, but if you ensure that your toddler's diet is varied and fresh, he'll be getting everything he needs.

BEWARE OF...

After your child turns one, you can start introducing most foods into her diet. There are however, some foods that aren't appropriate until a little later. These include:

◆ *Raw or partially cooked eggs*: because of the risk of salmonella poisoning. This is one reason why you shouldn't allow children to eat uncooked cake batter, or anything with unpasteurised eggs, such as homemade mayonnaise.

◆ *Whole or chopped nuts of any kind*: Until the age of five, these remain a choking hazard. Because of the high incidence of peanut allergies, introduce peanuts (in ground or 'butter' form first) cautiously.

◆ *Shark, swordfish, marlin or tilefish*: contain high levels of mercury, which affects a child's developing nervous system. Don't serve more than 300g (12oz) a week of tuna, shellfish, tinned fish, small ocean fish or farmed fish for similar reasons.

Raising a healthy eater

So what happens when you can't get your toddler to eat all this 'good stuff'? You can train your toddler to be a 'good eater', but this is definitely where you need two important skills from your backpack: *Patience* and *Persistence*.

In 20 years, I've never had a 'fussy' eater. According to the law of averages, you'd think I'd have had at least one, in two decades of childrearing, right?

DIPPING WHEN ALL ELSE FAILS

Encouraging your kids to try new foods – or even eat at all – can be very taxing. As much as young children like to dip fruit in the yoghurt and veggies in the hummus, a lot of you parents have succumbed to placing ketchup on absolutely everything. Now don't get me wrong. Anyone who knows me knows I like a bit of ketchup. But please let me leave you with these tips: Don't give her the squeeze bottle or she'll end up squeezing half the bottle on the plate. Rather, pour an amount that would fill half an egg cup on her plate (roughly 30ml), and let her dip. When it's all gone, it's all gone. The same goes for any other dressings.

So what's going on? The truth is that parents create the 'fussy' eater – the 'he'll only eat macaroni' eater. Or what about the 'our child only eats food that's on the children's menu' eater? The children's menu is meant to offer properly-sized portions, not a whole different range of food! It doesn't mean because your toddler is a child that she shouldn't be eating a lean piece of chicken and some stir-fried vegetables. It doesn't mean the only thing she can eat is a drumstick with SpongeBob's head on it.

You create your child's eating habits, which means you can raise a healthy eater. Here's my advice on how to do it:

Offer variety

Giving your toddler a variety of textures and flavours is incredibly important to expand her palate. If you're enthusiastic about trying different foods, write down your recipes and incorporate them in your meal planner (see Part III). Take it slowly, though. Your child's digestive system will need to adapt to a wide range of new foods, so it's a good idea to offer a few new things at a time.

Offering a variety of textures and tastes also keeps your toddler interested in eating. When you've graduated her from eating purees to finger foods, you may find that she starts to play with her food and then lose interest. The reason for this is that it takes more time to eat with her fingers, and she becomes bored. When you make the transition from 'baby food' to fare that is appropriate for toddlers, you may also find that your little one loses weight.

That's why I advise giving her food with a consistent texture, alongside her finger food. This way, she'll have to use a spoon to eat it, and she can get on with the job. Things like chicken risotto, spaghetti or another pasta dish, or even a nice fish pie fit this brief perfectly. If she's got food on the spoon that contains the right blend of nutrients, and healthy food to pick up and eat with her fingers, she's very likely to get the nutrients she needs for healthy growth and development. Most importantly, she's less likely to become bored.

Keep trying

A very common thing I hear from parents is that their children don't 'like anything'. When I'm troubleshooting this very common problem, I will go into their pantry and fridge to see exactly what she does like, because the cupboard and fridge don't lie.

Like anything else, don't give up too soon. 'I tried it once and she didn't like it,' parents say. Once? That's not good enough! I've given the same food to kids between 12 and 15 different times over several weeks, because that's how much time it takes for the palate to get used to a taste. And remember, a child who says she doesn't like it means she doesn't like it *now*. Keep trying. You can also try offering the same food in a different form as she might be rejecting the texture and not the taste.

Try or finish?

Be clear if you are asking her to try something or to finish it. To try something is to take a bite. To finish it is to eat the whole thing.

If you see that your child eats well most of the time, but you want her to have one of the food groups she's missed, ask her to 'try it'. If you want her to finish it, you have to be specific in your request: 'Please eat both pieces of cauliflower.' Parents also commonly make the mistake of asking, 'Are you finished?' – rather than stipulating how much more they need to eat before they can get down. Parents have become too liberal! It's not being a tyrant to insist that your toddler finishes the healthy food on his plate. If you aren't over-feeding him, and the portion sizes are right, there's no reason why he shouldn't eat it.

Don't mix your compassion with your realistic expectation of doing the right thing. If he was ill, you'd insist that he ate all of his chicken soup and that piece of toast. To remain healthy he needs to eat the proper amount of healthy foods.

Be firm

Sometimes a toddler will say she wants something. You give it to her, and then she changes her mind. As I wrote earlier, one- and two-year-olds don't understand what they're asking for – or what they really want. Often they're parroting back what they hear. Your eldest asked for toast, so your toddler says she wants some, too. Then she sees an orange and says she wants that. That's why I allow young toddlers to change their minds about food choices, because sometimes it's influenced by others.

However, by the time she reaches three, I encourage her to think hard about what she wants – and stay committed to it. At this point such switches are a control issue. If a three- or four-year-old said she wants something and I fix it – only to have her say, 'No, I want this instead' – I hold firm. 'No, this is what you asked for; this is what you'll have.'

I take the same stance with the child who says, 'I'm not hungry' at meal time and then ten minutes later is in the cupboard and sees the biscuit. Again, I'm firm and tell her she has to wait until the next meal or snack time.

Use a farmer's board

This is a board that you make – created to look like a vegetable patch – which can be used to encourage healthy eating (see box). I can't tell you how effective it can be to encourage an understanding of healthy food and to get kids to try new things.

MAKING A FARMER'S BOARD

◆ Have your child help you draw and colour a picture of a farmer's vegetable patch on a large piece of paper. Have it laminated and put up on the fridge or a board. You can then create a variety of vegetables to put on the board, using sticky-backed tape.

◆ When your toddler eats a vegetable, she puts a vegetable sticker on the farmer's board.

Don't offer bribes

I'm not against giving 'treats' to kids. By being responsible about the foods that your toddler is eating, you have the freedom to give a little 'treat' every now and then. However, if you give her something you call 'special' every day, then it's not a treat.

A bigger problem, however – and something I constantly caution parents against – is feeling like you have to offer a treat in order to get your child to eat her meal. That's creating a bad habit from the word 'go'!

Stop the cattle grazing

Don't let your toddler graze all day on snacks. She won't sit down and eat a balanced meal because she's already full on sweets and crisps. Definitely offer two to three well-spaced and nutritious snacks throughout the day. Just don't let her constantly open the cupboards and take whatever she wants. More than anything, it creates bad eating habits – and spikes and dips in blood-sugar levels. Store snacks away from little hands. It's worth remembering, too, that even 'healthy' snacks should be limited. Your toddler's main meals are designed to be well balanced, and contain a variety of foods that will supply her with the key nutrients she needs to grow, learn and develop. It's almost impossible to regulate her intake when she's snacking all day long, and she'll never be hungry enough to sit down and eat a full plate if she's been grazing.

Jo Jo No No: Reward for seconds

Don't reward your child with praise or treats for having seconds. 'Oh, you did well! You had two portions!' This could create an association in her mind between eating seconds and behaving well, leading to possible future problems with weight.

Be a role model

I know your life is so busy, but it's good to have a goal of having at least one meal a day as a family – at the very least, a couple times a week. Toddlers model your behaviour. She'll watch you eat and then want to eat. She'll also see if you're on the phone or not focused on her. Be conscious of the messages you're sending. Make meals an important focus and your child will follow your lead.

Be careful how you label food

You don't want to say, 'That's bad food' or 'That's good food' because you don't want your child to associate the foods they eat in a particular fashion. If you're being conscious about buying food that is healthy for all of your family, no food will be 'bad' for your toddler, because she's eating a healthy, well-balanced diet. It's only what *you* feel about a food that you're rubbing off on your child – and that's what will be ingrained in her. Just because you don't like sweet potatoes doesn't mean she won't.

Relax – especially if she won't eat

Toddlers on the younger side are rapidly developing their different sensory tastes: bitter, sweet and sour. Sometimes she'll refuse to eat a particular food because the taste is too intense for her. Think about the vegetables your 18-month- to three-year-old likes to eat: cauliflower, peas, carrots, sweetcorn and broccoli. They're either bland or sweet. But as she gets older, around the age of four, refusal is often not about a like or dislike, but about control. Her tastebuds will be more sophisticated at this stage, and she should be ready and willing and enjoy a wider variety of foods. So it's not about taste at all!

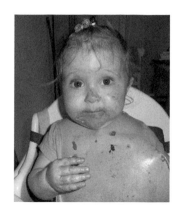

When your child rejects food and resists eating, you may feel an irrational fear of your child withering away. It's what I call the 'chicks in the nest syndrome'. We feed our young and when they don't eat, it creates anxiety because we know they need to eat to survive. So what we feel is real. And we know we don't want to force feed, because we know that's not right, either. This is where you have to go against your instinct. You want to force your child to eat, but you actually need to back off a bit.

Here's an example of what I mean. I once worked with Sophia, a mother who could not get her toddler Kieran to eat, and she was drastically losing weight. It had become very serious. Sophia was so worried about her daughter not eating that she shouted in panic – and at one stage started to force feed her until she gagged.

I suggested she start the meal with a different mindset and approach this problematic issue differently. She needed to still be firm with her expectations, but remove her obsession with food. Kieran had fallen into a routine of knowing that as soon as she sat at the table there would be a battle about her eating. This was a power play for control.

Instead, Sophia sat down and started talking to her about what they were going to do the next day. They sat at the table for 30 minutes. As Sophia distracted her by talking about things other than food, Kieran started to eat.

After a healthy pattern was established and a new approach adopted, change started to take place. All the snacks were removed so that we focused on her main meals. All the foods she had been surviving on – such as sweets and ice cream – were gone for the time being. So when mealtime arrived, she was hungry. Today Kieran has reached a healthy weight – an energetic child who is incredibly social, loves to engage in conversation and learn, and has a completely different relationship with her mother Sophia.

This was an extreme case, of course, and I share it to let you know that even when you feel there is no hope, never throw in the towel. Reach out for help. In this case, it made all the difference between Kieran being where she is today or being admitted into hospital with an eating disorder. Most food issues are about control, so if you remove the pressure and the emotion, you'll win the battle.

TIPS FOR AVOIDING MEALTIME BATTLES

- ◆ **Give clear warnings before each meal that it's nearly time to eat, so she can prepare herself to switch from what she's doing.**
- ◆ **Don't demand that she eats, if she complies with everything else. You can't really. Have faith that she won't starve and will eat when she's hungry.**
- ◆ **Refuse to cook separate meals on demand. Have her eat what you do.**
- ◆ **Use praise and encouragement for good table manners and when she tries new foods.**
- ◆ **Don't eat in front of the TV, but at the table.**
- ◆ *Relax.* **If you're tense about eating, your toddler will reflect that energy.**

Drinks

When your child is a baby, you give her milk to fill her up – and keep her healthy. But now that she's a toddler, you have to be much more mindful of the amount of milk and other fluids she's drinking. You definitely need to make sure that your child is well hydrated, but you also want to ensure that she's not drinking so much that she's not hungry enough to eat. You don't want her to miss out on getting the proper nutrition for her physical and mental development.

Milk and dairy products should be limited to about 400 to 600ml per day (about 16 to 24fl oz), and juice to between 120 and 180ml (4 to 6fl oz). If a toddler is drinking too much milk or juice, she won't be eating and getting essential vitamins and fibres he needs. Up to the age of five, she should be having whole-milk products; after this, you can move her on to lower-fat varieties.

I've seen speech delays from three-year-olds drinking eight beakers of milk a day. It does make sense if you think about it. When you eat, you have to chew. When you chew, you have to use your facial muscles. And your facial muscles help your pronunciation and use of words and language. If your child is just drinking, she's not getting the facial workout that helps with speech.

Jo Jo on Juices

Look for 100 percent fruit *juice* and not fruit *drinks*, as they contain loads of unhealthy sugar. In fact, giving your child water and then feeding her fruit is the best way to keep your child hydrated, as she'll get more fibre. I tend to dilute fresh juice when I give it to toddlers for two reasons: to stretch out the juice (a 180ml/6fl oz serving can be stretched to 360ml/12fl oz) and to reduce sugar intake. Always dilute with water – the lighter the colour, the better. Cranberry juice should go from being a deep red to almost blush pink.

I know drink boxes are convenient if you're on the go. But it's much better health-wise (and more environmentally friendly) to fill up a thermos, so that you can dilute the juice. Or, if your three-year-old is fixated on a fruit shoot, pour out half of it into a cup, and then dilute what remains with water.

If you do offer fruit juice, keep it to mealtimes. Not only will this help to protect her teeth (even fresh, natural juices contain sugars, albeit healthier than refined sugar), because the saliva that is created when she is eating helps to prevent decay, but also the vitamin C that it contains will help the iron in your toddler's meal to be better absorbed.

Jo Jo No No: Fizzy drinks

Undiluted, sugary fizzy drinks or fruit squash containing sugars can cause tooth decay. There are about 12 teaspoons of sugar in one can of fizzy drink. A penny will be stripped overnight in a glass of soda. Is that something you want to be giving your child?

TIPS FOR FLUID INTAKE

◆ In between meals, I constantly put a child's beaker or cup in front of him because at the age of two or three, he won't know he's thirsty. As he grows older – say, four – he'll know to say, 'Mummy, can I have a drink please?' At that stage he can recognise when he's feeling parched.

◆ When I'm feeding a toddler who is not eating enough, I'll just give half a cup of water or milk with his meal. Then, when he finishes his food, I'll give him more to drink.

Snacks

Consistent mealtimes create the cornerstones of breakfast, lunch and dinner. But, because of a toddler's need for fuel throughout the day, you'll need to supplement mealtimes with at least two snacks in between meals.

As I wrote about earlier, there's a big difference between snacks and 'snacking'. Healthy snacks keep your toddler going and actually help to stop him from grazing. With snacks, it's all about offering quality. It's easy to get into the crisps and biscuit habit, but these offer no nutritional value whatsoever.

Occasional sweets for snacks at parties are fine in moderation. However, I've found lately that even at birthday parties people are being more conscious about the food that they're serving. For your own toddler parties, consider offering food that is 20 percent sugar rather than 40 percent.

What time is snack time?

Look at your schedule as a whole to work out when your child will need to recharge and refuel. If he has breakfast at 7 o'clock, and you would normally do lunch around noon, his body needs fuel in between. The rule of thumb is every three hours or so – give or take a half an hour. Don't be militant with your time.

> **Avoiding night-time accidents**
>
> Apple juice, universally loved by toddlers, is actually a diuretic. You don't want to offer it to him right before bed.

The key is to observe your child. When do you notice his energy dip? Toddlers use up their energy very, very quickly. You need to observe your child and be flexible. If you have a morning activity where he's out running at the park for an hour, he'll probably need a snack straight after. You don't want to wait for a specific time – say, only snack at 10am – but, rather, pay attention to what he's doing. Because hunger is often a trigger for meltdowns, you need to get fuel back in his body sooner rather than later.

The same is true between lunch and dinner. Many parents tell me that their children start to drop around 3pm. Well then, that's snack time! In fact it's a good schedule to keep for the whole family.

Every healthy eating plan – no matter what your age – suggests having one or two snacks between meals to keep your energy levels up. What happens otherwise? We stretch ourselves (or, worse, skip meals) and then all of a sudden we're ravenous and need to eat right away. In those moments of hunger we might not make the best food choices.

You need the fuel to recharge yourself as well as your toddler. Have a piece of fruit or a slice of cheese as she has her snack. You'll feel better and be ready to handle whatever happens during the day.

HEALTHY SNACKING

- Offer choices, such as apples and peanut butter, cheese sticks, yoghurt, carrots, hummus and pitta bread, celery and cream cheese, orange slices, grapes … you get the idea.
- Don't provide crisps, biscuits, fizzy drinks or sweets.
- A snack should be palm-sized. It's not another meal.
- Who says a snack treat needs to be sweet? Consider using biscuit cutters and moulds to shape nutritious snacks like cheese or low-fat turkey into animals or hearts.

CREATE YOUR OWN SNACK BOXES

- ◆ Take a box, jar or paper bag and have your toddler decorate it.

- ◆ Tell him, 'You're making a special container for your snacks!'

- ◆ Each morning, give him a choice of what to put in the container. If he chooses something that needs refrigeration, put a drawing of it in the bag.

- ◆ By creating snack boxes in the morning, you've organised healthy food ready to grab and go when you need it.

Food allergies

Food allergies are real, can develop at any time, and can be dangerous. The good news? Many children outgrow them by the time they start school. However, for some like myself, it's a lifelong situation that you'll need to address, teaching your child to be aware of his allergies and in control of them as he grows.

In *Confident Baby Care*, I suggested giving only one type of food at a time, so you can watch for reactions. This same method should continue during the toddler years.

SIGNS OF FOOD ALLERGY

- ◆ Rashes, hives
- ◆ Swelling of the tongue, lips and face
- ◆ Stuffy or runny nose
- ◆ Wheezing and shortness of breath
- ◆ A tingling sensation on the tongue
- ◆ Abdominal cramps
- ◆ Vomiting and diarrhoea

COULD YOUR TODDLER BE DIABETIC?

If your child has the following symptoms, talk to your GP immediately: always tired and irritable, weeing frequently, constantly hungry and thirsty, sudden weight loss, blurry vision, and fruity, sweet breath. These could be signs of Type 1 diabetes.

If you have a family history of food allergies, discuss it with your child's GP. Your doctor will ask about what foods they eat and if you've noticed any symptoms or reactions from any particular food or food group. You may want to keep a food diary, noting down any reactions to foods – and, in particular, new foods, that your toddler tries. Even the mildest reactions, such as a rash, a little irritability or a runny tummy are worth noting down. Keep this to take to your GP, who may arrange for you to see an allergy consultant.

In children over the age of two, a skin-prick test can be undertaken. This involves scratching a small area of your child's skin (usually on the inside of his forearm) and placing a drop of specific food substances on the scratches. The welts that arise are measured, to assess whether your child has had an unusual reaction.

If there's a strong reaction, an allergy is diagnosed. There are also blood tests that can be done, where a blood sample is drawn to test for antibodies specific to certain foods.

Allergy symptoms can be mild or severe. Either way, they are not pleasant. If you notice even the mildest symptoms, call your GP right away.

If your toddler seems to be having trouble breathing, has swelling of the face or lips, or develops severe vomiting or diarrhoea after eating, call 999 immediately. Know where the nearest hospital is and get there right away. She could be suffering from anaphylactic shock, which is life-threatening. If you know she has allergies and have been given an EpiPen or Anapen, use it at once, and then call for an ambulance. See page 95 for instructions on how to use an EpiPen.

Because severe allergic reactions can be life-threatening, it's important to discover and prepare early on for any allergies your child has. Your GP can give you a prescription for an antihistamine or, in severe cases, prescribe an EpiPen or Anapen, which contains adrenaline to treat anaphylactic shock (see page 95).

Make sure everyone who comes in contact with your child – friends, carers, relatives, teachers and the parents of her own friends – is aware that she has a food allergy. Educate yourself and others on what to do in an emergency. It's absolutely critical to have a plan of action, and that all carers understand the severity of these allergies so that your child is protected from a potentially fatal reaction. When your toddler is about four, you can begin to teach her about her allergies so she can learn to be vigilant as well. It goes without saying, however, that a young child cannot make decisions that will affect her health. You'll need to make sure that everyone is looking out for her.

Be wary

Be aware of hidden sources of danger foods. Read every label and alert the waiting staff and kitchen if you are out for a meal. One thing you might not think of? Avoid ice cream served in ice cream parlours because of shared scoops. It might contain a bit of something, like a peanut, to which he's allergic. Cross-contamination is possible everywhere, so you'll need to be super-cautious, and even think about bringing your own meals when you are outside your own home. Birthday parties can be a minefield, too. You'll become the master of the fun packed tea!

Feeding your toddler on a restricted diet

If your little one has food allergies, or you have adopted a vegetarian or vegan diet, you'll need the help of a registered dietitian to be sure that he is getting everything he needs. For example, if your toddler is allergic to cow's milk, you'll need to find other sources of calcium. Leafy green vegetables are a good start, and so too are soya products and even fruit juices that have been fortified.

Similarly, if your child can't eat eggs, you'll need to find another good source of first-class protein and B vitamins, as well as many other nutrients, such as zinc and vitamins A, D and E. Animals products such as yoghurt, meat, milk and butter are good alternatives to eggs, and will provide protein as well as some vitamins B, A and D, and zinc. Wholegrains, pulses, seeds and brightly coloured fruit and vegetables are also good sources of many of the vital nutrients found in eggs.

FOODS TO WATCH OUT FOR

The majority of food allergies relate to these foods:

◆ **Cow's milk (and dairy produce)**

◆ **Eggs**

◆ **Peanuts**

◆ **Wheat**

◆ **Soya**

◆ **Tree nuts (walnuts, Brazil nuts, cashews)**

◆ **Fish (tuna, salmon, cod)**

◆ **Shellfish (lobster, shrimp, crab)**

◆ **Sesame seeds**

If your child is a vegetarian, protein is extremely important, so go for good sources in tofu and soya products, and in nut and seed butters (no whole nuts until your child is five, to prevent the risk of choking), dairy produce, pulses and wholegrains.

Most importantly, however, don't attempt to restrict your child's diet without the guidance of a trained dietitian. A toddler needs a wide range of key nutrients to grow and develop, and a shortfall of any can cause an imbalance that may lead to health problems, or poor growth and energy levels. The good news is that there are plenty of ways to ensure that even the most allergic child gets a balanced diet, and with a little help, she'll thrive like any other child.

Mealtimes can be a minefield for parents – if you let them! Remember that in most cases, food issues are about control, and if you stick to your guns and offer healthy, nutritious food, day after day, you'll create great eating habits that will provide the foundation for your toddler's healthy future. It's all about persistence and a belief that the food choices you make for your toddler really are crucial. Get that right, and you are off the starting block when it comes to good overall health and well-being.

10

Going out and about

No one says that you can't travel when you have a toddler – you simply have to look at the practicalities of different trips. And no one says you have to get cabin fever. It's not good for any of you.

If you're adventurous, your children will be encouraged to do different things as well. You're leading by example. It's important for their social skills that they learn how to behave properly at home *and* out in public. Exposing your toddler to different places and situations is a great way to build her confidence and make her feel comfortable in new environments. And, when it comes time to leave her at an activity or carer, it will be much easier if she's used to going places.

Families who go out and about to try new things also give their children the understanding that life is full of exploration and learning. Parents say to me, 'I didn't have a parent who gave me the time of day and was creative with me.' If this was true for you, break the cycle. Reach out for outside resources, talk to your partner about different experiences you want your kids to have, and do them.

Many people have a fear of taking their toddlers out to restaurants, shops – or even on holiday. But remember that everything that you do at home is practice for what you do when you're out. By setting realistic expectations for what your toddler can cope with, you'll help to pave the way for a smooth time out.

If there's one skill from your backpack that will help you the most as you take your toddler on errands, to appointments, restaurants, the shops – or even when you're travelling – it's to *Plan Ahead*. Proper planning is the key to happy adventures, whether you are walking around the block or travelling around the world.

Things to consider before setting out on errands:

◆ Choose the right time to go. You don't want to be out during meal-, nap- or bedtime.

◆ Make sure he's well rested and bring along snacks and a drink to tide him over. Raisins or sultanas, cheese sticks, or little breadsticks in a sandwich bag are ideal. I also bring a juice cup or a bottle of water.

◆ Set realistic expectations. He gets easily bored and distracted, so you can't plan to do three hours at a London museum. A hungry, bored, or tired toddler can lead to meltdowns.

◆ For the day-to-day running around, look at your whole week and pace yourself. You want to intersperse what you need to get done with fun activities and playtime. Try not to stack one errand on top of another; otherwise, there'll be a lot of popping him in and out of the car seat or long periods of time stuck in the pushchair.

◆ Try to walk when you can. It's nice to be in the fresh air and you don't have to deal with getting him in and out of his car seat multiple times.

MUMMY'S LITTLE HELPER TECHNIQUE

◆ When taking toddlers on errands, I find it helpful to buy or make a little sheriff badge or 'Mummy's Little Helper' badge, and give her a list of her duties, to be interactive in helping me complete the task.

◆ This is particularly effective with four-year-olds who declare, 'I don't want to go.' Tell her that if she helps you, she'll get a badge and, when you get back from your errands, you'll do something fun.

Trouble-free shopping with toddlers

The reality is that you need go to the shops at least once a week. Even with the advent of online shopping, it is important to get your toddler out to experience this aspect of life. I know many parents who avoid taking their kids to the shops because they're worried about their toddler misbehaving or freaking out.

I've met four-year-olds who have never been shopping. To me, 'Let's avoid the supermarket' marks the beginning of 'Let's avoid the park, let's avoid the activity centre, let's avoid going *anywhere*.' For some parents, ignoring these places is easier than addressing good behaviour. Taking your toddler to the supermarket is a great learning ground, where you can begin to get her interested in different types of healthy foods.

My rule for families with toddlers: When running errands or having a meal in a restaurant, remember that it's not a whole-day event. It's what I call 'in and out'. You'll get 30 minutes to an hour max before you need to switch activities.

Make it exciting for him by using the 'Involvement' technique. Having a list helps you get through the store fairly quickly. Again, toddlers do have a finite threshold – you probably have between 30 and 45 minutes to keep him engaged. Don't go right before a meal or he'll be hungry and begging for everything he sees. If it's around snack time, give him a healthy snack while you shop.

THE INVOLVEMENT TECHNIQUE

- **As you go through the shop, talk about the different foods on your list.**

- **With older toddlers, ask them to point out the different foods you're looking for: 'Look for the green grapes. Where are they?'**

- **This helps her start to identify colours, shapes, and the different fruits and vegetables. She also starts to see the variety of foods we're taking home for our meals.**

- **You can give her a mini version of your shopping list with pictures on it – three items that she's in charge of getting. Or, have her tick off each item on her list as you go. Some shops even have samples so she can try new things.**

I want it now!

You're in a long queue at the checkout; you're tired, in a hurry, and your child wants a sweet. And, of course, the shop has put the temptations right where he can see them. Sound familiar? What do you do when your toddler wants something that you don't want to give him? Here's my guidance: Don't use the word 'maybe'! And don't use the word 'later'. These words have no meaning for toddlers. What does 'maybe' mean? Yes or no? You haven't made up your mind one way or the other; you've just stalled the situation. What does 'later' mean? Five minutes, half an hour, five years?

Stick to your rules, especially for toddlers. Kids want everything they see all the time. I've seen too many parents fall into the habit of buying a treat for their toddler each time they shop, so there won't be a scene. But this just sets the expectation that every time you go to the shop – even it's just for milk and bread – you'll get him something. Talk about it *before* you go out to the store. Tell your toddler, 'We're going to the shops and Daddy needs to get a few things. We're not getting any children things today.'

Once you're there, he'll ask you anyway. Then you say, 'Remember what Daddy told you? We're not going to get anything for you today.' Hold to this statement and don't avoid the aisles. In fact, go down the toy or treat aisle on purpose. What you're teaching your toddler is an important lesson: You can't have everything you want. You can even tell him that when you get home you'll create a list of treats he wants but can't have right now.

Ultimately, it's all about follow-through. I can tell you what to say to your toddler and you can set up the rules and the explanations. But do you know what? Some day he may hear what you say and not like it. And then he'll go and have a meltdown anyway. That's when it's crucial that you follow through on your word! Mean what you say. Get in there and get out!

BREAKING THE 'GIVE ME' PATTERN

- What if you've already started the trend of giving in when he asks to avoid the meltdown? How do you change the pattern?
- Talk about it before you go to the shop: 'We're not getting something for you today.' In the shop, say 'no' and stick with it. You'll probably face a meltdown (or two) but he'll learn.
- Most importantly, don't avoid going to the shop with him.

Trips to hairdresser, dentist or doctor

At some stage or another, your toddler may have sat in the pushchair and watched you get your teeth checked or a quick fringe trim, while he had toys or books. You may not have found a babysitter, but you desperately needed a check-up because you had a toothache. Or you forgot about your hair appointment, and wow, there you go!

It's good if he's been with you to experience what he's now going to experience for the first time himself. Because you have set the tone. If he sees you enjoy it, he won't be anxious or worried. The more relaxed, casual, and happy you are, the more he will be, too.

Haircuts

◆ Depending upon how fast your child's hair grows, around the time that he turns into a toddler he'll probably be ready for that first haircut. You really want to make this a positive experience, as it will set the stage for future trips.

◆ Before you go, talk about how much fun it's going to be; it's a special thing for big girls and boys. You can even play-act a haircut in your home before you go, so he'll know what to expect.

◆ Bring something to distract him, such as a book or toy. Remember, however, that this is another 'in and out' event. You're either getting the fringe trimmed out of her eyes or you're having his hair cut because it's too long. It doesn't take long – five or ten minutes and you're done.

◆ If you go to your own hairdresser, you might be paying higher fees and it may take longer. Ask around for a recommendation for a stylist who cuts kids' hair all the time. These stylists know how to do two snips and they're finished; they'll also have experience in dealing with fidgety kids.

◆ If he's scared at the salon or barber, have him sit on your lap. He can also sit on a stack of telephone books or a booster seat.

◆ Bring a treat for afterwards, and remember to time the outing for a period when he's not too tired or hungry.

The dentist

◆ By three-and-a-half, all of your toddler's milk teeth should be in. You should probably take her to the dentist for the first time somewhere between her second and third birthday (although some dentists are now recommending that you go when your child gets her first tooth). This should be a quick 'in and out' event – just a check to make sure that all is well.

- If you haven't already done so – and it's possible – take her to one of your appointments before it's her turn. She can sit in the pushchair on the side of the dentist's chair. She'll see you sitting down (it helps to giggle and wink at her so she knows you're having fun).

- Afterwards, have her sit in the chair and put it up and down. Encourage the dentist show her the instruments, explaining what each one is for. Your toddler will be fascinated by the whole experience.

- Don't say things like 'Be brave'. She doesn't need to be brave; she just needs to have fun with it. There's no pain involved as long as she doesn't need fillings, which she shouldn't at this age.

- Make sure you take your toddler to the dentist if you have any concerns – or there are problems, such as a milk tooth being knocked out. Premature tooth loss can be a problem for speech development if it's a front tooth – and any tooth loss can cause other milk teeth to tilt or shift. Also see the dentist if your toddler chips a tooth or a tooth turns grey some time after a tumble.

The doctor's surgery

- Doctor's visits become tricky over the toddler years, because you're still going a lot for routine checks and vaccinations, and he definitely starts to associate the doctor with the pain of injections.

- Again, treat it very casually: 'We're just popping out over to here to do this little thing.' Set it up so there's no drama involved.

- Once you're there, try to relax him as much as possible. Have him sit on your lap, tell a story, or sing a song. Acknowledge what's happening, but do it in a way that reminds him how quick it is: 'Shot's coming but you'll get a fun plaster and it will be over quickly.'

- Let him know that as soon as you're finished at the doctor's, you'll go to the park or do something fun. Have him focus on what you're going to do after and not on the visit itself.

Happy restaurant experiences

- When you take your toddler out to a restaurant, be realistic about the type of place you choose – and how long you plan on staying there. If you pick a fancy restaurant with white tablecloths, chances are you'll be stressed. That's not setting things up for success.

◆ Choose a restaurant that's family-friendly. It doesn't have to be a fast-food restaurant, but it should be a place where you won't panic if food is dropped on the floor. Many great restaurants accommodate children dining by offering booster seats, a children's menu, and even coloured pencils and paper that they can draw on. A good thing to look for: Other families eating there. If you walk in to a fancy place full of couples and business people, it might not be the place for you.

◆ It's great to choose restaurants that have areas designed for toddlers to play while you're waiting for your food to come. A garden or conservatory is perfect. Fish tanks or indoor fountains are also great distraction devices.

◆ You probably won't have two hours, either. Place your order soon after getting there, and focus on your toddler. It's when you divert your attention by chatting with your friends that he acts up.

◆ Enjoy the experience. You want your child to see that it's a pleasant social experience with other toddlers, too.

Driving locally

◆ I find it helpful to keep a bag of toys and books that I can give as we're driving around.

◆ The best way to keep your child engaged? Interact with him by singing songs, telling stories, or pointing out what you're seeing as you're driving along.

◆ There is also great music, nursery rhymes and stories for toddlers that you can download onto your MP3 or iPod – or get a CD and play it in the car.

Air travel

I love to travel, so my experiences on aeroplanes with children were always pleasant, because I had a good attitude from the beginning. Here are my tips for you to have as much fun as I did:

◆ Consider the timing of when you go away. As soon as your child starts school, you'll be tied into school-holiday schedules. Now is the time to travel off-season. You can get better deals and you won't have as much overcrowding and delays.

◆ Pack the luggage two to three days ahead of time.

◆ Don't bring too much stuff. I learned this the hard way. There's no need to take a loads of clothing – you just end up lugging piles of baggage around. You can wash her clothes in the room with hand soap, or get a tube of travel detergent. For summer holidays, all you need are the staples: swimwear, a couple of T-shirts, shorts, plenty of sunscreen, and a pair of sandals. Going somewhere cooler, add one set of outdoor gear and a couple of changes of warmer clothes.

◆ To help me plan, I always wrote a list of what I was bringing and pinned it to the suitcase. I could quickly look at it and know what was going in the bag – and what needed to come home at the end of the trip.

◆ Pack a bag for the flight itself, with snacks, juice, water, toys and a change of clothes. I *always* packed a spare set of toddler clothes, in case of accidents on the flight – or baggage being delayed. Don't forget a bib, because you can just wipe it off and keep your child's clothes clean(er).

◆ Be prepared for lost baggage by having all medications and essentials with you on the plane.

◆ If it's an early-morning or night flight, I put her in her PJs before we leave the house. I want her to be as comfortable as possible, so she can fall asleep.

◆ Don't just load up on junk food. She'll feel better with a balanced meal. Pack things like picnic food or finger foods that can be put into sandwich bags.

◆ Get your toddler involved by having her pack a little carry-on backpack or suitcase on wheels with her favourite toys. I would say to my charges, 'What is it that you want to take on your holiday?' They would put all the things in the middle of the room and I would go through and eliminate various items: 'OK, if you can only choose ten things, what would they be?' This helps to narrow it down and make sure you're packing something dear to each one. Whether it's a little toy or a blankie, it helps to have something familiar for your toddler. The fact is that she's going somewhere new. What's more, by choosing her favourite things for the plane, she's helping to set herself up with entertainment for the journey ahead.

◆ This is something my Dad was a stickler about – and still is now! Get there early. But he was right. When you have got a child, you don't want to be the ones running to security to be told, 'I don't know if you'll make it.' Giving yourself extra time eases the stress of travelling with toddlers.

PREPARING FOR THE 'WHAT IFS'

I always prepare ahead of time for the 'what ifs'. What if he gets diarrhoea or throws up? What if you *are* stranded in a snowstorm? Stranded on the plane or the motorway? Pack a change of clothes, extra food, even a travel potty for the car. That way you won't be caught off guard if something happens.

Once on the plane

◆ Alert the flight staff to any special considerations or allergies. I have peanut allergies, so this is something that is always top of my mind when travelling.

◆ Plane rides are hard for toddlers. They're dealing with elevation changes, ears popping, loud noise and having to be strapped in – all in an unfamiliar environment. You finally get her to sleep, turbulence hits, the seat-belt signal dings on, and she starts crying. Unfortunately, as a society we've become less tolerant of kids just being kids.

◆ I think that the best thing you can do in these situations is to try to make her as comfortable as you can. That's why you've come prepared with your snacks and bag of activities.

◆ Giving her a sip of water or juice during take-off and landing can help to equalise the pressure in her ears.

◆ When you take her to the loo, leave the door open. It gives you more room to manoeuvre and privacy is not the number-one issue for a three-year-old!

◆ Just do the best you can. Ignore looks from intolerant passengers. And the next time you're on a plane and see a screaming toddler – pass on your tips.

> ### Jo Jo Travel No Nos
>
> ◆ **If you've already potty-trained your child, don't put a nappy on for the trip because you think it will be easier. You'll just be giving the wrong message and taking a step backwards.**
>
> ◆ **It's not OK for your child to use the seat in front as a toddler gym.**
>
> ◆ **Be considerate of the contained space. The volume needs to be firmly set to 'moderate'.**

Train journeys

◆ There are so many wonderful holidays that you can experience by train. The best part is that there are usually no security checkpoints or worrying about checking your bags.

◆ On a plane, you have the pressure of confined space. Trains give you and your kids the opportunity to walk freely through the carriages. You can even bring the pushchair, which is a familiar place for your child to fall asleep. You can also look out the window and engage your child in games like 'I See'.

◆ Use the same tips as for plane travel: pack ahead, bring snacks and activities, and go early so you're not rushing.

Road trips

◆ Travelling by car also gives you more freedom. You can take breaks and stretch out the legs. You can also use incentives, such as, 'At the next services, you can get out and run around for a bit.'

◆ I like to pack the car with clear storage boxes full of different things to make the trip more comfortable. If your toddler gets bored with what he's playing with, pull out a bin and change the activities. You also have more freedom to bring along more snacks and drinks from home – a cooler bag works well.

◆ Plan ahead. On a long trip, it works well to start off after rush hour – and after your toddler is fed. That way he'll fall asleep for much of the journey.

◆ Pay attention to how much time you spend in the car. If you're driving for six hours in one day, it might be hard to get him into his car seat to drive another six the next. Look for ways to break up the trip. Can you stay in one fun place for a day or two?

◆ Avoid having the trip escalate into a power struggle: 'I want out!' – 'No, you're staying in your seat.' Distract him by pointing to something out the window: 'Look at that car ahead – is it blue?' This might help to break the cycle.

◆ Make sure he's comfortable in his car seat – not too hot or cold. He might be prone to travel sickness. Talk to your GP or pharmacist before you go, to get some medicine that is suitable for toddlers.

◆ Above all, be realistic about how long he can sit. As much as you might want to get to your destination fast, schedule breaks for him to get out and run off some excess energy. Doing this can make your trip calmer and more enjoyable for the whole family.

ACTIVITIES FOR TRAVELLING

Keeping a little one entertained on a long trip can be daunting. You need to have a variety of activities on hand. Good things to pack include:

◆ **Colouring pads, crayons, sticker books, doodle pads and Etch-a-sketches**

◆ **Small puzzles, finger puppets and miniature pots of playdough**

◆ **Books and books on tape or CD**

◆ **Toddler-appropriate TV shows downloaded onto an iPod or a portable DVD player. With these, I recommend using over-the-ear headphones. Headphones that fit right into the ears are too much for his delicate eardrums and can cause damage. Remember to keep TV time limited.**

PART III

A day in the life of a toddler

TOUCHSTONES FOR THE TODDLER YEARS

1 Communicate clearly

2 Adopt a positive mindset

3 Repeat, again and again

4 Be consistent

5 Give encouragement

6 Establish routines

7 Have realistic expectations

8 Set boundaries

In this section, I will take you through a daily toddler routine, addressing the major issues you could encounter – and offering tips and techniques for a healthy and happy toddler (and parent!) from morning to night. Yes, it takes some tools from that backpack you've been carrying, but I assure you life will be easier.

- ◆ **Plan Ahead**
- ◆ **Energy**
- ◆ **Commitment**
- ◆ **Humour**

11

Why routine matters

I know that a lot of people cringe when they hear the word 'routine'. I believe that's because they see it as a schedule that's so rigid it can't be bent. That's really not what it is. A schedule should be flexible enough so that you have room to breathe.

A routine is a game plan, as far as I'm concerned. You're creating a structure for your day – but with wiggle room. Having a structure in place helps you plan ahead, while leaving room to adapt as things happen. For as much as some toddler behaviour is predictable, every day is certainly unpredictable.

Routines simply help you to better manage your time so you can juggle everyone's needs, including your own. You'll be better organised, as you understand what he needs and when, which leads to consistency in sleeping, eating and playing. He'll be well fed and rested, helping him be more open to learning and less prone to meltdowns. It helps you focus on the priorities, getting what you need done to manage your life and raise your family – as well as run a home. You have direction, and more focus to keep your eye on tasks that you need to follow through on. And if you've ever felt like the day was slipping by, you know a routine creates something more constructive.

A set routine also gives stability to your toddler. His short attention span – coupled with all the new skills he's learning – means he can easily be overwhelmed. Structure makes him more secure as he knows what's going to happen at each part of the day.

In case you haven't noticed, when a toddler feels rushed, he'll dig in his heels and throw a tantrum. With a routine in place, you can give him advance warning, as you shift from one activity to the next: 'Five minutes to bathtime.'

This helps to make him more cooperative. It's what I call the 'speaking clock', which helps a toddler transition in a routine.

JUMP INTO THE RHYTHM OF LIFE

A routine set around waking up, getting dressed, being active during the day and then settling down at night is an important life skill to teach children. Because that's the pattern most human beings follow!

Creating a routine

The routine I suggest in this section is only a sample. It needs to be customised to your family's needs. You may choose to go out with your toddler in the morning because he needs to burn off steam, and do quieter activities in the afternoon. Or perhaps it's easier to run errands in the morning. The point of going through each part of the day is to help you with the common issues that tend to arise at that time.

Many people become intimidated at the thought of creating a schedule. It's actually very easy to do. Start with the things that are necessary and go from there:

◆ Your toddler needs get *at least* ten or 11 hours of sleep each night. Work out from when he should go to bed to assess when he needs to get up. Perhaps he should go to bed at 7:30pm (for 11 hours of sleep). Now you know she's going to be getting up around 6:30am.

◆ Everything else can be scheduled between those two times: breakfast, getting ready, getting him off to nursery or daycare or having morning play, lunch, nap (if he's still doing it), play, dinner, bedtime routine, bed. In each of the following chapters in this section, I give you a sample schedule for that time of day.

◆ Make sure you give yourself more time than you think you'll need so you don't feel rushed – or have to rush your child.

◆ Now that you have your child's activities set out, see where you can fold in your own errands. It may be that you are playing with your toddler in the morning, then you get a little housework done while she naps, then you run an errand together, and then have playtime. The key point is to engage when you can, so you're not just moving from task to task.

◆ Pace yourself. Look at the whole week. You don't need to get everything done in a day and remember that you can't go, go, go all the time with a little one in tow.

◆ Eight 'ish', four 'ish' – the transition times in a routine are important because it allows you and the kids to breathe.

◆ Once you've created the routine, talk your toddler through every step. Routines work when they're backed up verbally and repeated over and over again.

◆ Post the schedule where you can see it so you'll have a visual reminder. It can be fun to create a routine that contains pictures of the activities. Older toddlers can move the pictures around once each activity is completed.

◆ Between the ages of one and four, your child will go through so many changes. You will need to continue to adjust times and activities according to what's best for each stage.

The routine is for your child

I've worked with many parents who will put certain parts of routines into place because it suits them and not their toddler. They'll set bedtime too late for their toddler so they can see him when they get home from work and spend more time with him. Or they set bedtime too early because they want evenings to themselves. You may ask what's wrong with that? And I would answer, what about your little one's body clock?

When you have kids, your life shouldn't be put on hold. But you certainly need to realise that you have to accommodate this little human being. This isn't about setting a schedule for you, but a schedule and routine that's best for your toddler. He requires proper amounts of sleep, food and stimulation throughout the day. The schedule won't work if you've decide all of the sudden that you want to do an activity when your child needs to sleep. That should never be compromised. When you do have a routine, you can predict what's happening when, and plan accordingly.

Schedules away from home

Creating a sense of consistency for meals, play and social time are good cornerstones for wherever you go. Going on holiday, or visiting a friend or a relative's house – the general routine is set to your child's body clock of sleep and eating. As your toddler becomes conditioned by the routine, you can begin to be flexible. You can go out to a restaurant and have that meal. You know your child will nap in the pushchair or car seat, holding on to her blankie. You can say 'yes' to that birthday party because you know that it's at a time when she's well-fed and rested, ready to play. You can also leave her more easily in the care of others, as the routine provides the continuity of care your child is used to.

Once you get really good at the daily routine, you know you can afford to allow your child to sleep an extra half an hour in the afternoon, so you can let her stay up later to see Daddy after he's been away all week. You'll know exactly where you stand and, most importantly, your toddler will, too. Let's look at how a sample routine works, and how to make it work for you *and* your little one.

12

Morning

Morning is here! Time to get your toddler up and ready for the day. You've created your routine, so you know how much time you have. You don't want to rush or make your child feel rushed; this will help to start the day off on the right foot.

What's the best way for your toddler to learn how to wash up and get dressed? By watching you or her older siblings. She'll see you do it and start to mimic what you're doing. To help the learning, talk her through every step as you go along: 'Right, we get up, go to the potty, wash up and then get dressed.' Talking through the steps helps with language development – and with learning to do the skill itself.

A SAMPLE MORNING ROUTINE

- ◆ Up, potty, brush teeth, wash face, brush hair
- ◆ Get dressed
- ◆ Breakfast
- ◆ Morning activities and play
- ◆ Snack
- ◆ Morning nap until 18 months, if need be
- ◆ Late-morning activities and play

TELL, DON'T ASK!

Whatever skill you want her to do, make sure you're telling politely, and not asking. This is a very important distinction. It's not 'Ready to brush teeth?' If you say this, you're leaving the door open for a big 'No!' It's 'Teeth now, please'. The quicker you learn this simple communication technique, the fewer power struggles you'll have with your toddler.

Brushing teeth

Setting the foundation of good oral hygiene habits is important to the long-term health of your child's teeth and gums. Teaching her now how to brush her teeth in the morning and at night establishes a routine that she'll follow for the rest of her life. It could also mean the difference between having tooth decay at a fairly young age – or not.

You've probably been dealing with teething for a while. By about the age of three, most of her first teeth should be in. I hope that as soon as your child cut her first tooth, you started to clean that tooth using your finger or a piece of soft cloth with a smear of toothpaste on it. As she got more teeth, you've transitioned to using a children's toothbrush with a pea-sized amount of children's toothpaste that contains fluoride. I want to remind parents that not only is it important to maintain oral hygiene to eliminate gum disease and decay, but it is also important to keep tooth enamel healthy, because that's what protects the tooth.

Throughout the toddler years, you need to brush her teeth – and make sure you do it properly (see opposite). As you brush her teeth, talk her through each step – or sing it as a song: 'We're brushing the back, and then the sides, and then the front.' Explain what you're doing: 'We have to get the food out.' The bottom line is that it just needs to be done.

Resistance will come during these years because your toddler will want to do it herself. That's independence rearing its head. Great. Just remember that she won't know how to do it properly. Let her do it first. Then you do it afterwards, so you can get to the hard-to-reach places. Only around the age of seven does a child have the manual dexterity to do it properly on her own.

Electric toothbrushes have become extremely popular as they, for a short period of time, take the stress out of getting kids' teeth brushed. They are OK to use, as toddlers often get excited by the noise or the characters. However, make sure she also learns how to brush her teeth manually, as it's an important life skill.

PROPER TOOTH BRUSHING

First...

To clean outer surfaces, tilt the brush so its bristles point toward the gums. Use short, side-to-side strokes, moving across your teeth in a circular motion. Also clean the gums.

Next...

To clean chewing surfaces of the molars, hold the brush flat. Gently scrub your teeth by moving the brush back and forth.

Then...

To clean inner surfaces of your back teeth brush in a circular motion at a 45-degree angle. And don't forget the gums. To clean the inner surfaces of your front teeth, hold the brush vertically and use gentle up and down strokes.

Jo Jo Teeth No Nos

- **Inconsistency with tooth brushing.**
- **Toddlers walking around with baby bottles full of juice hanging from their mouths.**
- **Any overconsumption of foods high in sugar and refined carbohydrates.**
- **Not enough water in between juices or milk.**

Change it up!

If you see your child stalling about brushing teeth before bed, is she associating, 'Brush teeth' with going to bed right after? It might well be. Toddlers know how to stall bedtime. And if it means messing up the ritual, so be it. Try brushing teeth before the bath. Or right after dinner.

Brushing hair

It's also important to keep your child's hair clean and tidy. You're not only helping her look presentable, but building the foundation of her eventual routine – one day she'll have to learn to get ready for the day by herself. You also initiate a pride in grooming, so she will want to look presentable.

Make it non-painful. As soon as you start pulling and she feels it hurt, it will make it that much harder to do the next time around. Here are my tips for pain-free brushing:

◆ Don't brush from the top of her head, all the way down. Go from the bottom, little sections at a time, and slowly work your way up.

◆ If you hold one hand flat on her head above the section of hair you're brushing, you stop the pull from the scalp, which is probably what she's complaining about.

◆ Use a detangler spray before you brush.

Jo Jo Hair No No

Please don't use curling or straightening irons on your toddler's hair. Not only can it damage her hair, but you could accidentally burn her.

Dressing for the day

As you well know, your toddler is active. You'll want to dress him in loose-fitting, comfortable clothes, in which he can easily run and play. And, as he loves to get into all sorts of things – including mud – it's a good idea to choose clothes that are easy to wash and care for. The good news is that toddlers' clothes are generally very practical – trousers with elastic waistbands that are easy to pull off and on (great for potty-training), scooped necks that are easy to pull over the head, and even Velcro shoes.

- ◆ **Persistence**
- ◆ **Patience**
- ◆ **Humour**

Have you noticed that your toddler knows how to take off his clothes before he learns how to put them on? You'll see he loves to pull his socks and shoes off in public; you can't keep a hat on his head. How many times has your toddler run around buck naked, as you chase him down? It's just a stage of development. Your job is to begin to help him learn to put clothes *on* as well as off.

When helping your toddler to dress in the morning, give yourself plenty of time. Remember: Rushing means resistance. The faster you want him to go, the more he'll slow down. In addition, you might not be as gentle as you should be when pulling on a jumper, for example –and you won't have time to coach him through the process, as you should be doing from the age of two.

At first you'll be dressing him all the time. Soon, with loads of practice, he will learn how to do it himself. Once again, the key is to talk him through the process as you're doing it: 'Let's put on your trousers, one leg and then the other. Good.' I find lots of praise and encouragement helps, too. Remember to use your happy tone of voice. If you make it fun, he'll think it's fun, too.

It can be boring to recite everything you're doing, over and over again. But, trust me, it really helps with language development and learning life skills. I promise that you won't have to be a parrot for the rest of your life! Try to see the humour in it, and load up on your patience for the next phase of 'Me do!'

As soon as he wants to start to dress himself, let him try. Between the ages of two and four, he'll be getting dressed with your help. By four, he should be able to do it himself.

Teaching your toddler to get dressed

- ◆ *Pull-over shirts and jumpers*: To help her know which is the front of a shirt or jumper, show her the tag and explain that it goes in the back. So when she puts the shirt over her head, she first feels for the tag at the back, where her neck is, and then pulls it over her head.

- ◆ *Tights and leggings*: Scrunch them up for her first, and then help her to put them over her toes and heels. Have her slowly wriggle them up her legs herself. Pull up the excess, if she needs help.

- ◆ *Trousers*: Have her sit down first, put one leg in and then the other – and then stand up and pull up the trousers. To tell front from back on pull-up trousers, teach her about the tag again. For trousers with zips, poppers or buttons, help her to learn that those go at the front, unless she wants to look like Zigzag, which was a popular band back in the 80s who wore their jeans backwards.

◆ *Outerwear.* One of my favourite tricks for helping three- to four-year-old toddlers learn to put a coat or jacket on is to lay it out on its back, with the sleeves out to the sides and the coat unbuttoned. Have him lie down on his back on top of the open coat and put his arms through the sleeves, then stand up. Voila, coat is on. This works well for button-up shirts and jumpers, too.

◆ *Zips:* A toddler needs to have good skills before being able to zip. It's not usually until about four years old, when you'll see her becoming more skilled at colouring and keeping things in line. This is a sign that the skill department is open for business. But don't discourage your toddler of any age from starting to mess around with the zip. Place the zip in the safety catch, and put your hands over hers – pull up the zip with one hand, while pulling down on the end of the zip with the other. It helps her to learn left and right, as well as coordination, in up and down.

Have fun with this stage – shirts going around and around till she finds the armholes, trousers on backwards. Giggle together, then get her to do it correctly. Even adults go out sometimes with their shirts inside-out!

And it's OK if she gets a bit frustrated because past frustration comes achievement. If you see her struggling, help her by giving a bit of showing and telling: 'No, try again. Put it in and then bring it up.' You're helping her learn perseverance – and the sense of accomplishment she experiences when she succeeds is priceless.

TIPS FOR BUTTONS AND POPPERS

◆ **Come behind him and put your arms around him so he's looking at the clothes, not you.**

◆ **With buttons, start by putting the button half through and letting him finish.**

◆ **With poppers, put your hands on his, put the knob inside the circle and push. Teach him how to prise them open by pulling the facings apart. Use words to go along: 'Push *in*, and pull *out*'.**

Tutus to the park?

Your toddler may offer resistance when you try to get her dressed – or she'll fixate on wearing something that you don't think is appropriate. I say 'you' because why would she think wearing a fairy-princess dress to the shops is weird? She doesn't and you shouldn't either. Superman capes, karate outfits, ballet tutus – I've seen them all become favourite outfits for outings. That's OK. Dressing up is part of a toddler's play and should be encouraged. I personally have no problem with dress-up items being worn outside – in fact, it delights me to see them. However, if she consistently picks shorts and it's snowing outside, pack away the shorts. Give her choices that are weather appropriate, but other than that, relax about what she's wearing. Who says bright pink and clashing red don't go together? And if it's not dirty, who cares if she wears her favourite skirt three days in a row?

What you do want to watch out for is what I call 'fad' dressing. This is when your child fixates on a particular item. I worked with one family where their three-year-old would only wear his PJs, all day, every day of the week! It's important to nip the fad dresser in the bud, otherwise the behaviour can continue for months.

If you have a fad dresser, don't offer any choices. Choose one set of clothing the night before that is not *the* item. Then, offer plenty of positive encouragement when she puts it on without a battle of wills. You can even use a reward chart for every day that she gets dressed without the fad – and without a fuss.

AVOIDING CLOTHES CONFLICTS

You choose outfit after outfit, and all you hear is 'No, no, *no!*' Let him feel like he's involved in the decision. Choose a couple of outfits the night before (two for two-year-olds or three for three- and four-year-olds) and let him choose which one he wants. Decision-making helps builds his confidence and encourages independence. Plus, choosing clothes the night before saves you time in the morning.

Shoes

First of all, buy the proper ones. When your toddler begins to walk, you really want him to walk barefoot first. It actually helps him to walk better as he'll grip the floor with his tiny feet. Walking barefoot also helps with balance and coordination, and encourages the development of his foot muscles. If you're worried about his feet getting cold in the house, put him in socks or slippers with non-slip soles.

Now, obviously your child can't go barefoot forever. About six to eight weeks after he's been consistently walking, you should get him fitted in proper shoes to wear when you go out. Children's feet grow so quickly and I know good shoes can be expensive. However, it's worth every penny to have him fitted in the correct shoes for his feet. You want the shoes to fit right, so his feet grow and develop properly.

The most important thing to do when buying shoes is to get his feet properly measured – the width as well as the length of each foot. Make sure that when he's measured, he's standing up and has socks on. Shoes should have about 1.3cm (0.5ins) beyond the toe, and be wide enough for all toes to lie flat. His heel should not be riding up. You should be able to put your thumb down on the front edge of the shoe, press down and still have room.

Choose shoes that are flexible, lightweight and *not* stiff in any way. They should be soft and easily bent. At this stage you don't need to worry about a thick sole. Don't go for the latest fashion trend or trainers. You could end up with a poor little Frankenstein who can't maintain his balance because the trainers are so bulky. In any shop that provides a good Start-rite shoe, you'll find staff who will be able to advise you.

Getting shoes on her feet

Putting on her shoes and socks is like other elements of dressing. First you do it, narrating what you're doing. Eventually she's going to want to try it herself. With socks, loosen the opening and bunch up the sock, holding it so she can slip in her toes first, and then her heel. You're going to have to straighten the seam yourself till she's four, I'd guess.

With shoes, loosen the laces, lift up the tongue and have her put her foot in while she's sitting down. Then have her stand up and push in her heel. If you've bought shoes with Velcro straps, which I highly recommend at this stage, she can even tighten them herself.

Tying shoelaces

Got a four-year-old who wants to learn to tie her shoes? Have her put her foot into one of your own tie shoes and practise on that. It's easier to learn with longer shoelaces. Even if she can't do it yet, there's no harm in trying. Don't squash her enthusiasm.

Breakfast

Now that he's dressed and washed, it's time to eat. Getting your toddler to eat a healthy breakfast preps him for the activities of the day. In other words, refuels him – after a long night's sleep, breakfast provides much needed nutrients for all the development going on in his body and brain.

A good line-up in the morning has all the food groups, and could, for example, include a combination of:

◆ Fresh fruit

◆ Natural yoghurt (taking care that it doesn't have too much sugar) or eggs

◆ Wholegrain cereal, toast, oatmeal or porridge.

Cereals are good in moderation. You don't have to choose the same type all the time; mix it up. Some kids favour the sweeter, chocolatey ones and parents tend to cave on this to get them to eat *something* at breakfast time. Do what I call a cereal cocktail, which is a healthy choice of cereal or muesli with a small amount of devil's delight sprinkled on top. I've also been known to flip a pancake or two and serve them rolled with a few raspberries. And that wasn't just for Pancake Day.

You should be teaching him to feed himself. See pages 255–259 for details on encouraging him to learn this essential life skill.

Morning playtime

After breakfast, it's time for play and stimulation – toddlers want to be challenged! It's no coincidence that many early-learning activities at nursery school take place in the morning, when your child is rested, alert and ready to be mentally challenged. Matching, sorting, building and problem-solving is all part and parcel of a good morning's learning.

You may have to go to work so he's going off somewhere else to play. Right now, however, I'm assuming that you're staying home with your toddler. In Chapter 5, you'll find a full list of ideas for mental and physical stimulation, as well as toys that are appropriate for each year of your toddler's life. Don't forget the books, either. You'll find my list of best books for toddlers on pages 293–295.

KEEPING MORNINGS POSITIVE

◆ After breakfast, I always encourage parents to spend the first hour in the morning with their toddler doing things that mentally stimulate him. You'll find that once you give your child that time first thing, he's happy just to go off and be more self-sufficient, giving you a chance to do some housework. And he gets a little rest.

◆ Kids are little energy junkies. Positive or negative: they'll respond to your energy. If your energy is not there, they'll create it by being naughty to get your attention. So, the more you can be positive when you play with him, the better his behaviour will be.

Play dates

Mornings are a great time to get together with your young toddler and other mothers, in an event commonly known as the 'coffee morning'. Play dates represent an opportunity for your toddler to develop her social skills – learning how to play with others, to share and cooperate. Socially, play dates are healthy for children *and* parents. If you've been living in a world where it's just you and your child, day in and day out, you need the interaction just as much as your child does, otherwise you'll feel you're going gaga.

Just as your toddler learns from watching you, they learn from watching other kids. For you, it's a time to talk about things that are happening in your life with your children – to talk to another adult, rather than just a two-year-old. It really helps to compare experiences, and it's very comforting to know what other parents go through. Most of all, it's fun – and stimulating – just to be in the presence of other adults.

The other important thing that happens when you get together with other parents is that you get to see how they deal with their toddler – what techniques they use to avoid meltdowns or how they step in and take care of problems when they arise. You can trade tips and learn from one another.

In my nannying days, I met regularly with a group of nannies and their little charges. It was something I looked forward to each week, just like my little ones.

Dealing with shyness

Toddlers are often shy of people they don't know. That's normal. The important thing to remember is that if you don't label it, but encourage her to participate, she most likely will. If she continues to be extremely shy, don't make a fuss or label her. Find even more occasions to expose her to the company of others, and help her learn what we do when we meet people by playing with dolls or soft animals. Explain what you're going to do before you go, and coach her once you're there: 'Say hello, darling.' Let her watch you confidently interact with others and don't let her draw you into her shy corner, paying attention only to her. That reinforces what you don't want.

The stages of play

During her first year, your baby began to amuse herself. From here, this evolves into playing alongside peers or siblings – what we experts call 'parallel play'. That's why, on a play date with two-year-olds, you'll see them playing alongside, not with, each other. Each one is happily doing his own thing (occasionally stopping to observe his little friend beside him) and then, of course, grabbing whatever he wants.

With hard-to-manage emotions and social skills that are still largely undeveloped, young toddlers may lash out physically to try to get what they want because they can't express themselves verbally. Depending on the temperament of the child, some will even try to intimidate others through grabbing, hitting or biting. That's one reason why you are closely supervising when toddlers are together – so that you can begin to teach your child proper behaviour.

FIGHTING ON PLAYDATES

If you have a toddler who is fighting on playdates or there are lots of tears, you must intervene. Children of this age are too young to work it out themselves. Here are the steps:

- **Warning: 'You are going to have to sit out if you don't stop fighting.'**
- **If she ignores the warning, have her sit on sidelines watching or institute the Naughty Step.**
- **Once she comes back in, be the referee – 'you get 5 minutes on the rocking horse, then it's Mika's turn.' You be the timekeeper. It's like going to the gym where you are asked not to hog the machines when it's crowded.**

THE SNATCH AND GRAB TECHNIQUE

If your young toddler grabs a toy, step in and firmly say, 'That is not how we play.'

- ◆ **Use short, simple words and explanations.**
- ◆ **Take the toy away and return it to the other child.**
- ◆ **Give your child another activity and encourage him back into the play.**

Cooperative play

Over time, as toddlers approach three, they begin to pay more attention to other kids, even copying some of their actions. This evolves into cooperative play where they are able to learn to take turns and to share – although it's still difficult at times.

Between three and four is when they really start to make friends – meaning that they like to play with a particular person. Their language skills have developed to the point where they're excited to be talking and interacting with other kids their own age, instead of just adults.

I love this stage! It's so sweet to see the affection that develops between toddlers. This is also the time of teaching the small pleasantries involved in hosting guests: 'Hello' and 'Let's say goodbye.' At this age, your child usually doesn't need you to watch him like a hawk for bad behaviour. He should know the basics by now. But, of course, you still do need to supervise. That way you can stop or divert problems before they erupt.

Learning to share

Sharing is important, as it shows we have the ability to develop our relationship with another person. Teaching a toddler to share is not something that will happen overnight. Part of it is linked to development, and your little one may not be there just yet. However, you're laying the foundation so that with repeated practice she'll eventually get the concept. Just understand that it can take years before she'll share without prompting, and you'll need to talk about it again and again and again.

- ◆ **Patience**

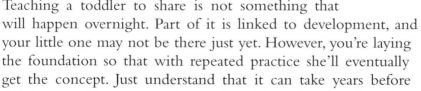

Your child's concentration and attention expands as she gets older. That's why it's better to distract an 18-month-old (who has a very short attention span) with another activity than it is to say, 'You just need to wait your turn.' By two-and-a-half or so, you should be teaching the concepts of sharing and taking turns. The best way to start is by making it a game between the two of you. It's much easier to practise cooperation with Mummy and Daddy before testing it out with peers who are also learning this life skill (see the 'Taking Turns' and 'Time Sharing' techniques, on the next page). The more you practise, the more she'll start to understand what it means to 'share' and 'take turns'.

THE TAKING TURNS TECHNIQUE

♦ **Set it up as a game.**

♦ **'Your Turn': give the puzzle or whatever you're playing with to your child.**

♦ **'Now my turn.' I do the puzzle.**

♦ **He'll see the switch back and forth, and how he has to wait until it's his turn. Eventually he will be able to do it with friends and siblings.**

By the time your toddler is three years old, she should understand the idea of sharing. Prep her before a play date even begins. Explain that her friend is coming over and it will be fun to play and share toys together.

If you're hosting a play date for your three- or four-year-old and she starts to become very possessive of her toys – 'But, it's mine! It's mine! It's mine!' – you need be firm and explain that she has a guest over and that it's good manners to share toys: 'If you went to her house she'd share her toys.' The same is true for sibling arguments over sharing. Explain that we share with our brother or sister.

Force sharing

I also like to reinforce sharing between siblings or toddlers on play dates by providing only one of something. I know this may be the opposite of your instincts. Parents often provide one of a particular toy or game to each child, to avoid conflict. But what does that teach her? How does a child learn to have compassion and become able to share with another human being? How does she learn to conform in school, where there's one set of crayons or there's only one ruler going around?

Toddlers need to learn to have patience to wait their turn! It's a really important life skill because we have to wait our turn as adults, as well. Sharing is a crucial social skill. So I believe in creating situations where toddlers have to learn it.

> ### Happy play dates
>
> Schedule play dates after breakfast and long before naptime, so your child is rested and ready to play.

If you're doing clay or painting, for instance, use objects that have to be shared, like one crayon of each colour. Everything is in the centre of the table and must go *back* to the middle after being used. Or I'll get a piece of paper and I'll cut it into a smiley face or some other object, and have children take turns colouring the same picture.

THE TIME SHARING TECHNIQUE

- ◆ **Have one toy and tell her you're going to share.**
- ◆ **Show her a timer and explains that when it pings, you will play with the toy.**
- ◆ **Give her the toy, set the timer for five minutes.**
- ◆ **When it pings, reset the timer for five minutes, and you play.**
- ◆ **Switch again when the timer goes off.**
- ◆ **This enables her to see that the time she has to wait is not endless, and she will get the toy back. This allows her to relax and share.**
- ◆ **Increase the time as she gets the idea.**

The special toy

There are times when a child may have received something about which he is incredibly sentimental: a special lovey, perhaps, or gift from a family member. This should be put away before the play date. Explain what you're doing: 'We're going to put that away and share your other toys.'

I've even told four-year-olds, 'You know that we're going to have friends around to play. Choose one thing you want to put away, and everything else we'll share.' That helps them understand that I respect that some things do belong to them. It also helps to teach them to look after their special belongings.

Troubleshooting sharing

If it's not working, ask yourself the following questions:

- ◆ Am I bribing my child to share?

- ◆ Am I buying two of everything to avoid the whole problem?

- ◆ Have I taken enough time to practise with my child before he has to share with others?

- ◆ Do I use a timer to help make the sharing fair?

BEING THE REFEREE

If you're at a play date or in the park, and children start to fight over a toy, you must referee. The same is true with siblings. Toddlers are too young to work it out on their own. Here's what to do:

- ◆ **Explain that they need to share and that each one will have to wait his turn.**

- ◆ **Tell them that each child will get the toy for a couple of minutes (you can set an egg timer or use your watch.)**

- ◆ **Acknowledge and praise your child if he shares the toy in question without being prompted.**

- ◆ **If your child refuses to share or play nicely, pick him up and walk away until he calms down.**

Play-fighting

There's a difference between play-fighting, skirmishes and outright aggressive behaviour towards another child. If a three- or four-year-old is play-fighting, he's just learning about his physical limits. On the other hand, aggressive behaviour is when a child is pinching, punching, hitting, biting or kicking someone. That is simply not acceptable.

If your toddler is old enough to understand that she's hurting another person (from about the age of two or older), then aggressive behaviour should be met with zero tolerance. Use the Naughty Step technique or the One Strike and You're Out technique for older toddlers who should know better.

Once you've made it clear through discipline that aggressive behaviour won't be tolerated, try to work out what is prompting the behaviour. What are your child's triggers? Is he hungry, tired or frustrated? Understanding what caused the aggression could help in preventing future outbursts.

Teaching empathy

Children aren't born caring about other people's feelings. They have to be taught to care. The best advice is to start talking to your toddler about other people's feelings when she is about two, being aware that she'll start to understand what you're saying at four. By five or six, she'll have grasped the concept and truly show and feel empathy for others. It's not about guilt-tripping her – 'You made her feel bad' – rather, when situations arise at home with you or at the playground, it's taking the opportunity to point out the effect: 'Look, that boy bumped his head. That must really hurt. Let's go see if he's OK.'

Playgroups and nurseries

If you are a stay-at-home parent, mornings are also a good time to expose your toddler to time away from you, so he gets used to not always being with you. There is a variety of options. See Chapter 3 for a complete discussion of how to choose the situation that is right for you and your child. Once you are happy with your choice, you can encourage your toddler to become a little more independent in stages. Not only will the socialisation do him good, encouraging him to practise some of the key life skills, such as sharing, but he'll learn to negotiate, interact and develop relationships with other children.

Play between siblings

If your children are close in age, the suggestions I offered for playing and sharing with friends will work for them as well. However, sometimes the gap in age is so great that playing together just doesn't work – at least not all the time. You may, for example, have a ten-year-old who is willing to play a toddler game once in a while, but he certainly isn't going to want to spend a whole day that way. In this situation, I suggest you look at things that you do as a *family*, like swimming and playing in the park, and also allow the older child to pursue his own interests and friendships.

Sibling battles

It's very natural and healthy for siblings to squabble and fight. It would be odd to expect kids *not* to fight – after all, adults do. There simply have to be ground rules and consequences in place regarding acceptable behaviour. If one intentionally hurts the other, then use the Naughty Step technique or One Strike You're Out technique. Of course, establishing what happened can be challenging. Give both of them a chance to tell their side. Don't be impatient. Don't try and guess what they're trying to tell you. *Listen* and let each tell you their side of the story.

   This can be quite tricky because, at this age, they often can't communicate well about what's gone on – and there's a tendency to believe the one having the stronger emotional reaction. The one making the most noise is not necessarily the injured party. The quiet one can often feel put-upon because they feel neglected. It has to feel fair.

Troubleshooting sibling battles

If it's not working, ask yourself the following questions:

◆ Am I treating both children fairly or am I favouring one over the other?

◆ Am I listening to the whole story?

◆ Do I know when my child is lying or being defensive? Can I read his body language?

◆ Does one of them always run in crying first, even when he's the one who's instigated and caused the trouble? Do I believe the one who's crying instead of trying to figure out what happened?

13

Afternoon

It's noon so the first thing on the afternoon schedule is lunch. I suggest approaching lunch for your toddler the same way that you approach breakfast – mindfully. Provide a balanced meal of protein, carbohydrate, healthy fats, veggies and fruit. Some lunch suggestions could include:

◆ Ham and tomato wrapped in a wholegrain tortilla, with fresh slices of apple and mango

◆ Chicken strips with brown rice, broccoli and sweetcorn

◆ Vegetable soup and a wholegrain roll

◆ Wholegrain pasta with fresh tomato sauce and grated cheese

◆ Cottage pie with peas and cauliflower

◆ Tuna, sweetcorn and cucumber mini-sandwiches

Add a few slices of fresh, raw veggies, such as strips of red pepper or sliced cucumber or carrots, a fresh fruity yoghurt for pudding, and you've got a perfectly balanced meal.

SAMPLE AFTERNOON ROUTINE

◆ **Lunch**

◆ **Nap for 18-month- to two-year-olds; quiet time for three- to four-year-olds**

◆ **Afternoon activities**

◆ **Snack**

◆ **Late-afternoon activities and play**

Naps or quiet time

Like eating and stimulation, getting enough sleep is an important part of your child's development. Around 18 months, most toddlers drop their morning naps, but they'll still need one in the afternoon (between one and two hours) until they're about three. Even then, I encourage quiet time for three-, and four-year-olds. They just can't keep going, going, going all the time. Have him look at books or do puzzles quietly for between 30 and 45 minutes or so – anything that is not running around and getting worked up.

Again, it's back to observing your child and interspersing being active with down time. Children between the ages of one to three need 12 to 14 hours of sleep; whereas three- to five-year-olds need between 11 and 13 hours. You'll want to make sure he's getting the total number of hours between his night-time and daytime sleeps. If you've had a busy morning, you'll notice he'll start to fade, and might even fall asleep in the car or pushchair. If your three-year-old falls asleep in the pushchair, leave him in it. It's not going to hurt him.

Pit stop

If your toddler is still napping in the afternoon or during an older sibling's rest time, try to rest as well. By that I mean put your feet up for a minute. You can hardly clock out and go and sit in the park for an hour-long lunch break! This is it!

Afternoon activities

Doing activities with your child in the afternoon is just as important as it is in the morning. Being engaged with and observing your child will help you to determine what type of activity you should do – and when. Take into account what you've already done today. Was it a busy, active morning? Does she need a quieter afternoon? Were you unable to get out in the morning, so she needs some physical activity to burn off energy? Do you need to do chores? This chapter includes ideas for involving your toddler so that she's being stimulated while you work, as well as setting up areas in your house for solo activities! But don't forget to get down with her and play for a while as well.

Here's the *Perspective* part: Enjoy this time. As your child gets older, she'll want her private time. When she's at this age, she still has the need to feel taken care of, to see what Mummy and Daddy are doing. Pretty soon, you'll be the one going, 'Come out, let's do something together.' She'll be in her room, not wanting to hang out with you.

◆ **Perspective**

Becoming familiar

When you take your toddler to a new activity around two or three years of age, she'll want to sit on you. That's OK. The situation is unfamiliar territory and she needs that security. But, as she gets older, you say to her, 'Sit next to me.' She's familiar with the situation now.

Activity areas

When you go to a nursery or childcare centre, you'll notice they have different activity corners: A place for a quiet time and reading, an art corner, or containers with blocks and other toys. You obviously aren't going to turn your house into a nursery, but it is good to have a quiet place where your toddler can curl up and unwind – perhaps with books on a shelf, or some puzzles she can easily reach. And you can keep different activities in baskets, making it easy to take them out and put them away. This helps her understand where things go. Crafts might be kept in a storage box or drawer that your toddler can't get into without you. Puzzles and other games might be in another cupboard she can reach.

TOY ROTATION

To help keep the mess down, as well as to prevent too many choices, try rotating toys in and out of view. Fewer options will actually help increase her ability to concentrate, and she'll be as excited to see old friends reappear as she is when you buy her something new.

I like to have books stacked on bookshelves because I like toddlers to get into the habit of opening up a book and looking at it – and then putting it back where it belongs. It's a good way to teach her cleaning up after herself, and how to respect her belongings.

Parents often ask me 'How do I teach that my living room space is not the playroom?' At this age, you certainly don't want to be cordoning off any part of your house. Fair enough that they do it in Buckingham Palace, but this is your own home. Closing off your office is one thing – or maybe you'll decide to do it with your bedroom – but communal areas should be just that: shared. You can, however, keep toys in a toy chest or a basket in these rooms, so that they are all contained. Teach her that whatever we take out, we put away – either as soon as we finish playing with it, or at the end of the day.

TOYS FOR MULTIPLES

- ◆ **Make a one-for-all a box, mainly because you really don't need two or three of the same toy. This allows your children to enjoy everybody else's toys that might not belong to them – but are age-appropriate.**
- ◆ **The rule is that if it goes in the box, everyone gets to play with it, whether it belongs to you or not.**
- ◆ **Special toys can be kept in each child's own box, and these are strictly off limits to siblings, unless permission is granted!**

Outside exploration and exercise

I'm a firm believer in getting kids out every day for a breath of fresh air. In fact, it's really for both of you. Your toddler needs to let off steam and move – and you benefit from a change of pace. It's important that your toddler gets at least one hour of physical activity a day, as part of a healthy lifestyle. Remember, that's what you're laying down for your child – the building blocks of a healthy lifestyle, which includes not only eating right, but moving regularly. Toddlers are naturally mobile, but with the rise of so many computer and video games aimed at little ones, even three- and four-year-olds are not spending as much time outside playing and running around as they should be. We want to establish a habit of physical activity that will last her a lifetime.

Of course, it's good for you too. Adults should also be moving for at least an hour a day, too! Why not go swimming with your kids on a Saturday? Go for that brisk walk around the block with your toddler. The more you can be active as parents, the more that you show your child this is just normal healthy living, and it will become habitual. If you're worried about your child running off, practice the 'Rolling' and 'Roaming' techniques in Chapter 3 (see page 88).

Take your child out to play in the garden or go to a local park. Going to the park is a great way to meet other parents – or see the ones you know. But do mix things up by going to different places. Try another park and feed the ducks, or play at a different playground with different equipment. Believe it or not, toddlers can – and do – get bored. And a bored toddler is more likely to have a meltdown.

TIPS FOR WALKING WITH A CROWD

I once worked with a family that had a six-week-old baby, a three-year-old, a four-year-old and a five-year-old. Yes, hard work. Going out to the park, I had the three- and four-year-olds beside the pushchair – one on either side – the baby in the pushchair, and the five-year-old adjacent to the pushchair. The oldest and most responsible one was put the furthest away, because I knew he wouldn't run off.

You can position your crowd the same way or, with multiples, use a cord and have each hold on, one after the other.

If it's raining or snowing, dress her in the appropriate clothes and head outside. After all, if we waited for the sun to shine for us Brits to go outside, we'd never see the light of day. If the weather's really bad, let her run in the house. Yes, she'll make a noise – that's OK. She needs a chance to be physically active. I see adults telling toddlers all the time to 'Quiet down!' While you don't want them to rampage through the house, I expect toddlers to make noise. I expect them to explore and use their imagination – deciding what they can do with a cushion, a sheet from your bed and a cardboard box – or a blanket draped over a table. That's a normal expectation for a three- and four-year-old.

Balancing watching and participating

There are times when you're involved in a game or activity – and then there are times when you can sit back and observe or supervise.

I suggest keeping art supplies in an art box or cupboard, because this type of activity can't go unsupervised. You can't just put out the paints for a toddler and say, 'Craft time'. You're teaching him to draw on paper, not the walls. You're watching that he's not putting glue, paint or crayons in his mouth (why wouldn't he? it looks good) and harming himself.

Out at the park, you may push him on the swings, and then sit on the bench and watch as he runs around. You learn a lot by simply observing how he interacts with other children. You're also ready to step in if quarrels erupt – or he runs off too far. Make sure you balance watching and participating. Toddlers love it when their parents play with them.

TAKE ADVANTAGE OF LOW-COST ACTIVITIES

- **Two-year-olds: playdough, drawing, cutting paper and baking with you**
- **Three-year-olds: face-painting, crafts, playing ball at the park, finger-painting, helping you in the garden and storytime at the library**
- **Four-year-olds: hide-and-seek, using a bat and ball, make-believe camping, riding the bus, baking together**

Scheduled activities

To avoid boredom (hers and yours), it also helps to look at your week as a whole and pace yourself with different, fun activities outside the house. That way you're not dependent upon the weather being nice. You can schedule library time – or maybe swim, music or toddler gym classes once or twice a week. For this age group, I try not to have too many 'lessons'; I just want them to play. If she does have a lesson, make sure it's not longer than 45 minutes and, when it's over, feed her a snack and have some free playtime.

Remember the salesman pitch and 'sell, sell, sell'. If you do sign your three- or four-year-old toddler up for an activity and, after the first lesson she says, 'I don't like it', keep going. Even at this young age, your child needs to learn to stick to things. Rather than give into 'Oh well, I hate it! I don't want to do it', your job is to coach and support by saying, 'Let's try it again next week.' How you respond to your toddler's resistance to an activity lays the foundation of how she will respond – at school and in life in general – to things she doesn't initially like.

Chores

You're at home and need to get some chores done. At what age do you introduce chores to your toddler? This is a question that I'm asked constantly. How do you move from doing everything for him, to getting him to help you, which in turn teaches him important life skills?

Toddlers shouldn't have set chores – they're too young. But you can get your child to learn chores through the 'Involvement' technique (see opposite). Show him how put his rubbish into the rubbish bin. Show him how to put his toys away, or how to place the talcum powder back where it belongs.

The Involvement technique is one of my favourites as it's such a positive way to help your toddler feel a part of the family, boosting his competence and confidence. Have him help you get the wash out of the tumble-dryer or even fold socks (matching and identifying which go together). The Involvement technique is easy because you're definitely at the stage where he

Cleaning fun

One thing I have done with older toddlers is to make animals out of old socks to dust with. What's needed? Old socks, some arts-and-crafts supplies, and needle and thread. Your toddler can wear them on his hands and have fun while dusting.

likes to do anything, as long as he's with you. He wants to be helpful, and doesn't discriminate. 'I don't like doing laundry' is something you won't hear him say for many, many years to come.

You'll be amazed at the conversations that will arise while doing household tasks. Get out your *Patience* from your backpack. He's not going to do it perfectly. It's about getting him started in on recognising where things belong and how he can participate in tidying up and putting things away.

◆ **Patience**

When a chore should not be a chore

Your toddler will react to your attitude about doing chores. Be mindful. Make it a game and make it fun. Some parents will time chores: 'Let's see if you can do it really quickly.' If you show excitement in your tone of voice, your toddler will get excited, too. If, for example, you're picking up books and you've got a positive attitude, then a chore isn't a chore. If you feel it's a pain in the neck, your toddler will mirror that reaction.

THE INVOLVEMENT TECHNIQUE

◆ **A toddler wants your attention and wants to help. So get him involved in whatever you're doing: carrying items at the grocery store, setting the table, sweeping the floor. Of course it will take longer, but that's not the point.**

◆ **Make sure you praise him and tell him what a good job he's doing in helping you.**

Teaching how to tidy up

Parents are always so shocked when they go into their child's room and find every toy out of the cupboard. Chaos everywhere! Toddlers have short attention spans – they'll play with one thing for five minutes and then move on to the next. If you say 'Put it all away', his little mind is thinking, 'Where does it go? How do I do that?'

I've had parents say, 'I have to ask my child 50 times to clean up. He won't do it. Why won't he listen to me?' Did you notice the tone of voice you were using? Did you say, 'Pick up your toys' and then proceed to do it yourself? You need first to show him how to do it, and then allow him to do it himself. It's the beginning of being more self-sufficient and taking responsibility (see the 'Clean-Up' technique, on the following page).

Gradually, as your toddler matures, and around the age of four, he becomes capable of tidying up his room and doing specific tasks by himself. If up to this point, you've never used the 'Involvement' or 'Clean-Up' techniques, you can't expect him immediately to know what to do. If you've been saying, 'Where do the socks go? See Daddy putting socks in the drawer' then, by the time he's four, you can legitimately say, 'Please put your socks away and grab some jeans to wear.'

THE CLEAN-UP TECHNIQUE

- ◆ **Like everything else, cleaning up has to be taught. You can't expect two- to three- years-olds to put stuff away without your help.**

- ◆ **Shadow your child and show her where things go: 'Mummy puts the car here. Now you put this car away. Mummy put this one away. There, you put this one away.'**

- ◆ **You need to show her step-by-step: 'Put the blocks here.' When she does that with you, then you say, 'Put the puzzle here.'**

- ◆ **Have specific places to put different kinds of toys: 'the big blue box is where cars go.' Through repetition of seeing where things go, she starts to remember.**

- ◆ **For really young toddlers, tidying up their toys can be overwhelming, so I create what I call little molehills, and then we do one molehill at a time.**

- ◆ **Through the repetition of showing and telling, your child starts to learn how to do it herself.**

Making tidying fun

Tidying up is tidying up – but you can make it a little bit more fun by jumping into a role. I worked for a family in an apartment in Manhattan, who would put builder caps on to do 'construction' – which was actually tidying up their rooms. Or turn it into a game: How fast can we do it?

14

Evening

The day is winding down. Evening can be a special time to regroup and reconnect as a family, as you all have a meal together and transition to quiet time.

SAMPLE EVENING SCHEDULE

- ◆ **Dinner**
- ◆ **Family time**
- ◆ **Bath**
- ◆ **Brush teeth**
- ◆ **Quiet time: read books**
- ◆ **Bedtime**

Dinner

I've helped many families whose mealtimes are fragmented. Parents are quickly feeding their kids, and then eating their own meals by the sink. Kids, even toddlers, are eating in front of the TV, or running around grabbing food and not sitting down to eat.

I want to really encourage you to sit down and eat dinner together. You can talk about what you did that day and your toddler can begin to learn how fun it can be to interact as a family. I know that with working schedules it's not always possible to do this, but it should be a goal to strive for at least a few times a week because it helps with social interaction and healthy eating habits.

If you need to feed your toddler a snack in advance, so she can hold out for dinner, fine. Just make it healthy. By eating at the table with your toddler, she's seeing firsthand how to eat and how to behave at the dinner table. It's never too early to start teaching basic table manners and etiquette. In fact, the whole meal is a learning experience for a toddler. She's learning how to be a big girl, eating at the table with everyone else – learning how to hold a fork or spoon, and try different types of food. She's learning how to be social.

- ◆ **Patience**
- ◆ **Perseverance**
- ◆ **Humour**
- ◆ **Plan Ahead**

Of course, that's the ideal. The reality is that dinnertime can be a period of stress for parents – and a battle for control by your toddler. But, it doesn't have to be that way. I'm going to help you have enjoyable dinners together – it's time for that old backpack again!

The Little Chef technique

Get your little one involved in preparing the meal and setting the table. I call this my 'Little Chef' technique. The key is to make the task something he can do – appropriate for his age. Your two-year-old can help with measuring or pouring. Your three- and four-year-old can help stir or mix. And an almost five-year-old can help you to come up with the menu, and get involved in the cooking or setting the table. Use lots of encouragement and praise for each task he completes.

Transition to dinner

Give a warning that dinner will be in five minutes, so your toddler knows what to expect. Help him wash up and then have everyone sit down together.

Keeping cool with mealtime madness

Parents often have trouble with various dining habits of toddlers. The following behaviours are quite normal – hopefully knowing what they are, and expecting them, will help you to keep your cool!

Yes, he wants what you have

No matter what he has on his plate, he'll inevitably want what's on yours. To me, it's another way to say: 'It's all mine: I want your time. I want your food.' My rule is: Yes, he can have a bite of your food, but first he needs to eat his own.

Yes, he'll throw his food on the ground

This is typical of very young toddlers. It's a game. Here's how I suggest you play it: He throws it, you replace it. You don't want him to think that by throwing his food on the ground he won't have to eat it. Replace it. A good tip: When you're creating your portions, always make another teaspoon so you're prepared.

If it's one of those drop-up, pick-up, drop-up, pick-up, drop-up, pick-up days, take away his plate for a little while and then bring it back again saying, 'Eat now. No dropping on the floor. That's naughty.' If he continues, take the plate away and offer no food until the next mealtime.

This behaviour should go away on its own. If he's still doing it at three, then you need to apply the Naughty Step technique.

Yes, food will be everywhere, at least at first

By the age of two, he should be feeding himself quite consistently. You don't want to fall into the habit of feeding your toddler because you don't want a mess. This is not the time to worry about messes. Guaranteed you'll be sweeping up your kitchen floor at least three times a day – and washing the table after every meal. That's a given. Put down a plastic placemat that's easy to wipe clean, and a large piece of plastic sheeting under his chair to make tidying up easier.

Follow my ladder for moving your toddler from being fed by you to self-feeding (see following page). Make sure to provide small utensils, not grown-up ones. I actually love this stage, when a child is learning to feed himself. At two, he's trying so hard to eat with a spoon, and food is everywhere. And, of course, he's not always using the spoon. Most of the food is going from hand to mouth (and floor!).

As he gets older, his fine motor skills will develop and he'll gain more control. This is when the mess will decrease and you can begin to teach table manners. Remember this is the age of finger-painting and mud pies. Just go with it.

Yes, he'll spit out food

Around the age of two, your toddler is making the transition from eating sloppier, lumpy food to whole pieces of meat or veggies. He's learning how to chew and swallow, which is why you cut up his food into small bites. Try to remember that when you see him put a veggie in his mouth, suck out all the juice and spit it out, he's not being naughty. He's just learning how to eat.

Meat's a big one for this. Toddlers often spit it out because the texture is too difficult to manage. When I introduce meat for the first time, I always give poultry first, then fish, and then red meat. Even then, I'll cut the meat up into small pieces and mix it in with a some vegetables and carbohydrates so that it's easier to chew and swallow. Through repetition – and over time – he will learn and the spitting stops.

How can you help with this transition? Consider serving risotto with tiny pieces of chicken, or fish with sweetcorn and mashed potatoes. Shepherd's pie is another great option: meat, veg and mashed potatoes all together. As you can see, these are all basic recipes, because going back to basics is what's necessary.

Conversation and manners at the table

Dinner is not a long, drawn-out affair with toddlers. It's reasonable to expect them to stay at the table for 20 to 30 minutes maximum. If you're repeatedly having problems with your toddler getting down, try my 'Stay at Table' technique (see opposite). This will help you keep to track of the time and you can make a game out of it for him.

As soon as your toddler can speak, teach him the basic manner words, such as 'please' and 'thank you' – and even 'down please'. Like everything else, you're teaching through repetition. Much of what you say in terms of manners won't register at first. But by four he can certainly learn to:

◆ Hold his utensils properly

◆ Ask you to please pass something he wants, rather than reaching and grabbing

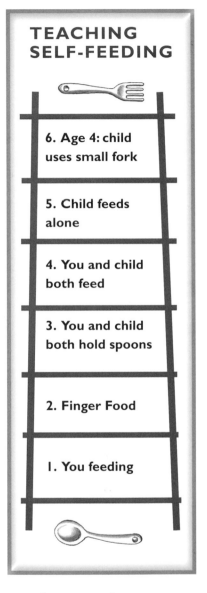

TEACHING SELF-FEEDING

6. Age 4: child uses small fork

5. Child feeds alone

4. You and child both feed

3. You and child both hold spoons

2. Finger Food

1. You feeding

◆ Wipe his mouth with his napkin

◆ Use the proper phrase for leaving the table: 'May I be excused, please?'

There is a balance here. The more you work during the day expanding his attention span doing activities, the longer he'll be able to stay at the table. If he can't sit still to do a puzzle for five minutes, he won't be able to sit at the table either … The more you work on focus and attention span, the less fidgeting you'll see.

I worked with a large family with both teenagers and toddlers, who never ate together. The older ones ate in their rooms while texting friends, the little ones in front of the TV. I helped them create a family dinnertime, and gave them a talking stick to promote conversation. The parents and the older ones would throw out a topic and, one at a time, each person would hold the stick and speak. Of course, the littlest ones couldn't say much, but they loved holding the stick when it was their turn and were helped with 'yes' and 'no' questions: 'Did you have fun today?' The whole family really came to enjoy this time together.

Lead by example

I remember helping a family who would all sit down at the table, and suddenly Mum would realise she'd forgotten the cream and jump up. Then she'd realise she'd forgotten the juice, and jump up for that, too. It went on and on. I helped the parents become mindful of how they ate and what they did at the table. Soon their children had better manners as well.

If you carry on getting up, it's no wonder that your toddler does, too. She's learning from your example – wiping her mouth with a sleeve because you didn't put any napkins down, talking with her mouth full because you do. Make sure you are a good role model for manners and polite conversation at the table.

THE STAY AT TABLE TECHNIQUE

◆ **Set a timer for 20 minutes (less for a child under four).**

◆ **Every time your toddler gets up, bring him back and sit him down. When the timer goes off, he can leave.**

◆ **Practise expanding his attention span – the longer you can engage your child during the day with sitting down and doing a puzzle for instance, the more able he will be to sit at the table.**

The evening routine

After dinner, you probably have an hour for family time, winding down and getting your toddler ready for bed. Actually, preparing your kids to go to sleep is also a sign for you that your day with them is coming to an end. You know that once you get them down to sleep, you'll have time for yourself and time to reconnect with your partner.

The evening routine is all about establishing an ambience that is effectively the wind-down to going to bed. The rituals you set now will last for many years to come. Even when they're older, you will probably have your most intimate talks at this time, as there is nothing else that has to preoccupy you.

You've set the time that your toddler should be in bed. Now work backward to make sure you have enough time to go through each stage of the routine. If you have about an hour to spend on bathing, getting pyjamas on, story time and into bed, you're in a good place.

Don't rush it. If you skip a stage in the routine, your toddler will feel cheated. Proper transitioning from day to night is essential to avoid night-time battles. As with any activity, give advance notice about what happens next. And praise her as she completes each stage without fuss. This also, quite simply, teaches your toddler the difference between night and day – and how we behave differently during these times of the day on a whole. Also, if you rush, it sends the message that you want to get rid of her. It's like you are trying to brush her off and she feels she's falling short with your patience.

Consistency is a skill that will serve you well here. Setting a consistent evening routine gives your toddler comfort and helps ease her into sleep. As you and your partner take turns putting her to bed, make sure you're both on the same page about how the routine goes.

Out late? Don't skip the routine

If you've been somewhere and it's late when you get back, don't skip the evening ritual entirely. You can let the bath go, but stick to brushing teeth and reading a book before bed. Keeping things consistent is so important to toddlers.

Bathing

The bath serves as a period of time to wind down before bedtime. Being in a warm bath actually relaxes your toddler's whole body and prepares her to sleep. But it's also a time to have fun – especially with a parent she may not have seen all day.

It goes without saying that bathtime is supervised – and at *all times*. Don't run and answer the phone or the door, or leave your toddler for a second. Check through the specific water-safety rules that you should bear in mind (see page 84). You really can't be too careful.

Most kids love getting into the bath and splashing around. Make bathtime fun with toys and games. Let her play with little plastic jugs and pots that she can fill and pour. Mirrors can be really fun, as she puts soap in her hair and makes different hairstyles (punk rebel is my favourite). If she doesn't have eczema or excessively dry skin, you can also add bubble bath. You can also have her put on goggles and play like a dolphin.

As she's playing, you're washing – getting soap on that sponge and making sure every body part is clean. Your tone should be very matter-of-fact. Identifying and then washing the different body parts is something toddlers learn through play: 'Where are your knees, where's your mouth? Let's wash your ears.'

When your toddler reaches 18 months, you should be telling your toddler what you are doing as you are doing it: 'Now we are washing our hair.' By about two-and-a-half to three, she'll want to do it all herself, and she probably knows how! However, just like brushing teeth, you can let her try – and then do it all over again, so that it's done properly! Make sure that you thoroughly rinse off all the soap, bubble bath and shampoo with clean water. Soap left on her skin can irritate.

Dealing with shampoo screamers

According to my Mum, as a toddler I was a screamer, who hated getting my hair washed. Lots of toddlers feel this way. I'm glad to know this is normal. I did outgrow it and your child will, too. Meanwhile, there are things you can try to reduce the unpleasantness for both of you:

◆ First of all, listen to exactly what she doesn't like.

- Once you know exactly what the problem is, you can find a way to work around it.

- Talk to her about what you're doing and why you use shampoo and conditioner. Give clear warnings before you wash out the soap.

- If she hates leaning back, have her stand up and pour water from a bucket or cup on her head. Or use the nozzle. You can even put her in the shower.

- A flannel over her face might help her avoid shampoo and water getting in her eyes. Or use a specially designed shampoo eye and face shield that will keep her eyes clear.

- Use tear-free shampoo that doesn't sting.

- Finally, you don't need to wash her hair every night, as it strips away essential oils.

- Making her more confident around water, by introducing swimming lessons or being in the shower with you, may help.

> ### In the tub
>
> If your child stands up – or you put her in the shower - make sure you put a sticky mat in the tub so she won't slip.

Drying off

The most important thing about drying off is making sure it's done thoroughly. Get into every crease and fold. If moisture is left in sensitive skin areas – folds behind the ears and creases around her pelvis, for example – they can crack and hurt.

Don't be afraid to use a hair-dryer if you want to. He's used to noise! By two, he will have heard the Hoover coming near, the washing machine rumbling, and the liquidiser in the kitchen. It's the loud, abrupt noises that scare toddlers. Just talk to him before you turn it on.

After you've dried him off, it's nice to end with a massage – particularly if it is something he enjoyed as a baby. I used to love doing it with the kids I looked after. Kids love it! It's a really nice time because they're just relaxed from coming out of the bath and they're all warm and wrapped up in their cosy hooded towels. It helps them to relax and get into that wind-down zone.

Nail clipping

Keeping your toddler's nails clean and trimmed is important from a hygiene perspective. Don't forget that she's constantly playing in the garden and in the mud, and picking her bottom, ears and nose! She's constantly getting into things – and then putting her fingers in her mouth. Keeping everything nice and trim will help to promote good hygiene. The bath's taken care of the dirt; now it's the time to make sure her nails are short enough.

Ever since she was a little baby you've been clipping her nails. During the toddler years this doesn't stop. Have her sit on your lap (as if you were doing your own) and tell her a story to distract her. You can also count piggies for the younger ones: 'One little piggy, two little piggies.' Sitting on you is important for two reasons:

◆ She'll feel comforted building up trust to allow her to cut her nails. It can be scary seeing the scissors; and

◆ You can clearly see what you're doing so you don't accidentally nip the skin or cut her nails too short, which can cause infection.

You'll probably only need to snip her nails every one or two weeks. Practice makes perfect. The more you do it, the more confident you'll feel. Trust me, kids used to come over for play dates and for half an hour I was Jo Jo Scissorhands. Literally.

If your child is not interested in having her nails cut, or is at an age where she is easily distracted, having two adults can be helpful. While she's sitting on your lap and you're cutting, the other person can distract her.

15

Bedtime

Your toddler is out of the bath, dry, teeth brushed, massaged, and with her pyjamas on. She's relaxing – and so are you. You talk calmly and more slowly to quiet her down. It's time for bed.

I talk a lot about transitions in this book. Now you're creating an ambience to signal the transition between day and night. Draw the curtains, put on the nightlights, and create an energy and mood to encourage relaxation and sleep. It's enchanting – the magic hour has begun.

The environment you're creating is relaxed, soft and still. Her body is tired and relaxed, but you need to quiet her mind as well. When those lights go off, her mind can race with lots of different thoughts – so, you want a smooth, calm transition.

Turn off your phone and slow yourself down. Remember that this is about you winding down as well. Your toddler is tired and ready for sleep, and you realise: 'Ah! Three more hours and I'm in bed!'

NO ROUGH-HOUSING

Avoid stimulating activities right before bed. Rough-and-tumble play will just rev her up and make it harder for her to switch gears to go to sleep. This can be hard if a working parent walks in just as the bedtime ritual begins. Have him be the one to read the story, perhaps, so he's involved but not whooping her up.

The bedtime story

Reading books in bed is a lovely, peaceful way to bond with your child. You're spending quality one-on-one time with her. Encouraging a life-long love of books is also a wonderful treasure that will benefit her for the rest of her life.

Choose two or three books and let her choose which ones she wants to read. Keep it to just one or two books – you don't want this time to drag on or became a battle for more and more books, which is a common delaying tactic. Toddlers are comforted by reading a story they know, so she'll probably choose a favourite to read again and again. That's OK, for, as you know by now, she learns through repetition. Remember, this phase won't last forever! If you are stuck for ideas, I have provided a list of my favourite books for each age group at the end of this book (see pages 293–295). Your librarian is also a great resource. There are many bedtime-story books that complement a child's age. By this I mean that you can find five-minute bedtime stories, ten-minute bedtime stories and 20-minute bedtime stories – whatever suits your child's age and attention span best.

- ◆ **Patience**
- ◆ **Perspective**
- ◆ **Commitment**

Trust me on this one, too – your child has memorised the pages. If you skip a few – and what parent hasn't – she will be sure to know.

Storytelling

Another wonderful way to end the day with your three- or four-year-old is by storytelling. Storytelling works best when your child can identify and relate to the story. Start off by taking a character from one of her favourite books that you read all the time. That character then goes on the adventure with your toddler, and they bond together. I often include siblings and parents in the story as well. Every night is a new chapter. Add in different aspects of your child's life – or include stories that go along with the time of year, such as Father Christmas, the Easter Bunny or something in keeping with your family's faiths or traditions.

Sometimes I tell stories in bed, and sometimes in their rooms – wherever your child wants to sit. After storytime or reading, have a cuddle and talk a little bit about the day. This is a great time to give praise and reminders of good moments.

Home noise

Once your child is in bed, the house doesn't have to be dead silent. In fact, it's important that your toddler hears something – whether you have things going on in the kitchen or you're moving around downstairs. It's very settling for her. She can hear you're still there while she goes off to sleep.

Your life shouldn't stop when your children go to sleep. It's important for you and for your relationship with your partner that you carry on with your adult life. Don't be afraid to have dinner parties. If your toddler wakes up from the noise, simply put her back to bed again.

Lullaby toys

A lot of parents continue the baby-years tradition of offering bed toys that play soft lullaby music. If he likes it, keep it in there. But by no means should you be playing music like you're at some rock concert – or have iPods on. Remember that you're creating quiet. I was once helping a woman with her 20-month-old son, who would not go to sleep. When I went into his room, I noticed he had all these noise-making toys in his cot. This included a ringing telephone and a monkey who screamed, '*Eek, eek, eek*' when you pulled the tail. When he was a baby, it wasn't a problem, because he didn't know that pulling the tail made the noise. But he definitely had it worked out now. Noise is fun! The solution was easy: Take the toy out of the cot!

This is sleep-time, not playtime. If you do want to let him have toys to play with when he wakes up, make sure they don't make noise. Soft cloth books or one teddy are good options.

Nightlights

Nightlights help in setting up a safe environment because, at a certain developmental point, toddlers can become afraid of the dark. Around the age of three his imagination will peak, and he can develop a whole host of fears that didn't exist before. A soft, dim light with a very low voltage can ease his fears, as he opens his eyes and sees his familiar room. It's also a good way to ensure that he can see where he's going if he needs to visit the loo in the night – and for you to see as well, if you come to lift him. You don't have to go with traditional nightlights. Obviously candles are a fire hazard and out of the question, but novelty nightlights and glow stars on the ceiling can produce just the right level of comforting light.

> ## A NEW ROOM
>
> If you've just moved and your child is just getting used to his room, make sure you spend time playing there during the day. The more time you spend in a room, the more you make your mark on it. He'll feel more comfortable when it's time to sleep.

Getting toddlers to sleep

You're creating an environment in his bedroom that promotes sleep, and you want your toddler to feel a sense of ownership: 'This is where I go to bed.' But just setting up a nightlight and providing cuddly, warm blankets won't make him fall asleep. You've still got to do the work.

For many of us, it's not that easy. In fact, sleep is one of the top concerns about which parents of toddlers ask me: 'How do I keep her down at night?' and 'What do I do if she just won't go to sleep?'

Throughout these years, you're dealing with transitioning your child from a cot to a bed. And then you also have to deal with separation anxiety, the ongoing quest for independence – and the developmental stage of fear of the dark and monsters coming from everywhere, because of that active little imagination going into overdrive. This can translate into resistance to going to bed, getting out of bed, night-time fears, and the ever-present 'monsters.' I'll provide solutions for all of these issues because, at the end of the day, both you and your toddler need to make sure you're getting enough sleep.

No bottles at bedtime

If you are still giving your toddler a bottle to go to sleep, it's time to stop. It's not good for her teeth. Her last fluid intake should be during dinner and before teeth-brushing. If she cries because she wants her bottle, use the 'Sleep Separation' or the 'Stay in Bed' techniques.

The importance of sleep

First of all, let's look at how much sleep your child needs each night. In a 24-hour period, 18-month- to three-year-olds should be getting between 12 and 14 hours of sleep; three- and four-year-olds need between 11 and 13 hours. What about you? Adults need about seven hours, but ideally eight.

Everyone in the family – and that includes you – needs to get the proper amount of sleep. The benefits of sleep do not just involve resting and restoring our bodies. Sleep helps regulate mood and is important for mental and physical development. When your child enters into deep sleep, important growth hormones are released and her little body get much-needed downtime to repair and reset. She'll then have more energy the next day for learning and exploring. Lack of sleep can affect her mood, behaviour and appetite. In short: a well-rested toddler is immeasurably happier.

Why can't I stay up?

At some point you are undoubtedly going to find your toddler pushing to stay up later. Every child says he's 'not tired', whether he is or not. You know the reason why he's saying this, but you also know that he needs a certain number of hours of sleep in order to function at optimum level. Full stop. It's important to maintain this line and follow through on what you know is the necessary bedtime for his age.

This can be particularly difficult when he has older siblings who are staying up later. The truth is, however, if you've got siblings of different ages, the younger one is *always* going to be asking, 'Why can't I ...?' That's part and parcel of having siblings. If you are letting the younger one stay up too late – or making the older one go to bed too early – to avoid a clash, recognise there are some issues that need to be addressed. Proper bedtime is proper bedtime, regardless of age. Explain to your toddler that when he gets to that age, he can stay up, too. Then put him to bed at the right time.

Transitioning from cot to bed

It's all part of the progression of life: womb to Moses basket, Moses basket to a cot, and then cot to a single bed. Parents see their toddler start to climb out of the cot and think: 'It must be time for him to sleep in a bed.' No, that just means he knows how to climb. He's learned to stand on his bumper and climb over. Lower the cot sides so he doesn't hurt himself, and use the 'Sleep Separation' technique I describe later in this chapter (see page 273) to teach him that he has to stay there until he's old enough for a big bed.

I like to move kids from a cot to bed when I see that their cot is too small. Look at the length and width of your child as he's in the cot. Does he have enough space? If not, then you should move him to a bed. Depending upon his verbal skills and level of understanding, I like to wait until he's about three for this transition. At two, the move might lead to night-time anxieties, because he's lost something that's familiar and comforting.

By three, you can involve your child in the process because he's capable of talking and understanding. Talk about it ahead of time and let him choose his new sheets. Be excited and explain all the wonderful things about sleeping in a big-boy bed. Whether you go for a toddler bed or a single bed, it doesn't really matter. However, if you decide to use a single bed, do put up a guard-rail. This will stop her from falling or rolling out of bed.

To make the bed feel smaller and cosier, take a quilt or blanket and roll it up on the side without the rail, and place another rolled blanket at the bottom. Having the blankets in place offers reassurance during the transition. His toes can feel the end of the bed. He doesn't need a pillow for his head, but at this age you can offer one if you want to.

Sharing a room

Sharing a room is not detrimental to your children's sleep. You simply need to look at how you handle the night-time routine. Every child deserves quality one-on-one time with her parent. Putting her to bed and reading a story is a great time to do that. Depending on the ages of your children, you can stagger the bedtime. Your partner can do the bath with the older child, as you put the younger one to bed.

If your little ones are close together in age — two and three, for example — it makes sense to put them down at the same time and do one story together. Find other times for one-on-one. If you have a toddler and a baby, get the baby down first. If your baby and toddler are sharing a room, you have to make sure that your toddler can understand — and will listen to you. You don't want him jumping into the cot or waking up the baby. When your baby is really young, I suggest she shares a room with you instead of your toddler. It's easier to do nightly feedings and it prevents any dangers your toddler might otherwise present through ignorance or over-enthusiasm, like climbing into the cot with the baby and accidentally smothering her.

It's fine for kids to share a bed together if the room fits only one; however, I like to make sure that they sleep head-to-toe. Why? Because if their faces are right next to each other, they're more apt to talk and stay awake. However, it's your choice.

Sleeping with you

There are loads of books on the pros and cons of attachment parenting and co-sleeping. I've met several families who believed in the benefits and have been happy doing it. But usually, even when the family co-sleeps, a child has been moved out to her own bed by the age of two.

In the long run, I think that most parents see that it's healthy for toddlers to have own space – and for a couple to have some time and space for themselves and their partnership. If for no other reason than kids move around a lot in their sleep. How can you get a good night's rest with a toe in your mouth?

If you say that you co-sleep and it works for you, fantastic. I simply suggest that if you are co-sleeping and not getting the quality sleep you need, you might consider that it's time to move her to her own bed.

Why is your toddler in your bed?

I caution against using co-sleeping as a way to avoid dealing with a sleep problem that your toddler is having. Kids need to learn how to self-soothe and fall asleep on their own – and they need to learn this without you as their human dummy, always by their side. It creates healthy detachment for your child to sleep on her own, in her own bed under the same roof as her family. It enables her to begin to develop a sense of independence that will allow her to sleep over at a friend's house when she's older, and to go to nursery or childcare comfortably and confidently.

I've also seen single parents move their kids in to fill the gap of the big bed. I really don't think that's a good idea. Your toddler will start to get used to this, and claim ownership of the bed and the room. If and when you bring in a new partner, it can cause problems. Not only is your child dealing with sharing her parent on an emotional level – but the actual space in the bed as well.

By all means let your toddler come to bed with you if she's ill. There's nothing better when a little one feels poorly and needs some TLC. Snuggling on the weekends or taking an occasional nap together in the afternoon – this is all fine as well. You just want to ensure she's in her cot or bed for the majority of time that she's sleeping.

Dealing with sleep issues

- ◆ **Commitment**
- ◆ **Patience**
- ◆ **Perseverance**

With toddlers, it's all about getting them to stay in bed when you put them there – and then sleep through the night. The following problems are those about which I hear constantly from parents. The three sleeping techniques I suggest here work really well if done consistently, using *Patience* and *Perseverance*.

The Time-controlled Crying technique

If your 18- to 20-month-old is still crying in the night, either when you put him to bed or when he wakens in the night, do the 'Time-controlled Crying' technique. After about 24 months, I suggest you use the 'Sleep Separation' technique, as it takes into account the separation anxiety he'll likely be going through.

In my *Confident Baby Care* book, I refer to this technique as the 'Controlled Crying' technique. However, some folks have confused it with sleep techniques that involve leaving the room and not returning. I don't believe in doing that. I leave, then come back in a few minutes to soothe, then double the time before I go back again – until gradually he soothes himself to sleep. The technique works because you go back; you're not leaving him there to cry it out. He has the security of knowing that you're still there. That's why I'm now calling it the 'Time-controlled Crying' technique.

The technique also works because he's getting lots of love, attention and stimulation during the day. In essence, you are creating a healthy balance that will allow your toddler to recognise that there are times when he simply needs to go to sleep.

THE TIME-CONTROLLED CRYING TECHNIQUE

Practise this during nap times, too. You are teaching your toddler how to soothe herself to sleep without you.

♦ **Place your toddler in her cot, say 'night-night' and walk out.**

♦ **The first time she cries, go in, put your hand on her tummy and say 'shhh', without making eye contact, then leave.**

♦ **Wait five minutes and, if she's still crying, repeat the routine. If she still cries, go back in ten minutes and then, if necessary, 20.**

♦ **Do not pick her up or she'll think she's getting out of bed. Be consistent.**

Note: This technique has never taken longer than seven days and the shortest time in which it has worked is two.

Troubleshooting the Time-controlled Crying technique

If it's not working, ask yourself the following questions:

♦   Is my child sick or going through a big life transition, such as starting childcare, moving house or divorce? If so, this is not the time to start this technique. Wait a couple weeks until she's healthy and her life is more stable.

◆ Is she getting the right amount of food and fluids during the day so that she's not hungry or thirsty now? Did I put her to bed too late so she's overtired? Establishing healthy eating and sleeping patterns before doing this technique is important.

◆ Are you cheating on the time – going back before time is up? Like my other techniques, this one only works if you follow the steps exactly.

Getting older toddlers off to sleep

There was a family whose daughter was not able to fall asleep without one of her parents lying down with her. Night after night they would stay with her until she fell asleep. Sound familiar?

If so, just like this little girl, your child needs the 'Sleep Separation' technique below. This involves remaining in the room to reassure her that you're still present without engaging with her – either through conversation or eye contact. Eventually you'll be able to put her down and leave with a simple 'Good night'.

A lot of parents ask me if they are going to psychologically damage their child by not responding. Of course not. You're teaching her a valuable life-long skill: How to put herself to sleep. And your presence speaks for itself.

THE SLEEP SEPARATION TECHNIQUE

◆ **Complete your usual night-time routine. After your cuddle, say good night, and tell her it's time to close her eyes and go to sleep.**

◆ **Turn the lights off, leave the door open and sit next to her bed or cot – out of arm's reach. Do not get into bed with her.**

◆ **Have her turn her face to the other side; you don't want to make eye contact, as she'll try to talk to you.**

◆ **Stay sitting in silence until she goes to sleep. If she tries to talk or get out of bed, stop her or just put her back silently.**

◆ **Repeat the same steps the next night but, this time, sit a little further away, until eventually you are sitting outside the door with the door open. Soon enough, you won't have to do it at all.**

Troubleshooting the Sleep Separation technique

If it's not working, ask yourself the following questions:

◆ Am I talking to her? Staring at her? No interaction is crucial.

◆ Is my body language speaking volumes? Do I become fidgety and create a distraction? You need to be still.

◆ Do I lie on the floor and fall asleep so I end up staying there all night? Each night, you have to move yourself closer to the door and then out.

Staying in bed

I once helped a family who had successfully boasted to me – and rightly so – that they had managed to transition their toddler from a cot into a bed with ease. Their son was absolutely delighted because he had a Spiderman pillowcase, a Spiderman duvet, and lovely little gold stars on his ceiling. Bedtime was no problem. However, within two weeks, the novelty wore off, and he found quite a few excuses for why he shouldn't remain in his bed.

Sound familiar? Trust me, toddlers will find *every* excuse in the book to avoid going into their own bed – and sleeping in their own bedroom. I have heard absolutely hundreds! It starts off with needing to go to the loo – and then he's hungry and thirsty, his leg is sore, and then his tummy hurts and there are monsters … The excuses just multiply and multiply until you get so fed up that you end up relenting and letting him get into *your* bed.

To cut this short, eliminate as many excuses as possible before bed. He's had dinner, so he's not hungry. He's had a sip of water, so he's not thirsty. He's been to the potty and, unless he's older, he's now in a nappy. You've taken care of the monsters (see page 278). If he insists that he has to go potty, give him the benefit of the doubt, but don't talk and put him straight back into bed afterwards.

However much troubleshooting as you do, he'll is still likely think of some other excuse. That's when it's time for the 'Stay in Bed' technique (see box opposite). It's a great way for you to reassure your child that he's perfectly fine to jump back into his Spiderman bed and sleep in his own room, for the sanity of all.

With this technique, I stress **perseverance** and *patience* because you may have to deal with your toddler getting up 20 times in one night, making it a two-hour struggle. It's the same concept involved as doing the Naughty Step technique. Stay strong and keep putting him back.

The key to the success of this technique is to make sure that the parent who put the child to bed is the one to takes him back when he gets up. If you need to use the technique over multiple nights, you can switch off – but be consistent in the night itself. You don't want your toddler to play one parent off the other. Eventually he will learn.

As you do this technique, your child may say, 'Why are you not talking to me, Mummy? Why are you not talking to me?' And you may feel, 'Oh my god, I'm ignoring him!' You are ignoring, but mindfully. Actively. You're teaching him that there's a cut-off period, and this is a healthy boundary: 'It's bedtime now. It means that we don't talk, we go to sleep. Tomorrow we wake up and we have a happy day.'

You can talk about it next day as well: 'When it's bedtime, you have to stay in bed. We're not going to have a conversation in bed.'

THE STAY IN BED TECHNIQUE

- **When your child gets up, take him back to bed with a simple: 'It's bedtime, darling'. Ignore excuses, except the potty – and that only once.**

- **The next time he gets up, usher him back with a simple: 'Bedtime'.**

- **By the third time he gets up, put him back without saying a word. Stay calm. Avoid eye contact, as your eyes speak volumes. Don't communicate in any way at *any* cost. He'll say, 'Why aren't you talking to me?' Say nothing.**

- **Repeat again and again, if need be; sooner or later he'll give up.**

- **If you choose to, use a reward chart to tick off trouble-free nights. When he gets to four, he can have a reward. But agree something small – you don't want him acting up to get a prize.**

Troubleshooting the Stay in Bed technique
If it's not working, ask yourself the following questions:

- Is this the right technique to use? If your little one is only two-and-a-half, and in the midst of separation anxiety, I would use the Sleep Separation technique instead.

- ◆ Have we recently moved? You will need to help him get used to his room in the day, and use the Sleep Separation technique instead until he's comfortable.

- ◆ Am I falling for the thousand excuses? You must ignore these requests.

- ◆ Am I getting into long explanations and conversations? You need to follow the steps exactly. Copy and post them somewhere prominent, if necessary.

Waking up in the night

In the middle of the night, there are times when you'll hear a cry of, 'Mummy, Daddy.' He might be having a nightmare, feeling poorly or calling you because he needs to visit the loo. There are also certain situations that cause sleep disruptions, to which you'll need to be sensitive, including illness, divorce, a move or even a new baby.

If your child comes to you in the middle of night, offer comfort and then put him back to bed. Give a quick hug and then, 'Good night.' If he has a problem settling down or you think his sleeplessness is because of a transition with which he's having trouble, use the 'Sleep Separation' technique. This reassures him that you're still there. Repeatedly getting up in the night for no reason should be dealt with by using the 'Stay in Bed' technique.

If your child is crying, having a nightmare or calling out to you, it is natural and right that you go to him to find out what's going on.

THE CHIMES TECHNIQUE

What if your child sneaks into your bed at night and you don't notice until the morning? Break the habit by using the 'Chimes' technique. Put wind chimes or a bell on a string on your bedroom door. That way you'll hear him coming in. Don't be tempted to bring him into your bed unless he's ill. Get up and take him back to his bed.

Night terrors

Night terrors can be particularly unsettling for parents. They often begin in toddlerhood. Suddenly your child is screaming and thrashing as if in true agony. Try to remember she's not awake and is having what some sleep experts call a 'content-less nightmare'. Advice varies as to what to do. Some sleep experts say not to wake her up, just make sure she doesn't hurt herself. She'll eventually stop. Others say try to waken her enough so that she stops screaming, then console her and put her back to bed. I say try both and see which works better. Take heart in the fact that children usually grow out of these by school age.

Monsters and ghosts

Around the ages of three and four, when toddlers' imaginations are running at full force, you may start to hear about monsters and ghosts: in the room, under the bed, or in the cupboards.

When you were young, your parents might have said to you: 'There are no monsters! Now back to bed!' That's being logical, but kids don't understand logic at this age. It's not until six or seven that they develop the ability to begin to be rational. You have to realise that to a toddler the monsters are real. So it's much better to acknowledge her fears and deal with them: 'OK, there are monsters, now let's get rid of them.' This will make her feel safe and ease her worries. I call this my 'Magic Dust' technique.

Here's how it works. When my friend's daughter was three-and-a-half, she had serious trouble sleeping. For about a week she'd go to bed about 7:30pm and then waken at 2am, unable to go back to sleep. Her Daddy asked her why she couldn't sleep and she said that there were trolls under her bed. Her dad said, 'Well, I wish you told me that earlier! I have a spray that the trolls don't like and it makes them run to their Mummies!'

He went in with Febreeze spray and spayed her whole room. It worked! It became part of their ritual after that. Every night before she went to bed, she would spray the whole house with Febreeze. I must say it smelled fantastic. And there were no more problems with monsters.

One family I worked with had a little boy who told me that he had two ghosts in his room – Rudolph one and Rudolph two. 'No problem,' I said, 'I'll get out the ghost dust and use my magic wand to make them leave.'

I grabbed a glass jar with a top and put a crystal in it. I turned to his Mum and said, 'Just go with it.' We went into his room and waved the wand around and chanted, 'Dear ghosts, we will not host you here – go back to ghost town where you belong.' Like a pair of Ghostbusters, we looked under the bed and in the cupboard, and chanted some more. Mum opened the jar and made a shaking motion, as if she was catching the ghost.

'Got it,' she cried. She then ran outside, opened the jar and let the ghost go.

We finished by taking the crystal and putting it near his door. 'Now, you have the charm to protect you every night.'

See how it works? Whether it's ghosts, monsters or clowns, you make your toddler feel safe by entering her world and act like a superhero to banish her fears. Kids see their parents as invincible. And that's great. She'll get a good night's sleep with the reassurance that you're there to protect her. Don't worry, you're not reinforcing her belief in monsters – you're validating her feelings and taking her seriously. You've entered the story she has and given it a happy ending.

THE MAGIC DUST TECHNIQUE

♦ **If your child is afraid of monsters, jump into the story: 'Really, where?'**

♦ **Reassure her that you can get rid of them with your magic.**

♦ **Use some item – a wand, glitter or non-toxic room spray – to banish the monsters.**

♦ **Celebrate together that they're gone.**

Early waking

No two ways about it: toddlers waken early. Long mornings in bed are a thing of the past for parents, at least for a while. At the same time, there's early and then there's the middle of the night. If she's up at 4 or 5am, escort her back to bed, tell her that it's too early to get up, and that she can play quietly in her room until you come in. This is like the 'Stay in Bed' technique in that you're limiting her access to you at certain times.

Sleep issues and adopted children

Sleep problems are more common for adopted and foster children. In deciding how to deal with them, you need to look at your child's history. This will help you to identify what underlying circumstances might be causing the problem. You can then adapt the techniques and suggestions I've made in this chapter in order to give her a sense of safety and security.

For example, a friend of mine adopted a little girl from China. Her daughter had horrible night terrors and problems going to sleep. All of the books were telling her to let her daughter cry through the night and eventually she'd get it. But, knowing her daughter's history – she was abandoned in the night and left on the doorstep of an orphanage – my friend knew that letting her cry it out would be the worst thing she could do. She'd feel abandoned again. Instead she opted for co-sleeping until her daughter gained a sense of security.

If you have an adopted or foster child who has been neglected, I would not do the 'Time-controlled Crying' technique because you need to build up her trust. Instead, I would look at tweaking the 'Sleep Separation' technique so that you are in the room with her longer before you end up outside the door. Or do as my friend did above.

We all need sleep, and if there is one important thing that you can do to make your life as a parent to a toddler easier, it's to ensure that he's getting it – and so are you! Take heart: sleep problems may abound as toddlers grow in independence and push their boundaries, but, like everything else, if you stay firm, employ persistence and parent consistently, your little one will soon get the message and snuggle into sweet dreams.

The journey continues ...

So, how do you feel after reading this book? I hope what you're feeling is an increased sense of your ability to parent your toddler with confidence. I do hope you are feeling more empowered. Just look at how much you've learned about yourself, your partner and your child.

Let's face it: At the end of the day, your little cherub needs you, his parents. Sometimes you have to read between the lines and take the time to work out what's going on – and how to resolve a situation. Your toddler needs you to create healthy patterns for him and to be responsive to his every need. He also needs you to be firm, consistent and loving, which will provide him with the boundaries he needs to feel secure in his ever-expanding world.

As you now know, you will be wearing many a hat in any 24-hour period. It's so important to be receptive to learning each day. But, it's equally important not to be your own worst critic. Remembering what you've learned gives you the know-how to make great decisions. If you happen to make a wrong one, remember that you are human, too. That's all part of the lesson.

There are two very strong emotions involved in parenting: fear and love. I hope that you're now making choices out of love of your child – not the fear of the unknown. If that's the case, you have an amazing journey ahead. You are now holding in your hands *Confidence, Patience, Perseverance, Energy, Commitment, Planning Ahead* and a good dose of *Humour*, as well as all the advice, tips and techniques I've given. Don't hesitate to go back through the book and refresh your memory about certain techniques or solutions as you encounter issues during these challenging, yet fun and rewarding years. Which means that if this book fails to find itself smudged with a tea stain, some pasta sauce, or a 4pm cupcake, you've not used it enough!

Know that you can nose-dive back into these pages for specific topics that will be of relevance to you at any particular time. But also know that it will become very automatic for you to do what makes sense because *you* will know what's best for your child and that's what counts. Congratulations on parenting confidently … your eyes are wide open.

Fondly,

PART IV

Useful resources

In this section, you'll find all sorts of helpful resources – some of my favourite nursery rhymes and books, emergency first aid, common medical ailments and what to do about them, and helpful websites and organizations.

Wonderful nursery rhymes

These are my favourites, and in my eyes, no toddler should emerge from his childhood without knowing at least a handful! Nursery rhymes are fantastic for encouraging the development of language skills, and they offer an opportunity for interactive play between you and your toddler.

This Little Piggy

(As you say each line, point to one of your child's toes, starting with the big toe and working down. When the last little piggy cries 'Wee, wee, wee, wee,' trace a line up your child's body and then tickle her under the chin.)

This little piggy went to market.
This little piggy stayed home.
This little piggy had roast beef.
This little piggy had none.
This little piggy cried 'Wee, wee, wee, wee!'
All the way home.

Rain, Rain

Rain, rain, go away;
Come again another day;
Little [name of child] *wants to play.*

Incy Wincy Spider

The incy wincy spider
Climbed up the water spout;
Down came the rain
And washed the spider out;
Out came the sun
And dried up all the rain;
And the incy wincy spider
Climbed up the spout again.

Baa, Baa Black Sheep

Baa, baa, black sheep,
Have you any wool?
Yes sir, yes sir,
Three bags full;
One for the master,
And one for the dame,
And one for the little boy
Who lives down the lane.

One, Two, Three, Four, Five

One, two, three, four, five,
Once I caught a fish alive,
Six, seven, eight, nine, ten,
Then I let it go again.

Why did you let it go?
Because it bit my finger so.
Which finger did it bite?
This little finger on the right.

Polly Put the Kettle On

Polly put the kettle on,
Polly put the kettle on,
Polly put the kettle on,
We'll all have tea.

Sukey take it off again,
Sukey take it off again,
Sukey take it off again,
They've all gone away.

Pease Porridge

Pease porridge hot
Pease porridge cold
Pease porridge in the pot
Nine days old.
Some like it hot
Some like it cold
Some like it in the pot
Nine days old.

Hickory Dickory Dock

Hickory, dickory, dock,
The mouse ran up the clock.
The clock struck one,
The mouse ran down!
Hickory, dickory, dock.

Pat-a Cake

Pat-a-cake, pat-a-cake, baker's man,
Bake me a cake as fast as you can.
Roll it, and prick it, and mark it with a 'B'
And put it in the oven for Baby and me!

Two Little Dicky Birds

(Hold your two forefingers out in front of you. Make one disappear behind your back, then the other, then bring them back out in front one at a time.)

Two little dicky birds sitting on the wall
One named Peter, one named Paul
Fly away Peter! Fly away Paul!
Come back Peter! Come back Paul!

Twinkle, Twinkle

(make a diamond shape with your hands)

Twinkle, twinkle, little star,
How I wonder what you are.
Up above the world so high,
Like a diamond in the sky.
Twinkle, twinkle, little star,
How I wonder what you are.

Pop Goes the Weasel

All around the mulberry bush
The monkey chased the weasel.
The monkey thought 'twas all in fun.
Pop! goes the weasel.

Pussycat

Pussycat, pussycat, where have you been?
I've been to London to visit the Queen.
Pussycat, pussycat, what did you there?
I frightened a little mouse under her chair.

It's Raining, It's Pouring

It's raining, it's pouring;
The old man is snoring.
He bumped his head
And he went to bed
And he couldn't get up in the morning.

I'm a Dingly Dangly Scarecrow

When all the cows were sleeping
And the sun had gone to bed,
Up jumped the scarecrow
And this is what he said:
I'm a Dingly Dangly Scarecrow.
With a flippy floppy hat.
I can shake my hands like this (shake hands).
I can shake my feet like that (shake feet).

When all the hens were roosting
And the moon behind a cloud,
Up jumped the scarecrow
And shouted very loud:
I'm a Dingly Dangly Scarecrow.
With a flippy floppy hat.
I can shake my hands like this (shake hands)
I can shake my feet like that (shake feet)

Mary Had a Little Lamb

Mary had a little lamb,
little lamb, little lamb,
Mary had a little lamb, its fleece was
white as snow.
And everywhere that Mary went,
Mary went, Mary went,
and everywhere that Mary went, the
lamb was sure to go.

The Grand Old Duke of York

(Try this with your child on your knees)

The grand old Duke of York, he had ten
thousand men
He marched them up to the top of the hill
(knees up)
And he marched them down again.
(knees down)
When they were up, they were up
(knees up)
And when they were down, they were
down (knees down)
And when they were only halfway up
(knees partway up)
They were neither up nor down. (knees
up and down quickly)

London Bridge

London Bridge is falling down,
Falling down, falling down.
London Bridge is falling down,
My fair lady.

Take a key and lock her up,
Lock her up, lock her up.
Take a key and lock her up,
My fair lady.

How will we build it up,
Build it up, build it up?
How will we build it up,
My fair lady?

Build it up with silver and gold,
Silver and gold, silver and gold.
Build it up with silver and gold,
My fair lady.

Simple Simon

Simple Simon met a pie man
Going to the fair;
Said Simple Simon to the pie man
'Let me taste your ware'
Said the pie man to Simple Simon
'Show me first your penny'
Said Simple Simon to the pie man
'Sir, I have not any!'

I'm a Little Teapot

I'm a little teapot, short and stout
Here is my handle (one hand on hip),
here is my spout (other arm out
    straight)
When I get all steamed up, hear me shout
Just tip me over and pour me out! (lean
    over and tip arm out like a spout)

Jack and Jill

Jack and Jill went up the hill
To fetch a pail of water.
Jack fell down and broke his crown
And Jill came tumbling after.

Ring-A-Ring O'Roses

Ring-a-ring o'roses,
A pocketful of posies.
A-tishoo! A-tishoo!
We all fall down.

Humpty Dumpty

Humpty Dumpty sat on a wall.
Humpty Dumpty had a great fall.
All the king's horses and all the king's men
Couldn't put Humpty together again!

Banbury Cross

(Do this while bouncing your child on
your knee)

Ride a cock horse to Banbury Cross
To see a fine lady upon a white horse.
Rings on her fingers and bells on her toes,
She shall have music wherever she goes.

Five Little Ducks

Five little ducks went out one day
Over the hill and far away
Mother duck said
'Quack, quack, quack, quack.'
But only four little ducks came back.

Four little ducks went out one day
Over the hill and far away
Mother duck said
'Quack, quack, quack, quack.'
But only three little ducks came back.

Three little ducks went out one day
Over the hill and far away
Mother duck said
'Quack, quack, quack, quack.'
But only two little ducks came back.

Two little ducks went out one day
Over the hill and far away
Mother duck said
'Quack, quack, quack, quack.'
But only one little duck came back.

One little duck went out one day
Over the hill and far away
Mother duck said
'Quack, quack, quack, quack.'
But none of the five little ducks came back.

Sad mother duck went out one day
Over the hill and far away
The sad mother duck said
'Quack, quack, quack.'
And all of the five little ducks came back.

Five in the Bed

There were five in the bed (hold up five
fingers)
And the little one said,
'Roll over, roll over'
So they all rolled over and one fell out.

There were four in the bed (four fingers)
And the little one said,
'Roll over, roll over'
So they all rolled over and one fell out.

There were three in the bed (three
fingers)
And the little one said,
'Roll over, roll over'
So they all rolled over and one fell out.

There were two in the bed (two fingers)
And the little one said,
'Roll over, roll over'
So they all rolled over and one fell out.
There was one in the bed (one finger)
And the little one said,
'Goodnight!'

Little Miss Muffet

Little Miss Muffet sat on a tuffet,
Eating her curds and whey;
Along came a spider,
Who sat down beside her
And frightened Miss Muffet away.

Hey! Diddle, Diddle

Hey! diddle, diddle,
The cat and the fiddle,
The cow jumped over the moon;
The little dog laughed
To see such sport,
And the dish ran away with the spoon.

The Farmer in the Dell

(This can be played as a circle game if
you have a large group: the children
join hands in a circle and dance around
the *farmer*, who stands in the centre.
At the end of the first verse, the *farmer*
chooses his *wife*, who joins him inside
the circle. At the end of the next verse,
the *wife* chooses a *child*, and so on, until
the last verse when everyone is in the
circle except the *cheese*, who stands
alone. Whoever ends up being the *cheese*
becomes the *farmer* for the next round.)

The farmer in the dell
The farmer in the dell
Hi-ho, the derry-o
The farmer in the dell

The farmer takes a wife
The farmer takes a wife
Hi-ho, the derry-o
The farmer takes a wife

The wife takes a child
The wife takes a child
Hi-ho, the derry-o
The wife takes a child

The child takes a nurse

The child takes a nurse
Hi-ho, the derry-o
The child takes a nurse

The nurse takes a cow
The nurse takes a cow
Hi-ho, the derry-o
The nurse takes a cow

The cow takes a dog
The cow takes a dog
Hi-ho, the derry-o
The cow takes a dog

The dog takes a cat
The dog takes a cat
Hi-ho, the derry-o
The dog takes a cat

The cat takes a rat
The cat takes a rat
Hi-ho, the derry-o
The cat takes a rat

The rat takes the cheese
The rat takes the cheese
Hi-ho, the derry-o
The rat takes the cheese

The cheese stands alone
The cheese stands alone
Hi-ho, the derry-o
The cheese stands alone

One, Two

One, two, buckle my shoe;
Three, four, knock at the door;
Five, six, pick up sticks;
Seven, eight, lay them straight;

Nine, ten, a good fat hen.

Little Jack Horner

Little Jack Horner
Sat in a corner,
Eating a Christmas pie.
He stuck in his thumb
And pulled out a plum,
And said, 'What a good boy am I!'

Old MacDonald

(Make up additional verses using other
animals and their sounds.)

Old MacDonald had a farm,
Ee i ee i oh!
And on that farm he had some chickens,
Ee i ee i oh!
With a cluck-cluck here,
And a cluck-cluck there
Here a cluck, there a cluck,
Everywhere a cluck-cluck
Old MacDonald had a farm
Ee i ee i oh!

Old MacDonald had a farm,
Ee i ee i oh!
And on that farm he had some dogs,
Ee i ee i oh!
With a woof-woof here,
And a woof-woof there
Here a woof, there a woof,
Everywhere a woof-woof
Old MacDonald had a farm
Ee i ee i oh!

Old MacDonald had a farm,
Ee i ee i oh!

And on that farm he had some turkeys,
Ee i ee i oh!
With a gobble-gobble gobble-gobble here,
And a gobble-gobble gobble-gobble there
Here a gobble-gobble, there a gobble-
gobble,
Everywhere a gobble-gobble
Old MacDonald had a farm
Ee i ee i oh!

Old MacDonald had a farm,
Ee i ee i oh!
And on that farm he had some cows,
Ee i ee i oh!
With a moo-moo here,
And a moo-moo there
Here a moo, there a moo,
Everywhere a moo-ooo
Old MacDonald had a farm,
Ee i ee i oh!

This Old Man

This old man, he played one
He played knick-knack on my thumb
With a knick-knack patty-whack, give a
dog a bone
This old man came rolling home

This old man, he played two
He played knick-knack on my shoe
With a knick-knack patty-whack, give a
dog a bone
This old man came rolling home

This old man, he played three
He played knick-knack on my knee
With a knick-knack patty-whack, give a
dog a bone

This old man came rolling home
This old man, he played four

He played knick-knack on my door
With a knick-knack patty-whack, give a
dog a bone
This old man came rolling home

This old man, he played five
He played knick-knack on my hive
With a knick-knack patty-whack, give a
dog a bone
This old man came rolling home

This old man, he played six
He played knick-knack on my sticks
With a knick-knack patty-whack, give a
dog a bone
This old man came rolling home

This old man, he played seven
He played knick-knack up in heaven
With a knick-knack patty-whack, give a
dog a bone
This old man came rolling home

This old man, he played eight
He played knick-knack on my gate
With a knick-knack patty-whack, give a
dog a bone
This old man came rolling home

This old man, he played nine
He played knick-knack on my spine
With a knick-knack patty-whack, give a
dog a bone
This old man came rolling home

This old man, he played ten

He played knick-knack once ag'n
With a knick-knack patty-whack, give a
  dog a bone
This old man came rolling home

Hokey-Cokey

You put your right foot in,
You put your right foot out;
You put your right foot in,
And you shake it all about.
You do the Hokey-Cokey,
And you turn yourself around.
That's what it's all about!

Chorus:
Oh, the hokey cokey cokey
Oh, the hokey cokey cokey
Oh, the hokey cokey cokey
Knees bend, arms stretch, rah! rah! rah!

You put your left foot in,
You put your left foot out;
You put your left foot in,
And you shake it all about.
You do the Hokey-Cokey,
And you turn yourself around.
That's what it's all about!

Chorus

You put your right hand in,
You put your right hand out;
You put your right hand in,
And you shake it all about.
You do the Hokey-Cokey,
And you turn yourself around.
That's what it's all about!

Chorus

You put your left hand in,
You put your left hand out;
You put your left hand in,
And you shake it all about.
You do the Hokey-Cokey,
And you turn yourself around.
That's what it's all about!

Chorus

You put your right side in,
You put your right side out;
You put your right side in,
And you shake it all about.
You do the Hokey-Cokey,
And you turn yourself around.
That's what it's all about!

Chorus

You put your left side in,
You put your left side out;
You put your left side in,
And you shake it all about.
You do the Hokey-Cokey,
And you turn yourself around.
That's what it's all about!

Chorus

You put your nose in,
You put your nose out;
You put your nose in,
And you shake it all about.
You do the Hokey-Cokey,
And you turn yourself around.
That's what it's all about!

Chorus

You put your backside in,
You put your backside out;
You put your backside in,
And you shake it all about.
You do the Hokey-Cokey,
And you turn yourself around.
That's what it's all about!

Chorus

You put your head in,
You put your head out;
You put your head in,
And you shake it all about.

You do the Hokey-Cokey,
And you turn yourself around.
That's what it's all about!

Chorus

You put your whole self in,
You put your whole self out;
You put your whole self in,
And you shake it all about.
You do the Hokey-Cokey,
And you turn yourself around.
That's what it's all about!

Chorus

Great books for toddlers

I can't over-emphasise the importance of reading to your child. Not only is it a comforting, nurturing activity that you can easily share, but starting early – and continuing throughout childhood – will encourage her language skills, her vocabulary and her imagination. With a bit of luck, you'll be instilling a lifelong love of reading. Can there be anything better? Here are some of my favourites for each age group:

Eighteen months to two-and-a-half years
The Very Hungry Caterpillar by Eric Carle
First 100 Words by Roger Priddy
Each Peach Pear Plum by Janet and Allan Ahlberg
Peepo by Janet and Allen Ahlberg
The Baby's Catalogue by Janet and Allan Ahlberg
Noisy Farm by Rod Campbell
Dear Zoo by Rod Campbell
My Presents by Rod Campbell
It's Mine by Rod Campbell
I'm Hungry by Rod Campbell
Oh Dear! by Rod Campbell
That's Not My series by Fiona Watt and Rachel Wells
Brown Bear, Brown Bear What Do You See? by Eric Carle
Polar Bear, Polar Bear What Do You Hear? by Eric Carle
Wibbly Pig series by Mick Inkpen

Meg and Mog series by Helen Nicholl and Jan Pienkowski
Noisy Animals by Felicity Brooks and Stephen Cartwright
Night, Night, Baby by Marie Birkinshaw and Kate Merritt
Baby 'touch' and 'touch and sing' books by Ladybird Press

Two-and-a-half to four years

I Want My Potty! by Tony Ross
We're Going On A Bear Hunt by Michael Rosen and Helen Oxenbury
Topsy and Tim series by Jean Adamson
Where's That Monkey? by Dan Crisp
Usborne First Experiences series
The Usborne Book of Nursery Rhymes
The Gruffalo by Julia Donaldson and Axel Scheffler
Guess How Much I Love You by Sam McBratney and Anita Jeram
The Gigantic Turnip by Aleksei Tolstoy and Niamh Sharkey
Monkey Puzzle by Julia Donaldson and Axel Scheffler
Room on the Broom by Julia Donaldson and Axel Scheffler
The Smartest Giant in Town by Julia Donaldson and Axel Scheffler
Five Minutes' Peace by Jill Murphy
Elmer by David McKee
The Very Bouncy Bear by Jack Tickle
The Tiger Who Came To Tea by Judith Kerr
The Mog Collection by Judith Kerr
Cops and Robbers by Janet and Allan Ahlberg
Goodnight Moon by Margaret Wise Brown and Clement Hurd

Four to five years

The Jolly Postman by Janet and Allan Ahlberg
Hairy Maclary From Donaldson's Dairy by Lynley Dodd
There Was an Old Lady Who Swallowed a Fly by Pam Adams
The Lion Book of Five-Minute Parables by Charlotte Ryton
Aliens Love Underpants! by Claire Freedman
The Odd Egg by Emily Gravett
Thomas the Tank Engine by Wilbert Awdry
The *Mr Men* series by Roger Hargreaves
Tabby McTat by Julia Donaldson and Axel Scheffler
Giraffes Can't Dance by Giles Andreae and Axel Scheffler

Alfie and Annie Rose series by Shirley Hughes
What's the Time, Mr Wolf? by Annie Kubler
Who's in the Loo? by Jeanne Willis and Adrian Reynolds
The Usborne First Bible
Don't Let the Pigeon Drive the Bus by Mo Willems
Max by Bob Graham
Whatever Next! by Jill Murphy
Oliver Who Would Not Sleep by Mara Bergman and Nick Maland
The Beatrix Potter collection
Winnie the Pooh by A.A. Milne
The Dr Seuss collection
The Little Prince by Antoine De Saint-Exupery

Emergency treatment

Toddlers can easily choke, fall into water and stop breathing, or otherwise need emergency treatment. I can't encourage you strongly enough to take a class in emergency first aid, including CPR (cardiopulmonary resuscitation), in which you will practise, rather than just read about, what to do. Every parent should know basic first aid, and this section should not be treated as a substitute for proper training. For a reminder of the basics, take a look below.

Choking

Unfortunately, choking is quite common in toddlers. It can be the result of an illness or occur when an object becomes caught in her airway. In case of an emergency, follow these step-by-step guidelines.

STEP 1. Quickly assess the situation

If your child is suddenly unable to cough or speak, something is probably blocking her airway, and you need to get it out. She may make odd noises or no sound at all, and her skin may turn blue or bright red. In this case move on to step 2

If she's coughing or gagging, her airway is only partially blocked. Encourage her to cough, which is the best way to dislodge a blockage. If she can't clear her airway by coughing, help her to dislodge the object using the techniques in step 2.

If you suspect that your child's airway is closed off because her throat has swollen shut due to an allergic reaction or an infection, call 999 immediately – and if you have an EpiPen or Anapen, use it now.

STEP 2. Try to dislodge the object

If your toddler is conscious but can't cough, talk or breathe, or she's beginning to turn blue, shout for help and get someone to dial 999. Kneel behind her. Place one arm diagonally across her chest and lean her forward, with her head down if possible. Firmly strike her between the shoulder blades with the heel of your other hand. Give up to five of these blows to her back.

If the back blows are unsuccessful, wrap your arms around your child's waist. Make a fist with one hand and place the thumb side against the middle of your child's abdomen, just above the navel and well below the lower tip of her breastbone. Grab your fist with your other hand and give up to five quick thrusts into the abdomen.

Continue alternating up to five back blows and up to five abdominal thrusts until the object is dislodged, your child can breathe or cough forcefully, or she becomes unconscious. If you're alone, give three cycles of back blows and abdominal thrusts before calling 999. If your child becomes unconscious, she'll need modified CPR (see step 3).

STEP 3. Give modified CPR

Open your child's mouth and look for an object. If you see something, attempt to remove it carefully with your fingers. If you cannot, place your child on her back. Give her five rescue breaths by pinching her nose with your fingers and blowing into her mouth. If you don't see her chest rise, reposition the head and try again. If there is no response, proceed to chest compressions: place the heel of one hand on her breastbone at the centre of her chest. For a toddler, you should be able to give enough pressure with one hand; for a larger child, you should place your other hand directly on top of the first hand. Try to keep your fingers off her chest by interlacing them or holding them up. Give 15 compressions by pushing your child's sternum down one third to one half of the depth of her

When to go to hospital

If your child is choking, there is no time to drive him to hospital. Call 999 and use the steps on this page to help him clear the blockage. If you need to use abdominal thrusts or give modified CPR, or if you have administered adrenaline, your child must be checked over by a medical professional, even if he appears to have made a full recovery.

chest. Allow the sternum to return to its normal position before starting the next compression. Repeat the cycle of giving 15 compressions, checking for the object, and trying to give two breaths (15:2) until the object is removed, your child starts to breathe on her own or emergency medical personnel arrive.

CPR

CPR stands for cardiopulmonary resuscitation. It is undertaken if your child has stopped breathing, to keep the blood that contains oxygen flowing to your toddler's brain and other organs until emergency medical personnel arrive.

STEP 1. Check your child's condition

If you suspect that your child is unconscious, *gently* shake her and call her name loudly. If she doesn't respond, have someone phone 999 – or if you're alone, give one minute of care, then call 999 yourself before continuing.

STEP 2. Open your child's airway

Swiftly but gently place your child on her back on a firm surface. Tilt your child's head back with one hand and lift her chin slightly with the other to open her airway.

Check for movement and breathing for no more than ten seconds. To check for breathing, put your head down close to your child's mouth, facing her feet. Look to see whether her chest is rising, and listen for breathing sounds. If she's breathing, you should be able to feel her breath on your cheek. If your toddler isn't breathing go to Step 3.

STEP 3. Give five rescue breaths

Pinch your child's nose shut, seal your mouth over hers, and blow gently for one second into her lungs until you see her chest rise. Pause to allow the air to flow back out, then repeat. You will need to give five rescue breaths in total before moving on to Step 4.

If your child's chest doesn't rise, her airway

is blocked. Her head may be positioned incorrectly. If after repositioning her head there is still no effect, consider giving her first aid for choking (see pages 296–7).

STEP 4. Give 15 chest compressions

Place the heel of one of your hands on your child's breastbone at the centre of her chest. For a toddler, you should be able to give enough pressure with one hand; for a larger child, you should place your other hand directly on top of the first hand. Try to keep your fingers off her chest by interlacing them or holding them upward.

To give a chest compression, push your child's sternum down one third of the depth of her chest. Allow the sternum to return to its normal position before starting the next compression. Give your child 15 chest compressions in total at the rate of 100–120 per minute. Then give her two more rescue breaths.

STEP 5. Repeat compressions and breaths

Repeat the sequence of 15 chest compressions and two breaths. If you're alone with your child, call 999 after you've given care for one minute. Continue the cycle of chest compressions and rescue breaths until your child shows signs of recovery or help arrives.

Even if your child seems just fine by the time help arrives, you will need to have her checked by a doctor to make sure that her airway is completely clear and that she hasn't sustained any internal injuries.

Heat stroke

Heat stroke is a potentially life-threatening condition that occurs when the body's temperature rises and its ability to cool down shuts off. Toddlers are especially vulnerable to this condition, so you'll need to keep a close eye on her if she plays outside in very hot weather – particularly if she becomes dehydrated or is dressed too warmly. Severe sunburn can also bring on heat stroke. Please note, too: heat stroke can occur in minutes if you leave your toddler in a parked car. This is yet another reason why you should never, ever leave your child alone in a car – even for a moment. The temperature inside climbs much higher, much faster than outside. Symptoms of heatstroke include:

◆ A temperature of 39.4°C (103°F) or higher, with no sweating

◆ Hot, red, dry skin

◆ A rapid pulse

◆ Rapid, shallow breathing

◆ Restlessness

◆ Confusion

◆ Dizziness

◆ Headache

◆ Vomiting

◆ Lethargy (not responding as strongly as usual when you call his name or tickle his skin, for example)

◆ Unconsciousness

If you see any of these symptoms, call 999 and work to bring your child's internal temperature down as fast as possible while you are waiting for the ambulance. Undress your toddler completely and lay him down in a cool room or in the shade if you can't get to a room. Sponge down his body with a flannel dipped in cool water, and fan him with a magazine or an electric fan. Talk to him reassuringly to keep him calm. Don't give him anything to drink or eat and don't offer any medication to reduce his fever (such as paracetamol or ibuprofen) because it won't lower a temperature caused by heat stroke.

Heat exhaustion

Heat exhaustion is milder than heat stroke. Symptoms include: thirst, fatigue, cool, moist skin, and leg or stomach cramps. Bring him indoors to an air-conditioned room, if possible, and offer plenty of liquids – avoiding drinks that are very sugary or cold, as these can cause stomach cramps. Give him a cool bath or shower and keep him indoors for the rest of the day. If he doesn't seem to be improving quickly, take him to your GP or A&E at your local hospital.

AVOIDING HEAT STROKE AND EXHAUSTION

Dress your toddler in lightweight, loose-fitting clothing. Make sure he drinks more fluids than usual on hot days, and don't let him play outside for long. When it's very hot, keep him indoors. If your house is very hot and you don't have air-conditioning, it's a good idea to visit somewhere that is cooler, such as a public library, shopping centre or leisure facility.

Mild sunburn

Your child should not become sunburnt if you are scrupulously careful about the amount of time he spends in the sun, and applying sunscreen regularly. However, if he does turn a bit pink after exposure to the sun, try this:

◆ Soak a clean flannel in cool water and gently place it on the sunburned area for ten minutes.

◆ Lather on plenty of after-sun lotion designed for toddlers – and don't forget to rehydrate him with plenty of fluids.

◆ If his skin begins to blister, it could mean he has a second-degree burn. Call your GP, who will advise you about the appropriate treatment.

Your toddler's first-aid kit

A first-aid kit is essential with toddlers in the house. Cuts, scrapes and bruises are almost inevitable as children clamber around, exploring their environment. A good first-aid kit contains the things you'll need to treat your toddler if she's under the weather, and should have everything you need to deal with minor medical problems. I consider the following to be the essentials of any good kit. You may also want to create your own mini-kit for travelling, or when you are out and about:

Hand sanitiser

Plasters in various sizes

Antiseptic cream for scrapes and cuts

A mild topical hydrocortisone cream for insect bites and rashes

Arnica cream or tablets for bruises

Cotton wool

Fever-reducers and pain-killers, such as paracetamol and ibuprofen. Never give aspirin to children, as it is linked to a serious liver disorder called Reye's syndrome.

First-aid manual

Small scissors

Gauze dressings to clean cuts and stop bleeding, and adhesive tape to hold them in place

Hydrogen peroxide for disinfecting cuts

Ice packs, small and large. Look for flexible ones that don't require freezing – just twist and they're cold!

Oral syringe or droppers for giving medicine

Rehydrating fluids, such as Dioralyte in case of diarrhoea or vomiting

Tweezers for removing splinters and glass, etc.

Rubbing alcohol for disinfecting tweezers

Digital thermometer

Health checks and visits

You'll be well aware of the systems in place to assess your baby's health and development, and the support that your local team of health visitors, along with your GP, can offer. Over the toddler years, your little one will continue to have developmental checks, as outlined in your 'Red Book' child health record, and you'll also need to pay a visit to your local baby clinic or GP's surgery for the next round of vaccinations. You can expect the following:

Between two and two-and-a-half years

Your child will have a health and development review. This is a chance for you and your partner to ask questions and prepare for the next stage of your child's development.

This review will be carried out by a member of the 'Healthy Child' team, who is usually a health visitor, nursery nurse or children's nurse. They'll encourage you to talk about how things are going and will listen to your concerns. You'll also be able to get advice on childcare or other support, if you are considering returning to work or training. The review may take place at your local clinic, GP's surgery or even at home. It's a great idea for both you and your partner to attend, so you are both up to speed on your baby's health and development.

The review will cover:

◆ general development, including movement, speech, social skills and behaviour, hearing and vision;

◆ growth, healthy eating and keeping active;

◆   teeth-brushing and going to the dentist;

◆   managing behaviour and encouraging good sleeping habits;

◆   keeping your child safe,

◆   vaccinations.

At school entry (four to five years)

Your child will have a full health review. This includes having their weight and height measured and their vision and hearing tested.

Once your child reaches school age, the school staff, in conjunction with your GP surgery, local health visitors and nurses, will help support to your child's health and development. They will work with you to make sure they are offered the right vaccinations and health checks, and will give you advice and support on all aspects of health and well-being, including emotional and social issues, if required.

Vaccinations

At around 40 months, your child will be given the pre-school MMR booster vaccine against measles, mumps and rubella, as well as the DTaP/IPV against diphtheria, tetanus and pertussis (whooping cough). The NHS reports that one in ten children will develop a fever between six and ten days later, as the measles part of the vaccine begins to work. Some also get the measles-like rash and go off their food. These reactions are typically mild. If you are concerned, speak to your health visitor or GP.

Common illnesses in toddlers

At some stage or another, your toddler will come in contact with other children and when he does, he will get colds and other illnesses as his immune system is maturing. While this can be worrying and frustrating for parents, it is a normal, healthy part of your toddler's physical development.

The best thing I can do is to familiarise you with the symptoms of common health conditions so you know best how to ease your toddler's discomfort – and yours! You'll need to know when to take your child to the doctor, and when to seek emergency help. When in doubt, I always say, call and go. A parent's judgment is respected by the medical profession, so don't hesitate to convey your worries or concerns to your GP or health visitor. Let's look at the most common childhood ailments, and see what you can do to help your child.

Chickenpox (Varicella)

Chickenpox is a virus that causes an itchy rash of blisters all over the body and even inside the mouth. These blisters can be anywhere from the size of the end of a pencil, to a five-pence coin, and may vary in distribution and extent. About 24 to 48 hours after the blisters emerge, the fluid within them becomes cloudy and they begin to crust over. At this stage, they can be very itchy and uncomfortable. The rash can be accompanied by a cough and runny nose, upset stomach, a mild fever and general malaise.

Chickenpox is highly contagious, from about two days before the blisters appear until they scab over, which can take up to two weeks. There is a vaccine against chicken pox, but it is not part of the immunisation schedule in the UK.

Helping hand

Because the condition is contagious before symptoms emerge, it's difficult to prevent your child from acquiring chickenpox if he's been in contact with someone with the virus. When chickenpox is about, some would argue to avoid contact with those who have it like the plague; others would say, 'Let's have a party.' Personally, I'm in favour of the party as it will help build your child's immunity earlier.

Treating chickenpox

Heat will make the itching worse, so keep your toddler cool by placing her in cotton clothing and bedsheets. Cotton breathes so it helps reduce sweating. Place a frozen flannel on the itchiest areas. Calamine lotion or calendula ointment can be applied to prevent itching and encourage healing, while her fever can be brought down with paracetamol or ibuprofen. Sleeping with fewer layers on also helps, perhaps just a vest and underwear. Plenty of fluids and foods like yogurt and ice pops that make a child feel like she's keeping cool are also good.

> ### Call your doctor
>
> Call your GP if your toddler's symptoms don't improve after a few days. Any signs of problems breathing or fever too high, go straight to A&E.

Your toddler is bound to scratch, but she'll do less damage to her skin – and be less likely to develop an infection at the site of the spots – if she has clean, well-trimmed fingernails. If she tends to scratch in her sleep, you may want to put an old, clean pair of socks over her hands to prevent her from making things worse.

JO JO ITCHING HINTS

- ◆ **Most motif pajamas are made of polyester, which can increase sweating at night, so I'd avoid those.**
- ◆ **While the rash is active, bathe only once a week. Instead of doing baths, do a wash down with a flannel.**
- ◆ **When you do the weekly bath, a lukewarm oatmeal bath can reduce itching.**
- ◆ **Keep calamine lotion in the fridge so it's nice and cold when you put it on skin.**

Colds

Your child has a cold. She's sniffling, sneezing, and has a runny or stuffy nose – perhaps even a slight fever. Colds are very common, particularly in toddlers who attend childcare facilities, where they're exposed to all sorts of germs. A cold is a virus, and no antibiotics in the world can do anything to help a virus. You'll simply have to wait it out, and ensure that your child is comfortable. There are vapours that you can put on her chest, and to clear the head, humidifiers can help, as can the good old steamy bathroom.

Helping hand

Eating healthy, balanced meals with plenty of fruit and vegetables rich in vitamin C, getting lots of sleep, and being moderately active will help to keep your toddler less likely to succumb to *every* cold that's going around. When she's got a cold, it's back to basic hygiene – encouraging her to throw used tissues into the bin, and covering her mouth when sneezing. This will help to prevent *her* from spreading the virus in your household. But as most parents know, we're so close to our kids that inevitably we catch it as well. That's just part and parcel of having little ones.

Treating a cold

Paracetamol and ibuprofen will help to reduce a fever, and reduce any pain from aching or swelling of the glands. If she's struggling to breathe through her nose and is uncomfortably congested, you can use a vapour rub designed for small children on her chest, and use a vaporiser in her bedroom. Keep her upright on pillows when she sleeps, which can make it easier to breathe. Plenty of TLC is the order of the week. And remember, she needs to recharge her batteries so only moderate play to ride out the illness!

Conjunctivitis

Conjunctivitis, or 'pinkeye', is an irritation or inflammation of the lining of the eyelids and the whites of the eyes. It's usually caused by a bacterial or viral infection that is passed from toddler to toddler, as an infected child rubs his eyes and spreads the infection to toys and directly to other children.

Symptoms include a red or pink eye, itchiness, a thick, sticky, yellow or clear discharge, and eyelids that are crusty or stuck together after sleep. Sometimes there is also swelling around the eye from excess fluid.

Helping hand

Good hygiene is the best way to prevent the infection from spreading amongst family members and your toddler's friends, and it will also stop it from recurring. Don't share towels or pillows, and wash your child's bedding and towels on a hot cycle. It's also important to wash your hands after having physical contact with your child.

GOOD HYGIENE

Teaching young children the basics of good hygiene can't be under-estimated. If your child is accustomed to washing her hands with hot, soapy water regularly, drying them thoroughly, throwing away used tissues, covering her mouth when she coughs – and her nose when she sneezes – she'll not only be less likely to acquire one of the many viruses and bacteria floating around, but she'll be less likely to pass them on, too. If you are out and about, you can get into the habit of using antibacterial wipes to keep her hands clean – and a hand sanitiser, when hot water and soap is not available.

Treating conjunctivitis

Suspected infections are treated with eyedrops or ointment containing an antibiotic drug. Viral conjunctivitis tends to get better without treatment. In either case, you'll need to see your child's doctor. You can help by cleaning her eyes gently – from the inner eye to the outer corner – with a cotton ball soaked in warm, previously boiled water. Use a new cotton ball for each eye. Put a little Vaseline on your child's eyelids and eyelashes at night, taking care not to get it into the eyes, to make it easier to remove crusting the following morning. Cold wet herbal tea bags over the eyes can also help the swelling. I lie her down on the sofa, have her close her eyes, then I apply the tea bags and read a story for 5 minutes.

Coughs

There are many types of coughs, some of which accompany a cold. Others are caused by other infections, such as ear and tonsil infections, excess catarrh, inflammation of the airways and many other things. If your toddler's cough is caused by a virus, there is little that can be done, other than to keep your child warm, dry, and set up with plenty of fluids, until he throws off the illness.

Coughs are necessary to expel foreign bodies and mucus from the trachea and airways of the lungs. Coughing is a symptom rather than an illness, and can indicate sinusitis, croup, bronchitis, pneumonia, flu and other viruses, the early stages of measles, asthma, whooping cough, or an excess of catarrh from the nose or sinuses, usually due to irritation or infection.

A dry cough may be caused by mucus from infections or colds, chemicals in the atmosphere, a foreign object – or even nervousness, which constricts the throat. A loose, wetter cough is caused by inflammation of the bronchial tubes produced by an infection or allergy. A constant night-time cough, or one which recurs with each cold, and is hard to get rid of, may indicate asthma.

Helping hand

Keeping your child's environment free of smoke is important, as is checking that she isn't suffering from allergies that are irritating her airways. Addressing the root cause of the problem is the key to relieving any type of cough, and this may require some investigation!

Treating coughs

As a little girl with asthma, I know this one. If there is reason to suggest a bacterial infection, antibiotics may be prescribed. Some doctors may advocate a cough suppressant, but this is not advised unless the cough is non-productive and truly exhausting your toddler. Paracetamol may bring down any fever, and reduce the discomfort, and ibuprofen can help to relieve inflammation. A vapour rub appropriate for little ones can be rubbed into her chest, and a vaporiser put into her bedroom to produce steam that will help her breathing at night. Keeping her in a slightly upright position while sleeping can help her to sleep, and reduce coughing fits. Warm honey and lemon drinks can soothe; make sure they aren't too hot, and that you use pasteurised honey.

Croup

Croup is an inflammation of the larynx and trachea, which causes a characteristic cough that sounds like your toddler is barking like a seal. It can be the result of a bacterial or viral infection, or even simply a cold, and symptoms seem to come on after midnight.

Helping hand

Croup is one of those conditions that seems to appear out of the blue.
Treating the symptoms of a cold can help to prevent the virus from affecting
her larynx but, in reality, if it spreads, it spreads.

Treating croup

Try turning on the shower and filling the
room with steam. Warm, moist air helps
to reduce the inflammation. Ibuprofen
has anti-inflammatory properties, and can
help to ease discomfort and swelling that
may be causing the 'bark'. Your doctor
may recommend a course of antibiotics if
the croup is bacterial, or one or two doses
of a steroid medication may be prescribed.

> **When to get help**
>
> If his breathing is very noisy, or
> takes great effort, or if he gasps
> or makes a whistling noise, call
> 999 or get emergency help
> immediately.

Diarrhoea and vomiting

Diarrhoea is common. It may be accompanied by vomiting and abdominal pain
and is usually due to an infection or toxin in the bowel, when it is known as
gastro-enteritis. Toddler diarrhoea is a type of diarrhoea in an otherwise well
toddler who continues to have a good appetite and gain weight. It often contains
undigested food particles.

   If your toddler is suffering from gastro-enteritis, she may also have a fever
and abdominal pain. Vomiting can also have a number of other causes, such an
ear infection, urinary tract infection, meningitis, over-eating, motion sickness or
even just a raised temperature. Some toddlers will vomit when they have a cough
or a cold, probably because of the excess mucus, and if vomiting is persistent,
and occurs after meals, a food allergy may be at the root of the problem. For this
reason, it's a good idea to see your doctor if vomiting doesn't stop after 24 to 48
hours; this way, the cause can be assessed and the appropriate treatment offered.

Helping hand

Once again, scrupulous attention to hygiene can help to prevent your
toddler from picking up this type of infection. In particular, she should be
encouraged to wash her hands carefully after visiting the loo. It's also important
to ensure that the food she eats has been thoroughly cooked and stored at the
right temperature. If she experiences vomiting or diarrhoea after eating out,
chances are she's suffering from food poisoning, to which little ones tend to be
susceptible.

CALL YOUR DOCTOR

Call your doctor immediately if your toddler:

◆ **has signs of dehydration, including a dry mouth, sunken eyes, scant, dark-coloured urine, and a lack of tears – particularly if he can't keep fluids down or has diarrhoea every hour or so.**

◆ **vomits green bile or blood, experiences sharp abdominal pain, or hasn't kept fluids down for more than 24 hours.**

Treating diarrhoea and vomiting

In most cases, your doctor will focus on ensuring that your toddler remains hydrated (see box). If the vomiting is severe, solid foods may need to be avoided for 24–48 hours, although if your toddler is hungry, it's usually a good sign. Stick to plain, bland food such as apple puree, ripe bananas, white rice and plain toast. If the condition continues, your doctor may suggest taking a stool sample to rule out an infection. If a bacterial infection is suspected, antibiotics may be required.

KEEPING YOUR TODDLER HYDRATED

Toddlers can dehydrate very quickly when they are ill, and this can cause serious health problems. You can check for dehydration by gently pinching your toddler's skin (on the arm, for example). If it springs back, he's probably keeping down enough fluid; if a pinch-mark remains, you'll need to work on improving his fluid intake, and offer rehydration fluid. For severe dehydration, a stay in hospital may be needed.

Rehydration fluid is made up of salts and sugars that help to restore your toddler's electrolyte balance. If you can't get to the chemist, you can make your own, creating a mixture of clean water (one pint), sugar (one tablespoonful) and salt (one small pinch). Flavouring such as lemon-barley juice, or blackcurrant, may be added if your child refuses to drink without it. Offer small sips, which are more likely to stay in her tummy. If she's not keen, you can try freezing them in ice-lolly moulds or an ice-cube tray, and encouraging her to suck. Sometimes a distraction, like a bendy straw or special cup, can help to encourage drinking.

Ear infections

One of the most common cause of earache in children are middle-ear infections. These are usually caused by the transmission of infection from the nose or throat via the Eustachian tube – which connects the middle ear with the back of the throat and normally drains fluid. Because this tube is short and small in babies and young children, it is easily blocked, and infection does not have far to travel to the middle ear itself. Ear infections can cause a great deal of pain, and the pressure may burst the eardrum, causing a discharge. There may be fever and a sore throat, and your toddler may tug at his ears. Children also complain of earache when they are teething, or if they suffer from sinusitis.

Prevention

If your toddler suffers from frequent colds, he'll be more likely to succumb to ear infections. Speak to your doctor about the appropriate treatment. Make sure no one smokes in your home – or near your toddler, as this has been associated with an increased risk of ear infections in babies and toddlers. Keep your toddler up to date with his vaccines, as the pneumococcal vaccine may help reduce the number of ear infections.

Treating ear infections

Ear infections may be treated with antibiotics, but some doctors are now less keen on using them, as some research has found that they aren't very effective. Instead, painkillers and anti-inflammatories may be suggested. Rubbing the area below your toddler's ear with some warm olive oil can help to ease discomfort.

Fevers

Fevers are a fact of life for most children. In most cases they are nothing to worry about, but it is important to monitor the symptoms closely and to seek medical advice if they persist. Fever has been defined as a body temperature elevated to at least 1°F above the 'normal' of 37.0°C (98.6°F). All fevers should be investigated if they last for more than 24–48 hours, particularly if your child's temperature rises above 38.5°C.

In most cases a fever is the body's reaction to an acute viral or bacterial infection. By raising the temperature it is helping to create an inhospitable environment for viral or bacterial invaders, and also stimulating the production of disease-fighting white blood cells.

A child with a raised temperature may feel hot or cold, may perspire or shiver, will feel hot to touch and usually look flushed. He will lack energy, wanting to flop around or sleep rather than run everywhere as usual, be miserable and off his food. If untreated, a high temperature may sometimes cause a child to vomit, and rarely he may have a fit (febrile convulsion).

Helping hand

There is no reason to prevent a fever, as it is a sign that your child's body is working well to fight off disease. See a mild or moderate fever as a good thing. It's what I call sweating it out!

Treating fevers

Paracetamol or ibuprofen can be offered to bring down a moderate or high fever, and you don't need to report a fever lasting for less than 24 to 48 hours, unless there are other symptoms, such as a stiff neck, sensitivity to light or a rash. Keeping your child cool is important.. You are better off dressing her in light, cotton clothing, and giving her a tepid (not cold or hot) bath. She'll need plenty of fluids to remain hydrated.

BED REST

No child wants to be in bed when they're ill, even though that's often the best place for them. Keeping them occupied in their beds with the same types of activities that they might be doing at playgroup or nursery can help. Print off colouring sheets from the computer, and set her to work. Use a breakfast tray and give her some small pots of playdough, and bring out all of her favourite, interactive books.

The most important thing is to ensure that she rests, and that her energy is used to get well again, rather than to play! Most toddlers love having a parent there to offer lots of support and attention, so if you can find a balance between quiet activities that she can do herself – and fun, comforting chats, stories, puzzles and even just cuddles with you – your toddler may find being relegated to the sofa or their bed a treat, and stay put. This is one time when I'll suggest the odd DVD or children's TV program. They come in handy now!

German measles (rubella)

This is a viral infection that primarily affects the skin and lymph nodes, which is usually transmitted by droplets from the nose or throat that others breathe in. It's a generally mild disease in children; the primary danger of German measles is infection of pregnant women because it can cause serious developmental problems in unborn children.

The incubation period is 14–21 days after being exposed, and symptoms include mild fever, sore throat and swollen lymph nodes, at the back of the neck or behind the ears. After a couple of days, a rash of pink or light red spots begins on the face and spreads downward. The rash can itch and lasts up to three days.

Helping hand

German measles is no longer common, thanks to the rubella vaccine. If your toddler is not immunised, chances are he will get it if it's about. Some immunised children can succumb, too, so don't rule it out if he has all the symptoms.

Treating German measles

Paracetamol or ibuprofen will bring down the fever and reduce discomfort. Creams and ointments including calamine and mild steroid preparations can be prescribed if the rash is very itchy. Frequent, tepid baths will help to relieve any itchiness and bring down a fever.

Glue ear

Also called otitis media with effusion, glue ear is a chronic condition affecting a large number of young children. It is characterised by a thick, often smelly mucus that builds up in the middle ear, impairing hearing, and causing the eardrum to perforate to allow the mucus to be discharged. The condition arises mainly because the middle ear is unable to drain its secretions into the nose via the Eustachian tube. Unlike the other common forms of earache, glue ear is not primarily caused by infection and will not respond to antibiotics.

It may be caused by chronic nose or throat infection, but can also be due to allergies or exposure to draughts. It may also be associated with chronically enlarged tonsils and adenoids causing Eustachian tube obstruction.

The condition is usually symptomless, apart from impaired hearing sometimes, which is not always apparent. Most children are unaware that anything is wrong, and may be accused of being inattentive.

Important Note

Passive smoking has been shown to be a major cause of glue ear, so it's essential that your toddler is not brought up in an environment where there is any smoke at all. It's also important to ensure that your child isn't suffering from allergies, which could exacerbate and even cause the condition. If you are a parent who smokes, be very aware of this because it should be of concern.

Treating glue ear

Glue ear is often treated by a simple operation in which a tiny cut is made in the eardrum and a small plastic drainage tube − a grommet − is inserted. This allows the pressure to be equalised on both sides of the drum and encourages the drainage of middle-ear secretions. You may be reassured to know that most toddlers outgrow the problem by the time they get to school.

Hand, foot and mouth disease (HFMD)

If small blisters suddenly appear on your toddler's soles, palms and the inside of her mouth, chances are she has HFMD, a very common viral infection among toddlers. Highly contagious, it most often occurs in outbreaks during the summer and autumn. The incubation period is three to five days, and cases are passed on by coughing and sneezing, which transmits the virus into the air.

Symptoms include a fever (sometimes high), spots that look rather like chickenpox, but which are sore rather than itchy, and a feeling of malaise. The fever and spots usually clear within a few days. The mouth ulcers may last up to a week and can be painful, often leading to reduced feeding.

Helping hand

Wash your toddler's eating utensils, cups and plastic toys on the hot-water cycle in the dishwasher to prevent the condition spreading to other family members. You may also want to wash her bedding at a high temperature. If there is an outbreak at nursery or her childcare setting, encourage her to wash her hands frequently.

Treating hand, foot and mouth disease

Because it is a virus, there isn't much that can be done to treat the condition, although you can help your child feel better by keeping her temperature down with paracetamol or ibuprofen, and offering plenty of tepid baths. Dab the sore spots with cotton balls soaked in very cold water to soothe.

Headaches

Most headaches in children are due to infections such as colds, ear infections, gastro-enteritis or tonsillitis. Some children also suffer headaches when they are stressed or upset, or when teething. However, headache and fever may also suggest meningitis (see page 319), so check the other symptoms to ensure that she's not in danger. It's always worth reporting any headaches to your doctor, as they can have a host of causes that may need investigation. Severe or persistent headaches in particular must be checked out. How can you tell that your little one has a headache? She may say odd things, like her 'hair' hurts, or rub her head a lot. You may need to read between the lines on this one.

Helping hand
Addressing the root cause is the best way to prevent headaches, so you may need to consider whether anxiety could be causing her headache, or food allergies, lack of sleep, inadequate fluid intake, tooth problems, sinus problems or even low blood sugar (which can be eased by giving her regular, healthy snacks between meals).

Treating headaches
Analgesics, such as paracetamol or ibuprofen, may be suggested for chronic headaches, but your doctor will investigate to uncover the cause before prescribing anything. A cool cloth on your toddler's head, and a gentle massage of her forehead, the back of her neck and her temples may ease discomfort.

Head lice

Lice are tiny parasitic insects that attach their eggs (called nits) to the base of the hair shaft. Head lice do not cause disease, but they can itch and irritate the scalp. Head lice is very common among children who attend nurseries or preschool; when their heads rest close together as they play or work, the insects crawl from head to head. Before long, a whole class can be infested.

Check for lice or nits by parting the hair in several spots and using a magnifying glass in bright light. You can also comb her hair on to a sheet of dark paper, to see what emerges. Head lice are very small, and look rather like dandruff. They don't, however, come off when you pick at the hair.

Helping hand

If there are nits in your toddler's nursery or playgroup, you'll probably be advised. Tie long hair back; the insects find it easier to travel between heads when hair is long. In my experience of treating children with head lice, washing the hair in tea tree shampoo with a few drops of lavender oil added is a great preventative.

Regularly apply conditioner to your toddler's hair, and use a 'nit comb' to carefully remove any eggs or insects that may have made their way to his head. Doing this frequently can prevent an infestation.

Treatment for head lice

A shampoo, purchased from your pharmacist, will be suggested to deal with the problem, but wash all towels, clothing and bedding in boiling hot water, and disinfect combs and hair brushes after treatment. There is some evidence that treatments containing organophosphates can cause some neurological damage in a small percentage of children, so it is worth consulting your doctor before purchasing anything.

Impetigo

This bacterial skin infection is very common in toddlers. It shows up as clusters of little bumps or sores that ooze fluid, forming a honey-coloured crust over them. It often appears first around the mouth and nose but can spread rapidly if other parts of the body are touched. It is contagious, so beware.

Helping hand

Wash your child's bedding and towels at a very hot temperature frequently to prevent it from spreading to other parts of the body, and to other family members. Encourage her to wash her hands frequently, and use an antibacterial handwash. Keep her fingernails short, as she may be tempted to scratch as the blisters dry up.

Treating impetigo

Treatment is by antibiotics, which can be offered orally and/or used topically in the form of a cream or ointment. Your doctor may also suggest a type of liquid soap that can sterilise the rest of the skin, where bacteria may be lurking. You can keep the area clean by bathing in cool, previously boiled water, and gently dabbing at the crusts with a clean cotton ball.

Measles

Measles is a highly infectious disease caused by a virus which is normally inhaled. The incubation period is about 14 days, and just before the rash appears, tiny spots can be seenon the inside of the cheek. It begins like a cold, with runny nose or cough, then a fever and occasionally conjunctivitis occurs. Fever tends to become high as the rash comes out. The rash is characterised by flat, brown-red spots, which begin usually behind the ears and on the face. The lymph nodes will become swollen and there will be little or no appetite, and perhaps vomiting and diarrhoea. Measles spots are not itchy, but your child will feel profoundly unwell. Complications of measles include pneumonia, middle ear infections and bronchitis, and in rare cases encephalitis.

Measles is a serious illness and can be fatal for toddlers. Call your doctor if you suspect she is suffering from this condition. She will need to be quarantined to prevent the spread of infection, and monitored for complications.

Helping hand

The MMR vaccine has had a massive effect on reducing the number of outbreaks, and the death rate has fallen significantly as a result. It is a highly contagious condition, so you are unlikely to prevent your toddler from catching it if he's unimmunised. You can, however, keep his hygiene up to scratch to reduce the risk of infection.

Treating measles

Fever is generally controlled with paracetamol and ibuprofen, and plenty of liquids should be taken. Antibiotics are not prescribed for the measles itself, but may be necessary if any additional complications develop. Offer plenty of fresh water to encourage flushing of toxins, and to prevent dehydration, particularly in the case of fever.

Like with chickenpox, you want to keep the rash dry. Calamine lotion can help, as can cotton pajamas and bedclothes, which reduce sweating. Bathe only weekly in a lukewarm oatmeal bath, and in between baths, wash down with a flannel.

MENINGITIS – BE AWARE

All parents should be aware of the symptoms of meningitis in children of all ages. In older children, look for:

- **fever**
- **neck stiffness (your child may find it hard or painful to bend his neck forward)**
- **headache, which may be severe**
- **photophobia (sensitivity to light)**
- **vomiting**
- **drowsiness**
- **a patchy rash that does not turn white when pressed (press down a clear glass over the rash; if it remains red, chances are your child has meningitis)**

These symptoms often develop rapidly over a period of hours.

In babies and young children the early symptoms of meningitis are not specific. They include:

- **fever**
- **irritability, which may be made worse by holding or hugging**
- **loss of appetite**
- **vomiting**
- **unusual lethargy or sleepiness**
- **your child may also resist bending his or her neck, even if you try to encourage him to look down or up.**

If your child suffers from any of these symptoms, dial **999** immediately and ask for an ambulance. It is crucial that your child receives immediate assessment and treatment.

Meningitis

Meningitis is not common, but as it is very dangerous I am including it here. It is an infection of the lining of the brain (menges), and it is a serious condition that must be identified and treated quickly. It affects people of all ages, but is most common in pre-school children. Meningitis can be caused by several different viruses or bacteria. The outcome can vary from a mild infection, which clears up after a few days' illness, to a serious and frequently fatal condition. If meningitis is suspected, it is important to contact a doctor immediately. Meningococcal meningitis with septicaemia may present with a non-blanching skin rash, which often is associated with a rapid deterioration, which can be life-threatening and needs emergency treatment.

Helping hand

Children are now offered the Hib and pneumococcal vaccine against two types of meningitis, which has significantly brought down the number of cases. There is still a risk, however, so be aware of the symptoms and on t h e alert. Meningitis cannot be caught from casual contact, and the bacteria does not live long outside the body; however, it can be transmitted by sharing cups or water bottles, for example, or chewing on the same toy! Keep your child's hands clean, and discourage her from sharing tissues, food or eating utensils.

Treating meningitis

The treatment for bacterial meningitis is antibiotics given directly into the vein. A drip is also usually used to keep your child well hydrated. Viral meningitis, which is less serious than bacterial meningitis, does not usually require specific treatment, over and above bed rest, fluids and painkillers, such as paracetamol and ibuprofen, although antiviral medication may be required. The most important thing you can do, however, is avoid panicking. Although you may be terrified to find your toddler so ill, she'll need you to be strong and supportive, and if she senses your anxiety, she may become more anxious, too.

Molluscum contagiosum

These very small skin-covered warts are easily spread from one skin area to another through contact, hence the name 'contagiosum'. The warts are almost always grouped together, perhaps on the side of the chest with another grouping on the skin of the inner arm where it has had repeated contact with the warts on the chest. While they may spread quickly and become fairly widely distributed, the cure is often worse than the problem.

Helping hand

This is an extremely contagious condition, which can run riot among children who regularly share the bath, towels, clothing or even very close regular proximity. Skin-to-skin contact can spread it. Some children seem to have a natural immunity, while others seem to be unable to shake it. Boil-washing towels, clothing and bedding can help to prevent the warts from spreading.

Treating molluscum

When there are relatively few warts, a corrosive medication works well with a minimum of discomfort. Other treatments include cutting them away with a sharp curette or burning them off with an electric needle. However, since recent studies show that molluscum eventually disappears on its own, you may want to choose to wait it out. If your child is itchy, apply a little calamine lotion to the warts; usually, however, they have few symptoms.

ADMINISTERING MEDICINE

Sometimes I let toddlers choose whether they want to take their medicine with a syringe or a spoon. If they have a little play with it first, they often find it less daunting. Kids are clever: they soon work out when you plan to head towards them with that medicine spoon! Although timing is important for many types of medication, such as antibiotics, a half an hour on either side of the appointed time is fine. So, I suggest that you slightly alter the routine, to catch them unawares – sometimes before breakfast, sometimes halfway through, and sometimes after!

Mumps

Mumps is a virus that can infect many parts of the body, especially the salivary glands towards the back of each cheek, in the area between the ear and jaw. These swell and become painful, making a child look like a hamster with food in its cheeks. Since the introduction of the MMR vaccine, mumps is no longer common.

The condition rarely occurs in children under two or three years of age, and takes about two to three weeks to incubate. It is infectious for a day before the glands begin to swell until about a week after they have gone down. Symptoms include a general malaise, and then a fever with headache and pains around the neck. Swallowing will be painful.

Helping hand

The MMR vaccine is designed to prevent this condition, and has been largely successful. Otherwise, keeping your child healthy and strong with a good food plan, , plenty of restful sleep, and good levels of exercise give her the best chance of fighting off any virus.

Treating mumps

Your doctor will suggest plenty of fluids, and paracetamol or ibuprofen for the pain and fever. You can apply cold compresses to the swellings to ease the discomfort (some children prefer them warm!), and offer ice lollies to soothe her throat and neck.

> ### Caution
>
> There are complications that can develop in teenage boys who contract mumps, so it's important that your child remains at home until she is well again. If the illness is followed by severe headache, stiffness or fever, see your doctor immediately, as complications affecting your child's brain can occur.

Pneumonia

If your toddler has a high fever and flaring nostrils and is wheezing or struggling to breathe, she may be suffering from pneumonia, an infection of the lung tissue caused by a virus or bacteria. This can be a serious illness, and she must be taken to the doctor urgently in case hospital treatment is needed. Symptoms can include: rapid, shallow breathing, chest pain, sore throat and headache, cough with mucus (occasionally blood), a dry cough, which becomes moister and more productive, high fever, sweating, shivering, and lethargy .

In children, pneumonia occurs following another respiratory infection, such as colds, flu, bronchitis or whooping cough, or after measles (bronchopneumonia). It is more likely to occur when your child has not recovered completely, or not rested sufficiently throughout the course of the illness.

ENCOURAGING YOUR TODDLER TO DRINK WATER

Water is by far the best way to keep your toddler hydrated when she's ill, but what happens if she's not keen to drink it? Try a squeeze of fruit juice, such as natural pear, which will make it more enticing. Try putting it into a fancy cup with a straw, which will fascinate her long enough to get at least a little inside her.

Helping hand

Some children are more prone to respiratory problems like pneumonia, and in others it can be the result of a consistently poor diet, lack of fresh air and exercise, pollution or passive smoking. Children who are chronically ill and taking regular medication may be more susceptible. Addressing these issues can help to keep the condition at bay. It's equally important to ensure that your child doesn't go back into her childcare setting – or preschool – until she has recovered from any illness, even something as simple as a cold or a cough. Pneumonia tends to be a secondary condition, so it's important that any illnesses are resolved with lots of rest, good, healthy food and attention.

Treating pneumonia

Bacterial pneumonia requires antibiotics, while no specific treament is generally required for the viral form of the disease. Paracetamol or ibuprofen may be given to reduce fever and in severe cases, oxygen therapy or artificial ventilation may be required. Using a vaporiser in your child's bedroom can help her to breathe more easily, and subsequently get more sleep. Rubbing her chest with a vapour rub may also help to open the airways.

Threadworms

Threadworms are tiny worms that live in the digestive tract, and look like little white threads. They are very common among young children, who acquire them when someone with threadworms scratches his bottom, gets the eggs under his fingernails and then touches a surface that your toddler subsequently touches. She puts her fingers in her mouth, the eggs go down into her digestive system and about a month later, the worms hatch.

The most common sign is itching around the anus. However, many children have no symptoms. Worms can sometimes be seen around the anus, or in the faeces, and they inflame the area of the bowel of rectum where they attach themselves. Threadworms are not dangerous, although they do tend to disturb sleep.

Helping hand

Worms are incredibly contagious, so you may need to get your whole family checked out. It's important that every family member is completely fastidious about hygiene. Worms thrive upon sugar, so cutting this out can not only help to prevent infestation, but prevent them from recurring. Boil wash the sheets and towels of anyone who suffers. Most importantly, however, discourage your toddler from putting her fingers in her mouth; not always easy, I know, but this is the single most efficient way for worms to be transmitted. If she is a finger-sucker, make sure she washes her hands frequently with hot soapy water, and is encouraged to scrub under her nails with a child-friendly nail brush.

Treatment

Over-the-counter preparations are available to get rid of worms. They actually don't taste that bad, like a cross between protein shake and a root beer (Yes, I've had to even deal with this in my day!). The medicines are called anthelmintic drugs, and they will be chosen according to the type of worm present. In addition to the medicine, keep your child's fingernails short, and discourage her from itching around her anus. If necessary, pop some old, clean socks on her hands before she goes to bed. It sometimes helps to put a little Vaseline, calamine lotion, or even creams designed for nappy rash around the area, to ease any inflammation and itching. Cool baths can also help reduce itching. It is usually good practice to treat the whole household.

Thrush

Thrush, or Candida albicans, is a fungal, or yeast infection. It is very common in toddlers, whose immune systems are still developing. There are two main types: oral thrush and vaginal thrush. It can occur in the nappy area, too, but usually only in babies. Oral thrush is characterised by sore, white, raised patches in the mouth. If you scrape one gently with your finger, it will be red underneath. In the genital area, you'll see a white discharge from your toddler's vagina, which may be itchy and even a little smelly.

Always read the label

It is important that you read the label of any medication before giving it to your child, and do not assume that familiar medicines are safe – both paracetamol and ibuprofen can cause serious side effects.

Helping hand

Eating a fresh, healthy diet and encouraging your toddler to get plenty of sleep will help to boost her immunity, and keep fungal infections at bay. In particular, a high-sugar diet – or one that is high in processed food – seems to be at the root of many cases. Sometimes it occurs after a course of antibiotics, when your toddler's balance of 'healthy' bacteria is upset. In this case, offering probiotics, which can be added in powder form to your toddler's meals, can help. Keeping your toddler's genital area clean, and avoiding the use of soaps, perfumed cleansers and even wipes and bubble baths can help to avoid irritation that could encourage thrush. Dab, rather than wipe, the vagina to prevent any irritation.

Treating thrush

Your doctor may prescribe an antifungal medication that can be applied to the affected area or taken orally.

Tonsillitis

Tonsillitis is an inflammation of the tonsils located at the back of the throat. It is generally due to either viral or bacterial infection (often by the streptococcal bacteria) and causes swelling and redness of the tonsils, possibly with white or yellow spots of pus. The adenoids may also become inflamed and infected.

Tonsillitis can occur at any time but is particularly common during childhood.

Your toddler may have swollen glands (lymph nodes), a sore throat with pain on swallowing, a headache, ear pain and general weakness. Most cases are accompanied by fever, and you may notice that your child's breath is bad.

Helping hand

If your toddler complains that her mouth hurts (often the way that a sore throat is described) it's worth having a peek in her mouth. Dealing with the first signs of inflammation can prevent the condition from becoming worse.

Treating tonsillitis

In most cases, antibiotics will be offered. If your toddler has recurrent attacks, his tonsils may need to be surgically removed. You can help to ease discomfort by offering plenty of cool drinks and fresh-fruit ice lollies, and giving paracetamol or ibuprofen to deal with the pain. Analgesic throat spray may also be used.

Urinary tract infections

A urinary tract infection occurs when bacteria get into the urinary tract from the skin around the rectum and the genitals, travelling up the urethra into the bladder. When this happens, the bacteria can infect and inflame the bladder, resulting in swelling and pain in the lower abdomen and side. This is called cystitis. If the bacteria travel further up through the ureters to the kidneys, a kidney infection can develop. Both types of infection are usually accompanied by pain and fever. Kidney infections are much more serious than bladder infections. Symptoms may include a high fever, irritability, abdominal pain, painful passage of urine, nausea and vomiting, and sometimes dark or smelly urine; however, not all children experience these. Your toddler is just as likely to have a mild fever and feel generally unwell.

The symptoms are not always obvious to parents, and younger children are usually unable to describe how they feel. Some children may make a face or grunt when they first pass urine or avoid weeing altogether. These may be signs of an infection. Recognising and treating urinary tract infections is important. Untreated, they can lead to serious kidney problems.

Helping hand

Keeping your child well-hydrated is the most important thing you can do to prevent urinary tract infections. Regular flushing helps to keep bacteria at bay. Girls should be taught to wipe their bottoms from front to back, to prevent faeces from coming into contact with their ureters. They should also avoid using soap in the area, or bubbles in the bath, which can cause irritation and inflammation that can trap bacteria.

Treating urinary tract infections

If you suspect a urinary tract infection, you'll need to take a urine sample to your doctor to have it analysed. Find a very clean jar and wash it with very hot water and soap, or put it in the dishwasher. When it is clean, encourage your child to urinate into the jar by holding it in the toilet bowl. Urinary tract infections are treated with antibiotics. It's also important that your child gets plenty of fluids, to flush out the bacteria. We now know that cranberry juice contains a substance that helps to prevent bacteria from settling in the urinary tract; drinking plenty of this (diluted, of course) can help to ease symptoms, encourage healing and prevent future attacks.

Whooping cough (pertussis)

This is a highly contagious bacterial disease that causes uncontrollable, violent coughing that can make it hard to breathe. Initial symptoms include a runny nose, slight fever and diarrhoea. It gets its name from the characteristic whoop when the child draws in his breath for the next bout of coughing, but the whoop may be absent in older children.

There may be as many as 50 paroxysms of coughing, which can be so severe that the face goes red or blue and the eyes bulge. There may be some vomiting with the coughing spells. The cough improves slowly over many weeks, often taking months to settle completely.

Helping hand

The DTaP vaccination protects children against whooping cough, but it does appear to make the rounds from time to time – even in immunised children. If there is an outbreak, ensure that your child is careful about washing her hands regularly with hot soapy water, and that she avoids 'sharing' food, drinks, cups or tissues.

CAUTION

There is a risk of secondary infection, in particular pneumonia and bronchitis. All cases of whooping cough should be seen by a doctor. If the cough is accompanied by vomiting, make sure there is adequate intake of fluid to prevent dehydration. Call your doctor immediately if your child becomes blue around the lips.

Treating whooping cough

Antibiotics are not particularly helpful, but may be indicated. If the illness is recognised early, however, erythromycin is often given, which appears to reduce your child's infectivity to others and reduce the length of the illness. A cough suppressant may also be prescribed. At home, you can use a vaporiser in your toddler's room to help ease her breathing, and keep her propped slightly upright when she goes to bed. If she doesn't use a pillow, place one under her mattress, or use a folded towel, to give her bed a slight incline. Rubbing her chest with a vapour rub may help to ease discomfort. Paracetamol or ibuprofen will help with the pain. Remember that your child may be very frightened by the coughing, so it's important to stay calm and reassuring, to help her to relax and get well.

DEALING WITH SKIN RASHES

- ◆ Avoid using soap or bubbles in the bath; in some cases, your **GP** will prescribe a bath additive that will help to ease symptoms and prevent itching.

- ◆ Don't bath her every day; instead, give her a 'wash down', the equivalent of a baby's top and tail.

- ◆ If your child suffers from eczema or psoriasis, make sure to cream her skin before bed every night. Make sure you cream top down, not up down as it can cause infection. It can be useful to do this directly after the bath, to seal in any moisture that is retained in her skin.

- ◆ If you don't have a prescription, make sure that you use a thick perfume- and dye-free emollient.

- ◆ Pat your child dry with a towel after the bath, rather than rubbing her.

- ◆ Place her in cotton nightwear, so that skin can breathe.

- ◆ Watch her diet. Many experts now believe that a large number of cases of childhood eczema are caused by food allergies. If her symptoms flare up after eating something specific, mention this to your doctor.

Further help

As your toddler grows and develops, different issues may arise requiring specialist support and advice. You may also find that you'd like a little more in-depth information about some of the subjects we've discussed in this book. In both cases, you should find what you need here!

Adoption

■ Adoption UK
www.adoptionuk.org.uk
(01295) 752240

Online and face-to-face support for adoptive parents before, during and after adoption.

Allergies

■ Allergy UK
www.allergyuk.org
(01322) 619898

Helpline and advice for allergies and allergic symptoms.

■ Kids' Allergies
www.kidsallergies.co.uk

Provides details of what a food allergy is, which children are at risk, what the symptoms of food allergy are, and what to do if your child has an allergy to food.

■ The Food Allergy and Anaphylaxis Network (FAAN)
www.foodallergy.org

Provides information on raising children with food allergies.

Bereavement

■ The Child Bereavement Charity
www.childbereavement.org.uk

Provides support and information for families dealing with loss.

Car Seats

■ Child Car Seats
www.childcarseats.org.uk
(01482) 575544

Provides information and resources on child car seats, including safety laws and guidance on choosing the right seat for your child.

Childcare

■ Sure Start
0870 000 2288

Offers free information about childcare services, including finding the right nanny or childminder.

■ National Childminding Association
www.ncma.org.uk
0845 880 0044

Provides information and resources on finding childminders and nannies.

■Working Families
www.workingfamilies.org.uk
0800 013 0313

Offers valuable information and advice on flexible working hours, childcare, and employment rights for working parents. Has local groups throughout the UK.

Dads

■ BabyCentre
www.babycentre.co.uk/toddler/dads

This general website has a special section for dads to share with one another and get support and information.

■ HomeDad UK
www.homedad.org.uk
(01938) 810626

A service devoted to fathers who choose to stay at home with the kids.

■ Dads at Home
www.dadathome.co.uk

Articles and advice for dads at home.

■ Fatherhood Institute
www.fatherhoodinstitute.org
0845 634 1328

Provides research, information, and support for fathers.

Dental Care

■ Dental Care of Infants and Toddlers
www.safedentistry.co.uk

Information and resources on dental care for infants and toddlers.

Emotional Support

■ Home-Start
www.home-start.org.uk

This charity is a network of parents helping parents struggling to cope for whatever reason – post-natal depression, loneliness, multiple births, illness, etc. You will be linked to a local group.

■ MIND
(National Association for Mental Health)
www.mind.org.uk
0300 123 3393

Confidential help for mental distress.

Exercise

■ Family Fitness Expert
www.familyfitnessexpert.co.uk
Exercises for toddlers.

General Wellbeing and Advice

■ www.jofrost.com

My website, where you can ask me questions, share your insights and ideas with other parents worldwide, and get support.

■ BabyCentre
www.babycentre.co.uk/toddler

Offers a wide range of resources, articles, community boards, and support for parents of toddlers.

■ A Healthy Me
www.ahealthyme.com

All kinds of information on parenting.

- Parentline Plus
0808 800 2222

Free confidential helpline for parents. Also offers parenting classes and other resources.

Grandparents

- Grandparents magazine
www.grandparentsmagazine.net

Online articles and resources.

- Grandparents' Association
www.grandparents-association.org.uk

The first UK charity devoted to grandparents.

- Good Granny
www.goodgranny.com

A website by and for grandparents, 'especially the young-at-heart grannies of today'.

- Seniors Network
www.seniorsnetwork.co.uk/grandparents

News, views, features on issues related to grandparenting.

Health Concerns

- NHS Direct
www.nhsdirect.nhs.uk
0845 46 47

24-hour nurse helpline.

- My Life, Diabetes UK
www.diabetes.org.uk

Kid-oriented site designed to teach kids about living with diabetes.

Multiple Births

- The Multiple Births Foundation
www.multiplebirths.org.uk
(020) 3383 3519
Information on the care, development

and special concerns of multiples, and a clearinghouse for other resources, like Home-Start.

- Twins and Multiple Births Association
www.tamba.org.uk
(01483) 304442

Information and support for parents of multiples.

- Twins Club
www.twinsclub.co.uk

By parents of multiples, for parents of multiples – find clothes and good baby equipment for multiples as well as lots of advice-sharing.

Nutrition

- Kids and Nutrition
www.kidsandnutrition.co.uk

Articles and tips on child nutrition.

- Food Guide Pyramid
www.foodguidepyramid.co.uk

Nutrition guidance for babies and toddlers.

- Healthy Start
www.healthystart.nhs.uk

Information on vouchers for free milk, fruit, vegetables, and vitamins – available to families on certain benefits.

Playgroups and Preschools

- The Pre-school Learning Alliance
www.pre-school.org.uk
(020) 7833 0991

Early years membership organisation – and one of the largest providers of childcare services in England.

- Wales Pre-school Playgroups Association
www.walesppa.org
(01686) 624573

Independent voluntary organisation that provides community based pre-school childcare and education in Wales.

- Scottish Pre-school Play Association
www.sppa.org.uk
(0141) 221 4148

SPPA is Scotland's largest voluntary sector provider of direct support services to community-led childcare organisations.

- Early Years
www.early-years.org
(028) 9066 2825

Non-profit organisation in Northern Ireland, providing information and training for parents, childcare providers, employers and local authorities.

Safety

- Child Accident Prevention Trust
www.capt.org.uk
(020) 7608 3828

All kinds of information and resources for keeping your child safe.

- Safe Kids
www.safekids.co.uk

Features articles and safety tips on keeping kids safe.

- Lead Paint Safety Association (LIPSA)
www.lipsa.org.uk

A non-profit organisation, LIPSA works to prevent unnecessary childhood and occupational lead poisoning.

Special Needs

- ComeUnity
www.comeunity.com
Clearing house for contact information for a wide variety of special needs support groups

and information. The place to start to find the group you need.

- Contact a Family
www.cafamily.org.uk
0808 808 3555

UK-wide charity that provides information, advice and support for families with special needs children.

Toys

- National Association of Toy & Leisure Libraries
www.natll.org.uk
(020) 7255 4600

Information about local toy lending libraries. Download their 'Good Toy Guide'.

- Toys Advice
www.toysadvice.co.uk

Reference site providing extensive advice on choosing toys for kids, including specific sections on toys that are suitable for toddlers.

- Early Learning Centre (ELC)
www.elc.co.uk

Shopping site offering a full range of toddler toys and activities.

- UK Recall Notice
www.ukrecallnotice.co.uk

Contains information and links regarding toy recalls.

Recommended reading

There is always more room for books on your shelves, and you may find that your ever-growing interest in your toddler and her growth and development will require further reading! Going into the details of every aspect of your child's life is clearly beyond the scope of this book, so I thought it would be useful to point you to the experts that I like to read.

Development

Child Development: An Illustrated Guide by Carolyn Meggitt. This book goes into great detail about a child's development from birth to eight, including gross motor skills, skills, sensory development, cognitive and language development, emotional and social development, and play.

The Sound of Hope by Rosie O'Donnell and Lois Kam Heymann. Great book on listening skills and how to help children avoid auditory processing disorder – and what to do if your child is diagnosed with this problem.

Food

The Top 100 Recipes for Happy Kids by Charlotte Watts and Gemini Adams. Wonderful, healthy, easy-to-follow recipes that avoid too much sugar and fat – and offer plenty of healthy grains, meats, fruit and veggies.

Feeding Your Baby and Toddler by Annabel Karmel. This great cookbook is written in sections based on age, with a discussion on feeding issues for each age group. There are delicious recipes and fun serving suggestions, too.

Children's First Cookbook by Annabel Karmel. Everything from simple treats to full meals that you can make with your child. A fun book for you and your three- and four-year-old, if you're willing to supervise carefully and get messy.

Vegetarian Kids' Cookbook by Roz Denny. Raising your child as a vegetarian? This collection of 350 recipes can help you prepare vegetarian versions of all-time family favourite dishes.

Health

Baby and Child Healthcare by Miriam Stoppard. An A–Z guide to children's illnesses, symptoms and treatment.

Guide to Your Child's Allergies and Asthma by the American Academy of Pediatrics is a valuable how-to book that covers everything from preventing attacks and explaining allergies to young children to best treatments.

Home management

Struggling to keep your household orderly with a toddler? *The Family Manager's Everyday Survival Guide* by Kathy Peel gives tips on everything from clearing clutter to cleaning and shopping.

Play

If you're having trouble working out how to fill the hours with your toddler, you might like *365 Activities You and Your Toddler Will Love* by Roni C. Leiderman and Wendy Masi and *The Toddler's Busy Book* by Trish Kuffner. Each is filled with a year's worth of ideas, most of which use materials you can find around your house.

Index